Society, Space, and Social Justice

Society, Space, and Social Justice

Geographies of Intersectionality

Edited by
Jennifer Y. Pomeroy and Vandana Wadhwa

LEXINGTON BOOKS
Lanham • Boulder • New York • London

Published by Lexington Books
An imprint of The Rowman & Littlefield Publishing Group, Inc.
4501 Forbes Boulevard, Suite 200, Lanham, Maryland 20706
www.rowman.com

6 Tinworth Street, London SE11 5AL, United Kingdom

Cover photo courtesy of Jennifer Y. Pomeroy, September 22, 2018. Edward McKnight Brawley (March 18, 1851–January 12, 1923), first African American student, studied at Bucknell University, Lewisburg, Pennsylvania. Later on in his life, he served as the president of Selma University and Moore College.

British Library Cataloguing in Publication Information Available

Library of Congress Cataloging-in-Publication Data

ISBN 9781498594806 (cloth)
ISBN 9781498594813 (electronic)

"To all the people who fight the good fight each and every day"

Contents

PART II: STRUCTURAL APPROACHES TO SOCIAL JUSTICE

Acknowledgments

Jennifer's Note:

This book speaks to ideas close to our hearts as we have often witnessed, encountered, and experienced inequality, inequity, and social injustice in our own lives. Given how close these topics are to us, we are very grateful to those who have worked with us.

First of all, I am appreciative to Kasey Beduhn, Alison Keefner, Zachary Nycum, and Lisa Dammeyer at Lexington Books who have provided us constant guidance and endless help and support addressing our inquires throughout the entire process. Thank you all very much from the bottom of my heart!

Second, I am so grateful to our contributing authors! I know each of you has spent a lot of time and taken extra efforts to make the changes and revisions many rounds. Without your true collaboration, perseverance, and patience, this book would not be possible. It is the knowledge and wisdom manifested in your insightful chapters that breaks the silence, raises awareness, ensures attention, and provides a platform for healthy debates in the coming years as disparity, inequality, and injustice will continue to rise and dominate the rapidly changing world.

Next, my deepest appreciation goes to my coeditor, Vandana Wadhwa. Thank you for your critical thinking, attention to detail, and thoughtful insights that made this book possible!

Last but not least, I would like to take this opportunity to thank my family for their support and patience.

Sincerely,
Jennifer Y. Pomeroy

Vandana's Note:

My first thanks goes out to Lexington Books (Rowman & Littlefield) for this wonderful opportunity. I have been working on social justice issues perhaps my entire life, whether or not I knew it at the time! This book has provided the means to finally give such efforts a formal shape and form. Of course, this would have all been for naught if not for the people who brought this opportunity to fruition: Kasey Beduhn, Zachary Nycum, Alison Keefner, and Lisa Dammeyer—I am deeply grateful to you all for your constant and unstinting support.

I would also like to thank all my collaborators in this endeavor: My coeditor and coauthor Jennifer Pomeroy, whose sheer will and determination were key to finishing this project! Thank you also to all the contributors to this volume—your hard work and patience with the process, and your passion for social justice was both humbling and inspiring—without all of you who collaborated, this work would not exist at all!

A special shout-out goes to my pal and sister-in-crime Deborah Metzel, who rescued us just in time with her wonderful critique and editing skills.

Thanks to my family for their belief in and patience with me: To my Dad, Wg. Cdr. J. L. Wadhwa—I will be ever grateful for your support and encouragement as I followed my heart, professionally and in personal life! To all my siblings (including those related by marriage!)—Mini, Nicky, Meetu, and Amul, you have been spectacular supports and I wouldn't trade you for all the world! To my mother-in-law—Amma, thank you for your love and thoughtfulness, and for taking upon yourself all the stress of moving house while keeping me fortified with your culinary delights!

And as ever, as it has always been in my every endeavor and in this one, I would never have come this far without the love, support, and irrepressible humor of my best friend and husband, Vikram—*Jaan*, thank you for being my rock, my nurse, and my chef as and when each was needed!

Sincerely,
Vandana Wadhwa

Introduction

Jennifer Y. Pomeroy

Strolling across the grounds of Bucknell University, I happened upon a sculpture with this quote: "Injustice anywhere is a threat to justice everywhere." The declaration was originally made by Dr. Martin Luther King, Jr. It is inscribed on a pedestal below a bust of Edward McKnight Brawley. Edward was first African American student who was enrolled at the university in 1871. The sculpture, featured on the cover of this book, sits at the periphery of Bucknell's Malesardi Quadrangle and was installed in 2017 to commemorate Brawley's graduation and the 1958 campus visit of Martin Luther King, Jr. Bucknell's early recognition of African American students like Brawley, who later served as president of Selma University and Morris College, left an important legacy. That it took until 140 years for this to be more fully celebrated shows that recognizing inequality remains a continuing challenge.

It is our hope that diversity is more fully appreciated as an integral and valuable aspect of society. And in attempting to craft a sustainable societal vision, it is recognized that a full embrace of a just, diverse society is critical. Even as substantial progress along these lines has been made, inequities, injustices, unfairness, and exclusion remain across many places and geographic scales.

Geographers have a long history of studying topics of inequality, differences, discrimination, social justice, and inclusion. Murdie (1969) examined residential differentiation, Brown and Moore (1970) investigated residential relocation, and Morrill and Wohlenberg (1971) studied poverty. While these studies set their research scenes in general, David Harvey's work, *Social Justice and the City* (1973), argues that the built physical environment, planning, and design of cities can exacerbate income inequality that results in unjust space where many urban dwellers are treated unequally and suffer involuntarily. Soja (1980) argues socio-spatial dialect is a "means of . . . social production of space" (207), and McDowell (1983) examines the gender division of urban space. Hayden's work (1984) focuses on the home space perspective and argues traditional home and neighborhood layouts are a mechanism of reinforcing gendered spaces and gendered roles. In *The Production of Space*, Henri Lefebvre (1991, originally 1974) emphasizes that social space and spatial relations are codeterminants that change in social relations does "require spatial reorganization, some new form of sociospatial practice that brings into being new possibilities, including new social spaces" (Smith et al. 2010, 6). Giddens's structuration theory critically frames the dualities of agent and agency in space formation and (re)creation of it in space and time. Such critical sociospatial views might be the beginning time that scholars start to engage in researching complexity embedded in inequality, inequity, and injustice issues. Some notable scholars are as follows: Crenshaw (1989) studied marginalization of black women and her 1991 work dealt with "multilayered and routinized forms of domination" (1245). Kobayashi and Peake in their 1994 work argued gender and race are socially constructed and being used for social identity creation and thus legitimization. Peake discussed the complexity of patriarchal urban spaces and overviewed the intersections of gender, secularity, and race (1993, 2010).

Along with other social sciences, inequality, inequity, and injustice have been studied primarily by a single dimension approach, whether it be class, gender, or race (Hopkins 2017; Valentine 2007). Such approaches are inadequate for studying today's issues of inequality, inequity, and injustice. This is because today's inequality, inequity, and injustice issues are more complex than the past, often mutually constitutive, with multiple identities, and have multifacets of oppressions at various points of intersection (Choo and Ferree 2010). Moreover, changes over these characteristics occur quickly and new characteristics and processes are emerging. Thus, studying today's inequality, inequity, and injustice issues requires a different framework, termed an intersectionality approach. Intersectionality is a multi-level analysis studying the complexity of social inequality, inequity, and injustice. This book is a collection of case studies that either implicitly or explicitly use the intersectionality approach. The unjust hegemonies of ableism, sexism, race, gender, and class are critically examined through a lens of environmental, legislative, societal/cultural, and infrastructural justice. Essentially, the questions that this two-part book seeks to answer are how marginalized, socially unjust spaces are constructed across multiple settings and scales, and what pathways forward can or should be adopted to advocate for and bring about a more sociospatially just society?

The first part of the book has five chapters and is devoted to exposing emergent forms of social injustice and inequalities along various social axes in the various geographic contexts. Each chapter presents a case study of the issues with new underlying processes, including hegemonic "ism" (ableism, racism, sexism) where inequalities and injustices are manifested, (re)created, renewed, and reinforced.

Chapter 1, "Community Starts at Home: Toward Equitable Housing for People with Disabilities," authored by Andrew Myers, Lillie Greiman, Brendan Hogg, Rayna Sage, and Craig Ravesloot, examines inequitable housing for people with disabilities in the United States. They describe an inaccessible space in the housing market for people with disabilities and investigate what factors cause such inaccessibility. Employing statistical regression, they uncover the factors of inequitable housing markets and the marginalization of people with disabilities. They conclude that home is a critical gateway for people with disabilities, and that adequate and affordable housing provision is not only the responsibility of those with disabilities but also a responsibility of the community in which people with disabilities reside. They suggest that making financial access easier and equipping homes with safer physical accessibility will help reduce inequity and create a more just housing market.

Chapter 2 is "Environmental Justice and Outdoor Spaces: Structural Racism's Persistence and the Dynamics of Change," written by Yonit Yogev. Yonit studies the structural racism in outdoor recreation. She focuses on the National Park Service (NPS) where routinized domination by whites and marginalization of people of color occurs. Through an in-depth qualitative analysis, Yonit helps give voice of her counternarratives and critical analyses and recommendations for overcoming those structural barriers. She recommends (1) having role models and mentors, (2) specifically targeted education, (3) youth leadership, (4) doing diversity training in "right ways," and (5) relevancy as structural mitigation strategies. In addition, she advocates that other outdoor agencies need to include grassroots organizations to diversify and staff their management and operation teams.

In chapter 3, "Subversion of Gender Justice: Public Policy on Sri Lankan Migrant Housemaids," Vidyamali Samarasinghe investigates how gender justice, patriarchy, and masculine hegemony threaded in to the Sri Lanka governmental policies regarding its large number of female overseas housemaids. Using multiple data sources, she analyzed how the shifting stances of Sri Lankan government and its policies occurred, and subsequent impacts by those public policies. She concludes that such deliberately created injustice over its female overseas housemaids is due to the failure of successive governmental policies that have deliberately created the layers of hegemonic masculinity. In combination with other already deeply rooted dimensions that suppress Sri Lankan women, her chapter implicitly applies an intersectional framework. Such intersected structure reinforces gender injustice.

Emmanuel Eliot's chapter 4, "Territorialization of Violence: Temporality and Scale—The HIV/AIDS Epidemic in Mumbai, India, in the Mid-1990s" focuses on the web of connecting patterns of scales that produced spaces for the HIV/AIDS epidemic to flourish in Mumbai during the 1990s. Specifically, Emmanuel characterizes the evolution of HIV/AIDS mortality patterns, and analyzes the underlying networks that are responsible for producing new spatialities of insecurity and resistance. He argues that spatial mismatches when combined with processes of injustice and marginalization, space and temporality can create territories of violence.

Chapter 5, "A Woman's Place: Examining Perceptions of Urban Social Space in India," authored by Vandana Wadhwa and Jennifer Y. Pomeroy, uses the 2012 Delhi gang rape case as the anchoring point in their in-depth examination of the continuing denial of the right for women to be included in Indian urban space. Despite rapid progressive development in Indian cities, many Indian women remain ignored, excluded, and invisible. They conclude that low respect and blindness to women's specific needs and desires to access urban space are deeply rooted in India's social structures, which results in physical design and construction of cities that are purposely created space for men. Conversely, urban form and design further solidify such patriarchal social structures.

Structures and systems are powerful agents that have a capacity for addressing unequal and unjust problems. The second part of the book offers structural approaches toward a more just society that is emerging in three geographic contexts. Together, they provide broader, interdisciplinary, and holistic understanding of structural approach is mitigating the tensions and conflicts in the encounter of inequality, inequity, and injustice. As Crenshaw (1991) states, "[I]ntersectionality might be more broadly useful as a way to mediating the tension between assertions of multiple identify an ongoing necessity of group politics" (1296). And Hopkins further emphasizes that "[i]ntersectionality is not only about multiple identities but is about relationality, social context, power relations, complexity, social injustice and inequalities" (2017, 1). Part II, "Structural Approaches to Social Justice," consists of case studies of Brazil, Johannesburg of South Africa, and Uganda that offer evidence of the effectiveness of using the intersectionality framework.

Chapter 6, "Intersectional Organizing as an Approach to Social Justice: Lessons from Brazil's Domestic Workers' Movement" by Caitlin M. Alcorn, focuses on the interlocking space of paid domestic workers in Brazil and their organizing of collective actions. Utilizing an intersectional way of thinking, she critically analyzes the legislative changes that were led by paid domestic workers' actions. She concludes that paid domestic work in Brazil is "an important yet overlooked" social institution in which, through gender, race, and class power structures, the unjust space is reinforced and reproduced across both public and private spaces and multiple generation. She argues that conceptualizing paid domestic work as a major social institution calls us to take seriously the movement that is attempting to remake it in a more just way. Her chapter expands feminist contributions to geographic research beyond "enduring state-centrism" (Pearson and Crane 2017) in the existing Latin American studies.

Luis Emilio Cecchi in chapter 7, explores the relation among freedom, justice, and space from an angle of the neo-republican concept of freedom and social justice. His chapter titled "Freedom, Justice, and Space: Infrastructure as a Driver of Spatial Justice?" argues that infrastructure is a leading driver of spatial justice. After he lays out the framework of the neo-republican theoretical approach, he then applies this in a case study of Johannesburg's transportation infrastructure—the "Transit-Oriented Development Corridor" to illustrate that spatial justice shares the same goal of injustice reduction with neo-republicanism. He concludes that "spatial freedom" should be used as a guide for the development of infrastructure by implementing a "neo-republican spatial agenda" that is spatially just because neo-republican freedom will provide dignity and justice to everyday life.

Lastly, in chapter 8, "AIDS and Aid in Uganda: PEPFAR—Social Justice or Structural Violence?" Vandana Wadhwa and Poojitha Kondabolu examine the impact of the U.S. President's Emergency Plan for AIDS Relief (PEPFAR) and probe the role of PEPFAR's effectiveness in addressing the HIV/AIDS epidemic in the context of Uganda. By systematically examining specific policy tenets, for example, provision of antiretroviral drugs (ARVs), they find that, during the implementation of the policy, PEPFAR in effect excluded "key" population groups ranging from commercial sex workers (CSWs), men who have sex with men (MSMs), lesbian, gay, bisexual, transgender, queer, and intersex (LGBTQI), to children and those in low income and rural and remote regions. They conclude such foreign aid policy is fragmented and deeply anchored in vertical structure that is conducive for structural violence. They conclude that in order to tackle such structural violence, Uganda's social context, especially existing inequitable health care context, needs to be considered.

In summary, all authors demonstrate that the intersectionality way of thinking helps uncover the "new space in processes of subject formation" (Valentine 2007, 10). Although the geographic settings in all case studies differ from one to another, they do encompass the six key ideas mentioned by Hopkins—social inequality; power relations across various dimensions; relationality; social context; complexity, and social justice (Hopkins 2018, 586) that are due to multiple axes. Such approach recognizes the overlapping space deeply rooted in our society, continuing to affect people's life. As Kimberlé Crenshaw advocates, bring to the center and front of the "lived experiences" of those who are being discriminated, mistreated, and oppressed provides a pathway toward a more equal and just society for all.

REFERENCES

Brown, Lawrence A., and Eric G. Moore. 1970. "The Intra-Urban Migration Process: A Perspective." *Geografiska Annaler: Series B, Human Geography* 52 (1): 1–13.

Choo, Hae Yeon, and Myra Marx Ferree. 2010. "Practicing Intersectionality in Sociological Research: A Critical Analysis of Inclusions, Interactions, and Institutions in the Study of Inequalities." *Sociological Theory* 28(2). https://doi.org/10.1111%2Fj.1467-9558.2010.01370.x.

Crenshaw, Kimberlé. 1989. "Demarginalizing the Intersection of Race and Sex: A Black Feminist Critique of Antidiscrimination Doctrine, Feminist Theory and Antiracist Politics." *The University of Chicago Law Review* 14:139–67.

Crenshaw, Kimberle. 1991. "Mapping the Margins: Intersectionality, Identity Politics, and Violence against Women of Color." *Stanford Law Review* 43: 1241–99.

Giddens, Anthony. 1984. *The Constitution of Society*. Berkeley and Los Angeles: University of California Press.

Hall, Edward, and Robert Wilton. 2016. "Towards a Relational Geography of Disability." *Progress in Human Geography* 41 (6). https://doi.org/10.1177%2F0309132516659705.

Harvey, David. 1973. *Social Justice and the City*. Athens: The University of Georgia Press.

Hayden, Delores. 1984. *Redesigning the American Dream: Gender, Housing, and Family Life*. New York: W.W. Norton.

Hopkins Peters. 2017. "Social Geography I: Intersectionality." *Progress in Human Geography* 1–11. https://doi.org/10.1177/0309132517743677. Accessed on March 23, 2019.

———. 2018. "Feminist Geographies and Intersectionality." *Journal of Gender, Place and Culture* 25 (4): 585–90. https://doi.org/10.1080/0966369X.2018.1460331

Kobayashi, Audrey, and Linda Peake. 1994. "Unnatural Discourse: 'Race' and Gender in Geography." *Journal of Gender, Place and Culture,* 1(2): 225–43.

Lefebvre, Henri. 1991. *The Production of Space*. Oxford, UK: T. J. International Ltd, Padstow, Cornwall.

Massey, Doreen, and John Allen. 1984. Geography Matters! Cambridge: Cambridge University Press in Association with the Open University.

McDowell, Linda, and Doreen Massey. 1984. "A Woman's Place?" In *Geography Matters!* edited by Doreen Massey and John Allen. Cambridge: Cambridge University Press.

McKie, Linda, Susan Gregory, and Sophia Bowlby. 2002. "Shadow Times: The Temporal and Spatial Frameworks and Experiences of Caring and Working." *Sociology* 36 (4): 897–924.

Morrill, Richard L., and Ernest H Wohlenberg. 1971. *The Geography of Poverty in the United States*. New York: McGraw-Hill.

Murdie, Robert. A. 1969. *Factorial Ecology of Metropolitan Toronto 1651–1961*. Chicago: University of Chicago Press.

Peake, Linda. 1993. "'Race' and Sexuality: Challenging the Patriarchal Structuring of Urban Social Space." *Environmental and Planning D: Society and Space* 11: 415–32.

———. 2010. "Gender, Race, Sexuality." In *The Sage Handbook of Social Geographies*, edited by S. J. Smith, R. Pain, S. A. Marston, and J. P. Jones, 55–57. London: SAGE.

Pearson, Zoe, and Nicholas J. Crane. 2017. "The Challenge of Feminist Political Geography to State-Centrism in Latin American Geography." JLAG perspectives Forum, 185–91.

Smith, Susan J., Rachel Pain, Sallie A Marston, and John Paul Jones III. 2010. "The SAGE Handbook of Social Geographies." London: SAGE Publications Ltd.

Soja, Edward W. 1980. "The Socio-Spatial Dialectic." *Annals of the Association of American Geographers* 70 (2): 207–25.

Valentine, Gill. 2007. "Theorizing and Researching Intersectionality: A Challenge for Feminist Geography." *The Professional Geographer* 59 (1): 10–21. 10.1111/j.1467-9272.2007.00587.x

Part I

EMERGENT AND EXTANT SPACES OF SOCIAL INJUSTICE

Chapter One

Community Starts at Home

Toward Equitable Housing for People with Disabilities

Andrew Myers, Lillie Greiman, Brendan Hogg, Rayna Sage, Craig Ravesloot

Home design, both in the United States and around the globe, is notoriously inaccessible (Greiman and Ravesloot 2016; Imrie 2004). Lack of accessible and affordable housing often forces people with disabilities to live in homes that do not accommodate their needs and abilities (Imrie and Kumar 1998; Stark 2001). For example, the absence of environmental supports (e.g., grab bars, raised toilets, shower chairs) in the bathroom limit daily activities like bathing (Bishop, Fienberg, and Holland 1978; Connell and Sanford 2001; Petersson et al. 2008; Stark 2001; Stineman et al. 2007). When people live in homes that do not accommodate their needs and abilities, they may experience a similar level of social isolation as people living in institutions (Gibson et al. 2012). While U.S. legislation such as the Fair Housing Amendments Act (FHAA) and the Americans with Disabilities Act (ADA) have helped improve access, many people with disabilities still live in inaccessible homes in the United States (Greiman and Ravesloot 2016).

Housing advocates in the United States have often drawn upon Lefebvre's (1968) "the right to the city" to advocate for more equitable housing policies and practices (Aalbers and Gibb 2014; Mitchell and Heynen 2009). The use of this concept to advocate for housing is rooted in an implicit association between housing and community: housing is a critical element of gaining access to local resources and opportunities to participate meaningfully in community life. While the importance of housing for connecting to community life is understood implicitly and anecdotally, there is limited empirical evidence that describes the specific role housing plays in providing access to community for people with disabilities. A better understanding about this relationship could provide evidence for creating policies and practices that promote housing that is more equitable and protects a person's right to their community.

We used a two-part approach to describe the state of housing for people with disabilities and explore the link between the home environment and community participation. The first part uses data from the American Housing Survey (AHS) to examine cost burden and housing quality. The second uses data from a primary data source, the Health, Home and Community Survey (HHC) to explore the association between specific home characteristics and participation in social and recreational activities. Together, these data tell a story of housing inequality for people with disabilities in the United States and why, as a society, we should care.

BACKGROUND

Access to the city is a fundamental human right (Lefebvre 1968). People with disabilities have recognized this right for a long time. They have also recognized the role that social and built environments play in restricting that right. Negative attitudes, inaccessible design, and systemic barriers restrict the opportunities and choices of people with disabilities to participate in their communities. For example, inaccessible buildings and infrastructure present barriers for people with disabilities from participating in recreational activities (Bedini 2000; Rimmer et al. 2004) and attending social events (Hammel et al. 2008).

In this chapter we utilize a feminist disability theoretical lens (Garland-Thomson 2002) to understand how housing (in)justice for people with disabilities is embedded in larger structures of power and culture that "saturates the particularities of bodies with meanings" (3) that have real consequences for one's ability to participate in community life. Integrating traditional feminist theory with newer work in disability studies, feminist disability theory highlights the dual roles of scholars in producing intellectual materials and participating in the promotion of social justice for people with disabilities. Going beyond traditional disability topics related to housing such as general physical accessibility and accommodation, a feminist disability theoretical approach reminds us to think critically about the experience of disability and housing justice. From this perspective, we consider issues such as medicalization of the body and home and how institutions governing housing policies and practices can constrain or enhance opportunities for people with disabilities.

Approximately 12 percent of people in the United States report some type of disability (von Reichert, Greiman, and Myers 2014). These individuals live within a "pervasive cultural system that stigmatizes certain kinds of bodily variations" (Garland-Thomson 2002, 5), resulting in gross inequalities. For example, people with disabilities often have substantial expenses that most other people do not, such as higher healthcare costs (e.g., hospital visits, prescription medications), expensive adaptive equipment (e.g., wheelchairs), and personal assistance services (Doessel and Williams 2011; Mitra 2006; Sen 1999). Yet, federal policies require impoverishment to qualify for subsidized health insurance and other supports (Stapleton et al. 2006), thus perpetuating inequality between disabled and able-bodied individuals. This is important because, on average, people with disabilities are less likely to be employed (35 percent versus 76 percent), earn less income in a year ($21,000 versus $31,000), and report higher levels of poverty (21 percent versus 14 percent) than people without disabilities (Kraus 2017). Together, this indicates that many people with disabilities are severely economically disadvantaged, which has important implications for how they spend their money.

Historically, service providers and policy makers oversimplified disability as a strictly medical condition (Siebers 2008). People with incurable disease or injury resulting in functional limitations were sent through rehabilitation, so they could live a "normal" life, or were sent to institutions where they would live excluded from society (Sage et al. 2018). Disability advocates began to challenge this medical model of disability in the 1960s through social movements like the disability rights and independent living movements (Dejong 1979; Wright 1960), which worked to disarm the cultural assumption that disability is an individual deficiency (Garland-Thomson 2002). These social movements led to landmark U.S. legislation such as the FHAA (1988) and the ADA (1991), which mandated basic access and freedom from discrimination in housing and public spaces. Going further, the Supreme Court's Olmstead decision (1999) stated that segregated housing (i.e., institutionalization) for individuals with disabilities qualified as discrimination and that people with disabilities should have the option to live in integrated community settings when appropriate. This legislation, though limited, marked a shift toward a different way of defining disability. Rather than viewing disability as something that must be cured (i.e., the medical model), policy makers and others recognized disability as an integral element of the human experience and something that is intimately tied to the social and physical environment. From this perspective, disability is an interaction between a person and the environment that limits opportunities to *participate meaningfully in community life* (World Health Organization 2001). This perspective is called the social model of disability.

Drawing upon the social model through a feminist disability lens, we use *participation* to describe engagement in the behaviors and activities that constitute community life. This may include obligatory tasks such as grocery shopping, discretionary activities such as going out to eat with friends, or more major activities such as employment or education. In this way, participation forms the foundation of social roles and community life (Heinemann

2005). Built environments, and the policies and institutions that influence how environments are built, are an important factor that shape opportunities to participate. While housing and home are often used interchangeably to describe a dwelling, in this chapter we use *housing* to refer to the general building and structure, and *home* to refer to the physical space where people live and form emotional attachments.

As important as built structures that comprise housing, are the environs that we call home. In addition to being a place of shelter, we often think of home as the place where we celebrate important events, bring people together, raise our families, and express our identities. However, home also plays an important role in community participation because it is where we prepare ourselves to go out (Imrie 2004). In this way, the home can act as a "springboard" to community participation (Greiman and Ravesloot 2016; Greiman et al. 2018). Home is popularly described as a place to rest, rejuvenate, and take care of one's self (Mallett 2004; Shahrom and Zainol 2015). Without a safe and comfortable place to take care of daily necessities, such as self-care, it can be extremely difficult to access community-based supports and participate meaningfully in society. Indeed, this notion is a key foundation for "Housing First" approaches addressing homelessness (National Alliance to End Homelessness 2016), and policy makers from around the world recognize the importance of home. For example, in 1948 the United Nations (UN) declared access to adequate housing as a universal human right (United Nations General Assembly 1948) with subsequent declarations (United Nations General Assembly 1966) further emphasizing each nation-state's obligation to ensure this right to its citizens.

While homes are clearly important, not all homes are created equal. Housing policy has long been an effective tool for keeping minority populations segregated and marginalized. For example, discriminatory policies in mortgage lending (e.g., redlining) encouraged and reinforced social segregation and laid the foundation for the spatial inequities we see today across the United States (Bruce and Franco 2018; Rothstein 2017). Later, officials often located public housing projects in these predominantly poor minority neighborhoods, perpetuating racial and economic segregation (Goering, Kamely, and Richardson 1997; Massey and Kanaiaupuni 1993). The poor-quality construction and maintenance of public housing projects has also been found to contribute to poor health outcomes among residents (Hynes et al. 2000), continuing the cycle of poverty and marginalization.

It is critical to understand that homes are complex social and cultural spaces (Blunt 2005). While popular culture often characterizes the home as a positive place, for example, "home is where the heart is," this idealized generalization does not accurately describe many people's relationship with their homes (Gibson et al. 2012; Mallett 2004; Wise 2000). For example, home spaces can be sites of social tension and even violence, particularly for marginalized groups such as women, LGBTQ individuals, and people with disabilities (Brickell 2012). Furthermore, as people's ability to meet expectations of their gendered or ageist cultural roles within the home and family changes with disability or illness, so does the meaning and functionality of the home environment (Crooks 2010).

Accessible and usable homes (i.e., homes that fit the needs and abilities of those living within them; see Research and Training Center on Disability in Rural Communities 2018) are an important element of promoting independence and community participation for people with disabilities (Dunn 1990; Iwarsson and Wilson 2006; Reid 2004). For example, the bathroom is one of the first places where people begin to experience difficulties in their activities of daily living (ADLs; Dunlop, Hughes, and Manheim 1997) and one of the most dangerous places in the home (Span 2009) due to bathing related injuries (Centers for Disease Control and Prevention 2011). The bathroom also plays a role in community access because most people perform some form of self-care prior to going out of the home, which usually takes place in the bathroom (Greiman et al. 2018). Home modifications (e.g., bathroom grab bars) are one way to help alleviate difficulties in the bathroom.

Finally, global policy also shapes housing justice for people with disabilities. The UN Convention on the Rights of Persons with Disabilities (CRPD) states that nation states must ensure that "persons with disabilities have the opportunity to choose their place of residence and where and with whom they live on an equal basis with others and are not obliged to live in a particular living arrangement." Additionally, they shall "have access to a range of in-home, residential and other community support services, including personal assistance necessary to support living and inclusion in the community, and to prevent isolation or segregation from the community" (United Nations n.d., 19). As of 2018, 177 nation states have ratified the CRPD, but the United States is not one of them. One of the oft-cited reasons for this is that the United States already has various laws protecting the rights of people with disabilities. While it is true that progress has been made in expanding access to suitable housing for people with disabilities in the United States, and by extension participation in community life, significant limitations remain.

Though the FHAA contains language aimed at addressing housing barriers, such as access and discrimination faced by people with disabilities, the policies themselves are narrowly defined and rather toothless. For example, accessible design requirements laid down in the FHAA apply only to housing of four or more units built after 1991, leaving a substantial portion of both old and new housing free from any accessibility requirements. Further, the Office of Housing and Urban Development (HUD), which administers the Act, has limited enforcement power and funding. Additionally, despite a federal mandate by the Obama administration that HUD "affirmatively further fair housing," under the Trump administration HUD has extended the timeline for communities to comply with this mandate (Capps 2018; Office of the Assistant Secretary for Fair Housing and Equal Opportunity, HUD 2018). In May of 2018, HUD announced the withdrawal of the Local Government Assessment Tool, which was used to assess implementation of fair housing law by local governments. Together, these limitations have resulted in state and local governments often ignoring fair housing regulations.

Just as housing is clearly important for connecting people to their communities, inappropriate housing may exacerbate exclusion. For example, it may not provide equitable access to community if the housing itself (as location and structure) is marginalized, or if the home (as a physical and emotional place) is unusable or unsafe. For people who experience disability, inappropriate housing can act as a major barrier to participating in community life. We use data from two different sources to explore the role of housing and home environments in accessing community.

METHODS

For the first part of the study, we examined data from the AHS (2017, N = 117,630). The AHS is collected every two years and administered jointly by the U.S. Census Bureau and the HUD. The AHS is the most comprehensive dataset on the state of housing in the United States, collecting information on housing occupancy, costs, quality, and neighborhood characteristics. It is a household survey that asks a single respondent to answer for all members of the home. For this analysis, we examined housing quality and housing cost for households with at least one person who reported a disability.

The AHS measures disability using a set of six questions asking about difficulty with hearing, seeing, cognitive functioning, mobility, self-care, and independent living (U.S. Department of Housing and Urban Development and U.S. Census Bureau 2015). While these questions do not measure disability directly, they are used as a proxy measure to identify people who likely experience disability.

The AHS defines housing quality through a three-tiered variable called "Housing Adequacy" ranging from "adequate," "moderately inadequate," or "severely inadequate." Housing is ranked from adequate to severely inadequate if they meet a set of criteria ranging from availability and use of utilities (i.e., electricity, heating, plumbing) to the presence/absence of pests (i.e., cockroaches and rodents), leaks, cracks and holes in the unit's structure (U.S. Department of Housing and Urban Development and U.S. Census Bureau 2015). Housing cost is reported as a percentage of monthly household income. For this analysis, we defined cost burden as any household spending over 30 percent of their monthly income on housing and severely cost burdened as households spending 50 percent or more. HUD uses these standards to determine worst case housing needs across the United States (Steffen et al. 2015). Data for this analysis was accessed using the AHS Table Creator using data from the 2017 survey, the most recent AHS data release.

For the second part of the study, our research team mailed 26,941 recruitment letters with return postcards to randomly selected households in a small western U.S. city (Missoula, MT) where approximately 13 percent of individuals report a disability. We used Dillman et al.'s (2009) methods for sampling and follow-up. We asked recipients (aged eighteen to seventy-five) who indicated they had a mobility impairment (i.e., serious difficulty walking or climbing stairs) to return the postcards if they were willing to complete a survey. If an individual did not return a survey within two weeks of our initial mailing date, we mailed a reminder letter. If we did not receive a survey after four weeks of the initial mailing, we mailed another reminder letter with an additional survey and after six weeks of no contact we mailed a third survey within a priority envelope. The initial survey included a one-time monetary incentive ($5). Informed consent was obtained from all participants included in this study. All respondent identifiers were removed prior to data analysis. The University of Montana Institutional Review Board approved these procedures for collecting primary survey data.

Overall, we received 658 postcards from eligible participants who subsequently returned 534 completed surveys (81 percent response rate). The average age of survey respondents was sixty-one (range: twenty-two to eighty); 64 percent were female; 94 percent white, 5 percent American Indian/Alaska Native, 1 percent Other, 3 percent Hispanic; 25 percent reported full-time employment, 11 percent part-time, 64 percent reported no employment. The average household income was $30,000 to $40,000; average education was "some college, but no degree"; 66 percent owned their homes while 27 percent rented.

Our HHC survey included basic demographic information (e.g., age, gender, race) as well as various other questions that query respondents about their home, health, and community engagement. We used a scaled version of the six-item measure of impairment used by the U.S. Census Bureau. While the original version uses a dichotomous ("yes" or "no") response, we chose to query respondents using a 0–10 scale (i.e., 0 = no difficulty and 10 = extreme difficulty). We reasoned that we would gather a more accurate sample of people experiencing mobility impairment because not everyone may feel that their limitations are severe enough to say "yes" on the dichotomous version. We used the Brief Community Engagement Questionnaire (BCEQ; Livingston et al. 2015) to measure community participation. Respondents use this measure to report on their community engagement over the last seven days including the number of errands (e.g., grocery stores, doctor's offices), number of social and recreational activities (e.g., religious activities, socializing), and minutes spent in major activities (e.g., employment or volunteering). The survey then queries respondents about the safety of their homes on a 1–5 scale (i.e., 1 = not at all safe and 5 = very safe). We specifically asked them to rate their level of safety while exiting/entering their home and while using the shower/tub to bathe. Finally, the survey asks respondents to rate their level of exertion (i.e., perceived energy use) throughout their home using the Borg Scale (i.e., 0–10) where 0 = nothing at all and 10 = very, very hard. Respondents were asked about their exertion using various areas of the home including the kitchen, living area, storage, bedroom, cleaning, toilet, shower/tub, and entrance. These analyses specifically focus on using the shower/tub and home entrance because we reasoned that they are more related to community participation.

Research assistants entered data from the HHC survey into an Excel spreadsheet programmed to restrict entries to valid values and then we checked data entry for accuracy. Descriptive analyses indicated that most study variables were not normally distributed, so we dichotomized variables and calculated logistic regression to examine the data for relationships between home experiences and community participation. First, we dichotomized home safety items by coding any response that was not completely safe as unsafe. We reasoned that any rating below "very safe" represents a concern for the individual. Next, we dichotomized the home exertion questions and participation variables using the median, creating high and low groups for each. We retained scaled mobility impairment and income as raw scores.

We computed separate logistic regression models for each predictor (bathing safety, bathing exertion, entrance safety, and entrance exertion) and each outcome variable (number of errands, number of social and recreational activities) to examine simple associations. Next, we included gender, mobility impairment severity ratings, and household income as control variables to examine the effects of home experiences on community participation not attributable to overlap with these variables. Lastly, we entered all four predictor variables into models for each of the outcome variables to examine the relative contribution of each when taken together and then computed these same three models with the same three control variables.

RESULTS

Table 1.1 shows the results from the AHS, which reveals that 22 percent of households in the United States have at least one resident with a disability. These households generally report worse housing conditions and greater cost burden than households without disability. For example, 7.9 percent of households with individuals with disabilities are moderately or severely inadequate compared to 4 percent of households without residents with disabilities. Further, nearly 42 percent of households with members with disability spend approximately 30 percent or more of their income on housing (approximately 22 percent spend more than half of income), compared to 32.6 percent of households without members with disability. These data show that households with members with disability use more of their income to pay for poorer quality housing than households without members with disability.

The AHS analysis highlights that people with disabilities live in inadequate housing, based on quality and condition of the building. Data from the HHC survey allow us to explore aspects of the home that are directly relevant to community participation for people with disabilities, such as bathroom and home entrance safety. These data show that for some people with disabilities, using the bathroom and entering/leaving the home feels unsafe. Among people who reported a mobility impairment rating above zero, 59 percent reported bathing as "less than very safe" and 48 percent reported their home entrance as "less than very safe." Therefore, while many participants do report feeling "very safe," a significant proportion report some safety concerns.

Table 1.2 includes the logistic regression results on the models tested for each of the four home-experience independent variables on whether the number of errands respondents reported was above or below the median for this sample. In general, participants that experienced bathing as unsafe and who were above the median on their exertion for home entrancing and bathing were about 50 percent less likely to be in the high errands group (odds ratios (OR) statistically significant and ranged from .564 to .499). Entering control variables truncated these relationships only slightly. We observed a similar pattern of results for the effect of home experience variables on social and recreational activities (see table 1.3). However, these analyses demonstrated

Table 1.1. American Housing Survey Data (2017)

Housing Stock Variable	With Disability (n=26,880)	W/Out Disability (n=90,750)
Total Households*	22.18%	74.88%
Adequacy		
Moderately Inadequate	5.99%	3.24%
Severely Inadequate	1.91%	0.78%
Total Inadequate	7.90%	4.02%
Cost Burden (% of income)		
Burdened (30–49%)	19.88%	18.17%
Severely Burdened (50%+)	22.11%	14.46%
Total Burdened (30%+)	41.99%	32.63%

*2.94% not reporting

Source: U.S. Census Bureau

Table 1.2. Home Experience Variables Regressed Separately on Community Errand Classification (High/Low) n=408

	Model 1				Model 2				Model 3				Model 4			
	OR	95% CI	OR$_{adj}$	95%CI	OR	95%CI	OR$_{adj}$	95%CI	OR	95%CI	OR$_{adj}$	95%CI	OR	95%CI	OR$_{adj}$	95%CI
Unsafe Entrance	.728	.490; 1.082	.898	.585; 1.380												
Entrance Exertion					.502*	.336; .749	.627*	.403; .976								
Unsafe Bathing									.499*	.330; .754	.563*	.364; .871				
Bathing Exertion													.564*	.378; .842	.705	.456; 1.092
Mobility			.953	.886; 1.025			.975	.904; 1.053			.967	.898; 1.042			.968	.897; 1.045
Gender			.830	.534; 1.290			.845	.547; 1.307			.843	.546; 1.316			.805	.521; 1.246
Income			1.081+	1.006; 1.161			1.074*	1.000; 1.155			1.073+	.998; 1.154			1.079*	1.004; 1.160
r²	.008		.035		.038		.050		.037		.053		.026		.045	

Note: *p< .05; + p<.10

Source: U.S. Census Bureau

Table 1.3. Home Experience Variables Regressed Separately on Social and Recreational Activities Classification (High/Low) n=408

	Model 1				Model 2				Model 3				Model 4			
	OR	95% CI	OR_{adj}	95%CI	OR	95%CI	OR_{adj}	95%CI	OR	95%CI	OR_{adj}	95%CI	OR	95%CI	OR_{adj}	95%CI
Unsafe Entrance	.498*	(.335; .740)	.628*	(.406; .971)												
Entrance Exertion					.421*	(.283; .628)	.596*	(.382; .940)								
Unsafe Bathing									.615*	(.412; .918)	.781	(.505; 1.208)				
Bathing Exertion													.565*	(.381; .839)	.822	(.529; 1.278)
Mobility			.857*	(.795; .924)			.869*	(.804; .940)			.855*	(.792; .923)			.858*	(.793; .928)
Gender			.960	(.614; 1.503)			.890	(.572; 1.384)			.907	(.583; 1.140)			.862	(.555; 1.338)
Income			1.093*	(1.017; 1.175)			1.086*	(1.010; 1.168)			1.099*	(1.023; 1.181)			1.100*	(1.023; 1.182)
r^2	.039		.125		.059		.126		.019		.113		.027		.113	

Note: *p< .05; + p<.10

Source: U.S. Census Bureau

clearer effects of home entrance experiences when we entered control variables. Lastly, the effects of home experience on major activities were smaller with only exertion entering demonstrating negative effects when we added control variables (results not shown, available via contacting author).

Regressing all of the home experience variables onto each of the community participation variables shows the relative contribution of each independent variable when taken together. Table 1.4 shows these results along with results when entering control variables. Those who rate their bathing as unsafe are approximately 43 percent less likely to be above the median in the number of errands they report (OR_{adj} = .567, p < .05). However, the effect of home experience appears to be different for social and recreational and for major activities. For these outcomes, exertion entering the home is associated with a 39 percent reduction in the likelihood of individuals being in the high social and recreation activity group (OR_{adj} = .606, p < .10). Similarly, they are 40.2 percent less likely to be in the high major activity group (OR_{adj} = .598, p < .05).

Overall, these results suggest that for people who report mobility impairment, bathrooms and home entrances that are unsafe and difficult to use reduce the likelihood of participating in community life beyond the effects associated with income and degree of mobility impairment.

DISCUSSION

This study adds to the call for housing justice for people with disabilities. Utilizing a critical feminist disability theoretical perspective (Garland-Thomson 2002) within the framework of the social model of disability, these results suggest that people with disabilities spend a greater proportion of their income on housing costs typically for lower quality housing than people without disabilities. This problem is exacerbated by the fact that people with disabilities are often poorer and less likely to be employed than their non-disabled peers meaning that people with disabilities typically have less discretionary income to spend. Participating in the community generally requires some discretionary funds to spend on food, entertainment, or transportation. A higher cost of living may exacerbate barriers to community life for people with disabilities, especially if they must choose between spending their money on rent or going out with friends.

The home experience results suggest that the home environment can be a barrier to community participation that is independent of income and severity of impairment. In these results (see table 1.4), safety and exertion appear to have differential effects for obligatory and discretionary activities when taken together. For example, most people must run errands to meet basic needs (obligatory). The adjusted OR for bathing safety suggests independent

Table 1.4. Home Experience Regressed onto Community Participation (n=408)

	Errands				Social and Recreation				Major Activity			
	OR	95% CI	OR_adj	95%CI	OR	95%CI	OR_adj	95%CI	OR	95%CI	OR_adj	95%CI
Unsafe Entrance	1.218	(.746; 1.989)	1.324	(.797; 2.201)	.723	(.447; 1.168)	.757	(.456; 1.256)	1.107	(.685; 1.789)	1.126	(.599; 1.412)
Entrance Exertion	.592*	(.360; .975)	.664	(.391; 1.125)	.507*	(.310; .828)	.606+	(.358; 1.026)	.577*	(.354; .942)	.598*	(.362; .988)
Unsafe Bathing	.597*	(.360; .989)	.567*	(.337; .954)	.932	(.565; 1.537)	.907	(.536; 1.535)	.962	(.587; 1.576)	.962	(.586; 1.580)
Bathing Exertion	.867	(.522; 1.442)	1.007	(.587; 1.725)	.875	(.527; 1.453)	1.146	(.661; 1.986)	.857	(.520; 1.413)	.913	(.548; 1.521)
Mobility			.982*	(.908; 1.064)			.876*	(.808; .949)			.966*	(.896; 1.042)
Gender			.829	(.528; 1.302)			.987	(.626; 1.556)			.920	(.599; 1.412)
Income			1.066*	(.990; 1.147)			1.088*	(1.011; 1.172)			NA	NA
r^2	.055		.064		.076		.134		.030		.033	

Note: *p< .05; + p<.10

Source: U.S. Census Bureau

negative effects of unsafe bathing on running errands. However, we do not see this effect for social and recreational or major activities. Instead, these discretionary activities are sensitive to exertion with entering and exiting the home. These results are consistent with Greiman et al. (2018) results that suggested when people with mobility impairment bathe less, they go out less often. Our results suggest that this effect may be greater for obligatory activities. In contrast, when people have a choice to engage in activities, then the effort required to go out impacts their choices. Hence, both effort and safety influence how and why people move between their home and communities, but in different ways. This level of detail may help shape the discourse on housing, participation and social justice for people with disabilities.

Toward Equitable Housing

Finding appropriate housing is a matter of social justice (Gibson et al. 2012). While the home is often described as a place that should promote rest and rejuvenation (Mallett 2004; Shahrom and Zainol 2015); for many people with disabilities, the home environment can be physically and emotionally demanding. Several studies have shown that when homes do not facilitate performing ADLs for people with disabilities (e.g., grooming and bathing), their level of participation decreases (Dunn 1990; Hammel et al. 2015; Stineman et al. 2007). As this study shows, home entrances and bathing safety have significant impact on some aspects of community participation, even after controlling for impairment severity, gender, and income.

To date, research about housing safety and difficulty has focused largely on elderly individuals, with an emphasis on fall prevention and home modification (Stark et al. 2017). When done correctly, home modifications can make daily activities like self-care in the bathroom safer and easier (Gitlin, Miller, and Boyce 1999; Hutchings, Olsen, and Moulton 2008; Petersson et al. 2008, 2009) and have a positive impact on individuals' independence, safety, and daily lives (Roelands et al. 2002; Sonn and Grimby 1994; Wang and Shepley 2008). However, only a few studies have examined how bathing may be related to activities outside the home among an older population (Pettersson, Löfqvist, and Fänge 2012; Stark et al. 2017; Tanner, Tilse, and de Jonge 2008; Thordardottir et al. 2018). Two studies specifically examined the effects of bathing and toileting on community trips: Like our study, they found that bathing had large effects (Hammel et al. 2006; Yang and Sanford 2012).

While home modifications can make the home safer, safety may not be the only important factor that links the home environment to community. Energy levels may also play a role. Our analyses show that entrance exertion has a statistically significant effect on errands and social and recreational activities, even after controlling for impairment, gender, and income. If a person must use a lot of energy just to leave their home, they may not have enough energy left for community activities, or they may need to save their energy for other in-home tasks.

Greiman et al. (2018) found that, when compared to people without a mobility impairment, people with a mobility impairment are less likely to bathe, dress, or groom. When they did perform these activities, they used more energy. People with mobility impairment were also less likely to leave their homes and go out into the community if they did not bathe, dress, or groom. This suggests that the amount of energy necessary to toilet and bathe may act as a barrier to community participation for people with disabilities. Indeed, other researchers have suggested that the time and energy necessary for personal hygiene may deter people from going out into the community, either because they don't have enough time and energy left for community activities, or because they are not willing to travel into the community without attending to their hygiene first (Yang and Sanford 2012). It seems possible that home modifications may not only make the home safer but may also reduce the amount of time and energy used throughout the home.

CONCLUSION

Home serves as the starting point for our daily lives (Greiman et al. 2018). This is where we groom, bathe, dress, and get ready to go out into our communities (Imrie 2004). However, housing stock and home design continues to marginalize people with disabilities and limit access to community. Equitable housing for people with disabilities should focus on providing the same opportunities that people without disabilities are afforded in their homes (Gibson et al. 2012), and as such, the same rights to community. Our findings suggest that making housing more affordable, safer, and easier to use can help work toward more equitable and socially just housing for people with disabilities.

While modifying the home environment to make bathing safer may increase the chances of going out into the community, there are numerous environmental factors in the community itself, including other people's homes, which may act as a barrier for people with disabilities. For example, even if a person has complete access to their own living spaces, they may still experience exclusion if they do not have access to the living spaces of family, friends, neighbors, or to public venues (Gleeson 2002). Other barriers such as inaccessible community features (e.g., curbs without curb cuts), lack of transportation, or negative attitudes may also act as barriers to community participation.

Clearly, the home is just the starting point for community access. However, without society-level action, people with disabilities may only have access to those spaces and places which they have the authority and resources to modify. Importantly, it should not only be upon people who experience disability to advocate for disability rights; other homeowners and tenants have a responsibility to support and protect the rights of people with disabilities as well (Shahrom and Zainol 2015). While there are aspects of personal choice and responsibility related to getting out into the community, there is also responsibility upon the community to provide opportunities for people to make those choices (Myers and Ravesloot 2016). Inclusive community development can foster these choices.

Within the social model of disability, environmental features (e.g., presence or absence of steps or curb cuts) are the focus of attention rather than the individual's ability (e.g., illness, impairment). This shift in framing places the responsibility upon the community as a whole while also creating new opportunities between people with disabilities, disability advocates, community developers, planners, architects, and builders to promote policies and practices that foster inclusive communities (Seekins 2006). For example, communities across the United States are advocating for state and local development to include *visitability* requirements to new housing developments (Maisel 2006; Nishita et al. 2007). Visitability is a development policy aimed at including basic accessibility requirements (zero step entrance, main floor bathroom, and thirty-two-inch wide doorways) to all new housing. This was developed as a reaction to the social isolation experienced by people with disabilities in the community as well as to the inevitable growth in the percentage of individuals expected to experience disability as the population of the United States ages (Smith, Rayer, and Smith 2008).

Homes are built in the context of communities that vary in terms of their values and need to comply with federal housing law. For example, sovereign tribal communities are not subject to federal housing laws. In other rural communities that are subject of federal law, there are stipulations that exempt certain housing types (i.e., housing complexes with fewer than four units). As a result, people with disabilities in rural places face unique challenges to finding appropriate housing. Future research should examine whether or not rural home access disparities relative to urban homes exacerbate rural community participation difficulties for people with disabilities.

When communities are designed in a way in which all people have the choices and opportunities to meaningfully participate and engage, we can call that an equitable community. From a feminist disability perspective, engaging in public spaces can enhance the power and influence of people with disabilities. Understanding how experiences in the home (and bathroom) shape community participation is critical for ensuring that these voices are included in community discourse and decision making.

ACKNOWLEDGMENTS

This work was supported by two grants from the National Institute on Disability, Independent Living, and Rehabilitation Research (NIDILRR) (University of Montana grant #90IF0111 and University of Kansas grant #90RT5043). NIDILRR is a Center within the Administration for Community Living (ACL), Department of Health and Human Services (HHS). The contents of this paper do not necessarily represent the policy of NIDILRR, ACL, or HHS, and endorsement by the Federal Government should not be assumed. Special thanks to Lauren Smith, Justice Ender, and other RTC: Rural staff for reviewing earlier versions of this chapter.

REFERENCES

Aalbers, Manuel B., and Kenneth Gibb. 2014. "Housing and the Right to the City: Introduction to the Special Issue." *International Journal of Housing Policy* 14, no. 3: 207–13. https://doi.org/10.1080/14616718.2014.936179.

Bedini, Leandra A. 2000. "'Just Sit down so We Can Talk:' Perceived Stigma and Community Recreation Pursuits of People with Disabilities." *Therapeutic Recreation Journal* 34, no. 1: 55–68.

Bishop, Yvonne M. M., Stephen E. Fienberg, and Paul W. Holland. 1978. *Estimating the Size of a Closed Population: Discrete Multivariate Analysis*. Cambridge: MIT Press.

Blunt, Alison. 2005. "Cultural Geography: Cultural Geographies of Home." *Progress in Human Geography* 29, no. 4: 505–15. https://doi.org/10.1191/0309132505ph564pr.

Brickell, Katherine. 2012. "'Mapping' and 'Doing' Critical Geographies of Home." *Progress in Human Geography* 36, no. 2: 225–44.

Bruce, Mitchell and Juan Franco. 2018. HOLC "Redlining" Maps: The Persistent Structure of Segregation and Economic Inequality." NCRC—National Community Reinvestment Coalition. March 20, 2018. https://ncrc.org/holc/.

Capps, Kriston. January 4, 2018. "Trump's HUD Just Suspended an Obama-Era Fair Housing Rule." *CityLab*. https://www.citylab.com/equity/2018/01/the-trump-administration-derailed-a-key-obama-rule-on-housing-segregation/549746/.

Centers for Disease Control and Prevention. 2011. "Nonfatal Bathroom Injuries Among Persons Aged ≥15 Years—United States, 2008." *Morbidity and Mortality Weekly Report*. 60, no. 22: 729–33.

Connell, Bettye Rose, and Jon A. Sanford. 2001. "Difficulty, Dependence, and Housing Accessibility for People Aging with a Disability." *Journal of Architectural and Planning Research*. 18, no. 3: 234–42.

Crooks, Valorie A. 2010. "Women's Changing Experiences of the Home and Life Inside It after Becoming Chronically Ill." In *Towards Enabling Geographies: "Disabled" Bodies and Minds in Society and Space*, edited by Vera Chouinard, Edward Hall, and Robert Wilton, 45–61. Ashgate's Geographies of Health Series. Farnham, Surrey: Ashgate Publishing Company.

Dejong, Gerben. 1979. "Independent Living: From Social Movement to Analytic Paradigm." Accessed December 2018. https://pdfs.semanticscholar.org/8e93/1ee3 a19f30ef0837de96bc37df1e3365f6f6.pdf

Dillman, Don A., Glenn Phelps, Robert Tortora, Karen Swift, Julie Kohrell, Jodi Berck, and Benjamin L. Messer. 2009. "Response Rate and Measurement Differences in Mixed-Mode Surveys Using Mail, Telephone, Interactive Voice Response (IVR) and the Internet." *Social Science Research* 38, no.1: 1–18. https://doi .org/10.1016/j.ssresearch.2008.03.007.

Doessel, D. P., and Ruth F. G. Williams. 2011. "Disabled People's Living Standards: Filling a Policy Vacuum." *International Journal of Social Economics* 38, no.4: 341–57. https://doi.org/10.1108/03068291111112040.

Dunlop, D., S. L. Hughes, and L. M. Manheim. 1997. "Disability in Activities of Daily Living: Patterns of Change and a Hierarchy of Disability." *American Journal of Public Health* 87, no. 3: 378–83. https://doi.org/10.2105/AJPH.87.3.378.

Dunn, Peter A. 1990. "The Impact of the Housing Environment upon the Ability of Disabled People to Live Independently." *Disability, Handicap & Society* 5, no.1: 37–52. https://doi.org/10.1080/02674649066780031.

Garland-Thomson, Rosemarie. 2002. "Integrating Disability, Transforming Feminist Theory." *NWSA Journal* 14, no. 3:1–32. https://doi.org/10.1353/nwsa.2003.0005.

Gibson, Barbara E., Barbara Secker, Debbie Rolfe, Frank Wagner, Bob Parke, and Bhavnita Mistry. 2012. "Disability and Dignity-Enabling Home Environments." *Social Science & Medicine* 74, no. 2: 211–19. https://doi.org/10.1016/j.socsci med.2011.10.006.

Gitlin, Laura N, Kathleen Swenson Miller, and Alice Boyce. 1999. "Bathroom Modifications for Frail Elderly Renters: Outcomes of a Community-Based Program." *Technology and Disability 10*, no. 3: 141–49.

Gleeson, Brendan. 2002. *Geographies of Disability*. London and New York: Routledge.

Goering, John, Ali Kamely, and Todd Richardson. 1997. "Recent Research on Racial Segregation and Poverty Concentration in Public Housing in the United States." *Urban Affairs Review* 32, no. 5: 723–45.

Greiman, Lillie, and Craig Ravesloot. 2016. "Housing Characteristics of Households with Wheeled Mobility Device Users from the American Housing Survey: Do People Live in Homes That Facilitate Community Participation?" *Community Development* 47, no. 1: 63–74. https://doi.org/10.1080/15575330.2015.1108989.

Greiman, Lillie, S. Parker Fleming, Bryce Ward, Andrew Myers, and Craig Ravesloot. 2018. "Life Starts at Home: Bathing, Exertion and Participation for People with Mobility Impairment." *Archives of Physical Medicine and Rehabilitation* 99, no. 7: 1289–94. https://doi.org/10.1016/j.apmr.2017.11.015.

Hammel, Joy, J. A. Sanford, D. Walens, J. G. Dahl, and L. Fogg. 2006. "The Impact of Home Modification on Community Living and Participation." presented at the 3rd International Conference on Aging, Disability and Independence, St. Petersburg, FL.

Hammel, Joy, Susan Magasi, Allen Heinemann, David B. Gray, Susan Stark, Pamela Kisala, Noelle E. Carlozzi, David Tulsky, Sofia F. Garcia, and Elizabeth A. Hahn. 2015. "Environmental Barriers and Supports to Everyday Participation: A Qualitative Insider Perspective from People with Disabilities." *Archives of Physical Medicine and Rehabilitation* 96, no. 4: 578–88. https://doi.org/10.1016/j .apmr.2014.12.008.

Hammel, Joy, Susan Magasi, Allen Heinemann, Gale Whiteneck, Jennifer Bogner, and Evelyn Rodriguez. 2008. "What Does Participation Mean? An Insider Perspective from People with Disabilities." *Disability and Rehabilitation* 30, no. 19: 1445–60. https://doi.org/10.1080/09638280701625534.

Heinemann, Allen W. 2005. "Putting Outcome Measurement in Context: A Rehabilitation Psychology Perspective." *Rehabilitation Psychology* 50, no.1: 6–14. https:// doi.org/10.1037/0090-5550.50.1.6.

Hutchings, B. Lynn, Richard V. Olsen, and Heather J. Moulton. 2008. "Environmental Evaluations and Modifications to Support Aging at Home with a Developmental Disability." *Journal of Housing for the Elderly* 22, no. 4: 286–310. https://doi .org/10.1080/02763890802458445.

Hynes, H. Patricia, Doug Brugge, Julie Watts, and Jody Lally. 2000. "Public Health and the Physical Environment in Boston Public Housing: A Community-Based Survey and Action Agenda." *Planning Practice and Research* 15, no.1–2: 31–49.

Imrie, Rob. 2004. "Disability, Embodiment and the Meaning of the Home." *Housing Studies* 19, no. 5: 745–63. https://doi.org/10.1080/0267303042000249189.

Imrie, Rob, and Marion Kumar. 1998. "Focusing on Disability and Access in the Built Environment." *Disability & Society* 13, no. 3: 357–74. https://doi.org/10 .1080/09687599826687.

Iwarsson, Susanne, and Git Wilson. 2006. "Environmental Barriers, Functional Limitations, and Housing Satisfaction among Older People in Sweden: A Longitudinal Perspective on Housing Accessibility," *Technology and Disability* 18, no. 2: 11.

Kraus, Lewis. 2017. "2016 Disability Statistics Annual Report." Durham, NH: University of New Hampshire. https://disabilitycompendium.org/sites/default/files/ user-uploads/2016_AnnualReport.pdf.

Lefebvre, Henri. 1968. *Le Droit à La Ville*. Vol. 3. Paris Anthropos.

Livingston, Nicholas A., Tannis. Hargrove, Lillie Greiman, Andrew Myers, Catherine Ipsen and Craig Ravesloot. 2015. "An Investigation into the Temporal Scaling of Community Participation Measurement." *Rehabilitation Psychology* 60, no. 4: 367–75. https://psycnet.apa.org/record/2015-53121-005.

Maisel, Jordana L. 2006. "Toward Inclusive Housing and Neighborhood Design: A Look at Visitability." *Community Development* 37, no. 3: 26–34. https://doi.org/10 .1080/15575330.2006.10383105.

Mallett, Shelley. 2004. "Understanding Home: A Critical Review of the Literature." *The Sociological Review* 52, no. 1: 62–89. https://doi.org/10.1111/j.1467954X .2004.00442.x.

Massey, Douglas S., and Shawn M. Kanaiaupuni. 1993. "Public Housing and the Concentration of Poverty." *Social Science Quarterly* 74, no. 1: 109–22.

Mitchell, Don, and Nik Heynen. 2009. "The Geography of Survival and the Right to the City: Speculations on Surveillance, Legal Innovation, and the Criminal-ization of Intervention." *Urban Geography* 30, no. 6: 611–32. https://doi.org/10 .2747/0272-3638.30.6.611.

Mitra, Sophie. 2006. "The Capability Approach and Disability." *Journal of Disability Policy Studies* 16, no. 4: 236–47.

Myers, Andrew, and Craig Ravesloot. 2016. "Navigating Time and Space: How Americans with Disabilities Use Time and Transportation." *Community Develop-ment* 47, no. 1: 75–90. https://doi.org/10.1080/15575330.2015.1111399.

National Alliance to End Homelessness. 2016. "Fact Sheet: Housing First." Na-tional Alliance to End Homelessness. http://endhomelessness.org/wp-content/ uploads/2016/04/housing-first-fact-sheet.pdf.

Nishita, Christy M., Phoebe S. Liebig, Jon Pynoos, Lena Perelman, and Katie Spegal. 2007. "Promoting Basic Accessibility in the Home: Analyzing Patterns in the Dif-fusion of Visitability Legislation." *Journal of Disability Policy Studies* 18, no.1: 2–13. https://doi.org/10.1177/10442073070180010101.

Office of the Assistant Secretary for Fair Housing and Equal Opportunity, HUD. Jan-uary 5, 2018. "Affirmatively Furthering Fair Housing: Extension of Deadline for Submission of Assessment of Fair Housing for Consolidated Plan Participants." Fed-eral Register. https://www.federalregister.gov/documents/2018/01/05/2018-00106/ affirmatively-furthering-fair-housing-extension-of-deadline-for-submission-of -assessment-of-fair.

Petersson, Ingela, Anders Kottorp, Jakob Bergström, and Margareta Lilja. 2009. "Longitudinal Changes in Everyday Life after Home Modifications for People Aging with Disabilities." *Scandinavian Journal of Occupational Therapy* 16, no. 2: 78–87.

Petersson, Ingela, Margareta Lilja, Joy Hammel, and Anders Kottorp. 2008. "Impact of Home Modification Services on Ability in Everyday Life for People Ageing with Disabilities." *Journal of Rehabilitation Medicine* 40, no. 4: 253–60. https:// doi.org/10.2340/16501977-0160.

Pettersson, Cecilia, Charlotte Löfqvist, and Agneta Malmgren Fänge. 2012. "Clients' Experiences of Housing Adaptations: A Longitudinal Mixed-Methods Study." *Disability and Rehabilitation* 34, no. 20: 1706–15. https://doi.org/10.3109/09638 288.2012.660596.

Reid, Denise. 2004. "Accessibility and Usability of the Physical Housing Environ-ment of Seniors with Stroke." *International Journal of Rehabilitation Research* 27, no. 3: 203–8.

Rimmer, James H., Barth Riley, Edward Wang, Amy Rauworth, and Janine Jurkowski. 2004. "Physical Activity Participation among Persons with Disabilities:

Barriers and Facilitators." *American Journal of Preventive Medicine* 26, no. 5: 419–25. https://doi.org/10.1016/j.amepre.2004.02.002.

Roelands, Marc, Paulette Van Oost, AnneMarie Depoorter, and Ann Buysse. 2002. "A Social–Cognitive Model to Predict the Use of Assistive Devices for Mobility and Self-Care in Elderly People." *The Gerontologist* 42, no. 1: 39–50.

Rothstein, Richard. 2017. *The Color of Law: A Forgotten History of How Our Government Segregated America*. New York, NY: Liveright Publishing.

RTC (Research and Training Center) on Disability in Rural Community, University of Montana. 2018. http://rtc.ruralinstitute.umt.edu/products-services-2/publications/.

Sage, Rayna, Bryce Ward, Andrew Myers, and Craig Ravesloot. 2018. "Transitory and Enduring Disability among Urban and Rural People." *The Journal of Rural Health* November Issue. https://doi.org/10.1111/jrh.12338.

Seekins, Tom. 2006. "Introduction: Disability and Community Development." *Community Development* 37, no. 3: 1–3.

Sen, Amartya. 1999. *Freedom as Development*. Oxford: Oxford University Press.

Shahrom, Siti Kalkhalah, and Rosilawati Zainol. 2015. "Universal Design in Housing for People with Disabilities: A Review." *Journal of Design and Built Environment* 15, no. 1: 33–42. https://doi.org/10.22452/jdbe.vol15no1.1.

Siebers, Tobin. 2008. *Disability Theory*. Ann Arbor, MI: University of Michigan Press.

Smith, Stanley K., Stefan Rayer, and Eleanor A. Smith. 2008. "Aging and Disability: Implications for the Housing Industry and Housing Policy in the United States." *Journal of the American Planning Association* 74, no. 3: 289–306. https://doi.org/10.1080/01944360802197132.

Sonn, U., and G. Grimby. 1994. "Assistive Devices in an Elderly Population Studied at 70 and 76 Years of Age." *Disability and Rehabilitation* 16, no. 2: 85–92.

Span, Paula. 2009. "The Most Dangerous Room in the House?" *New York Times.* May 28. https://newoldage.blogs.nytimes.com/2009/05/28/the-most-dangerous-room-in-the-house/.

Stapleton, David C., Bonnie L. O'Day, Gina A. Livermore, and Andrew J. Imparato. 2006. "Dismantling the Poverty Trap: Disability Policy for the Twenty-First Century." *The Milbank Quarterly* 84, no 4: 701–32. https://doi.org/10.1111/j.1468-0009.2006.00465.x.

Stark, Susan. 2001. "Creating Disability in the Home: The Role of Environmental Barriers in the United States." *Disability & Society* 16, no. 1: 37–49. https://doi.org/10.1080/713662037.

Stark, Susan, Marian Keglovits, Marian Arbesman, and Deborah Lieberman. 2017. "Effect of Home Modification Interventions on the Participation of Community-Dwelling Adults with Health Conditions: A Systematic Review." *American Journal of Occupational Therapy* 71, no. 2: 7102290010p1. https://doi.org/10.5014/ajot.2017.018887.

Steffen, Barry, George Carter, Marge Martin, Danilo Pelletiere, David Vandenbroucke, and Yung-Gann David Yao. 2015. "Worst Case Housing Needs: 2015 Report to Congress." 15. Worst Case Housing Needs. Department of Housing and

Urban Development. https://www.huduser.gov/portal/publications/affhsg/wc_Hsg Needs15.html.

Stineman, Margaret G., Richard N. Ross, Greg Maislin, and David Gray. 2007. "Population-Based Study of Home Accessibility Features and the Activities of Daily Living: Clinical and Policy Implications." *Disability and Rehabilitation* 29, no.15: 1165–75.

Tanner, Bronwyn, Cheryl Tilse, and Desleigh de Jonge. 2008. "Restoring and Sustaining Home: The Impact of Home Modifications on the Meaning of Home for Older People." *Journal of Housing for the Elderly* 22, no. 3: 195–215. https://doi .org/10.1080/02763890802232048.

Thordardottir, Björg, Agneta Malmgren Fänge, Carlos Chiatti, and Lisa Ekstam. 2018. "Participation in Everyday Life Before and After a Housing Adaptation." *Journal of Housing for the Elderly*, (April): 1–15. https://doi.org/10.1080/027638 93.2018.1451800.

United Nations. n.d. "Article 19–Living Independently and Being Included in the Community." Accessed August 13, 2018. https://www.un.org/development/desa/ disabilities/convention-on-the-rights-of-persons-with-disabilities/article-19-living -independently-and-being-included-in-the-community.html.

United Nations General Assembly. 1948. "Universal Declaration of Human Rights." United Nations General Assembly. Accessed December 2017. http://www.un.org/ en/universal-declaration-human-rights/index.html.

———. 1966. "International Covenant on Economic, Social and Cultural Rights." United Nations General Assembly. Accessed December 2017. https://www.ohchr .org/EN/ProfessionalInterest/Pages/CESCR.aspx.

U.S. Department of Housing and Urban Development, and U.S. Census Bureau. 2015. "Appendix A." In *American Housing Survey for the United States: 2015*, 47. https://www2.census.gov/programs-surveys/ahs/2015/2015%20AHS%20Defi nitions.pdf.

von Reichert, Christiane, Lillie Greiman, and Andrew Myers. 2014. "The Geography of Disability in America: On Rural-urban Differences in Impairment Rates." *Independent Living and Community Participation* No. 7. University of Montana.

Wang, Zhe and Mardelle McCuskey Shepley. 2008. "Site-Level Environmental Support of Active Behavior and Fall Prevention for Seniors." *Seniors Housing & Care Journal* 16, no. 1: 97–121.

Wise, J. Macgregor. 2000. "Home: Territory and Identity." *Cultural Studies* 14, no. 2: 295–310.

World Health Organization. 2001. *International Classification of Functioning, Disability and Health*. Geneva, Switzerland: World Health Organization. Accessed November 2017. http://psychiatr.ru/download/1313?view=name=CF_18.pdf.

Wright, Beatrice A. 1960. "Circumscribing the Problem." In *Physical Disability—A Psychological Approach*, 1–12. New York, NY: Harper & Row Publishers. https:// doi.org/10.1037/10038-001.

Yang, Hsiang-Yu, and Jon A. Sanford. 2012. "Home and Community Environmental Features, Activity Performance, and Community Participation among Older Adults with Functional Limitations." *Journal of Aging Research* 2012: 1–14. https://doi .org/10.1155/2012/625758.

Chapter Two

Environmental Justice and Outdoor Spaces

Structural Racism's Persistence and the Dynamics of Change

Yonit Yogev

AUTHOR'S NOTE

This chapter synopsizes research I completed in 2017 for a master's degree in environmental studies. Early stages of the research and literature review revealed the degree to which the voices of people of color have been excluded from outdoors-related decision-making processes as well as the dominant narrative of history. I also came to understand that given the importance of exposure to the outdoors for human health, the lack of equitable access for people of color should be seen as an environmental injustice.

I identify as a white, Jewish, middle-class woman, so while I can partially understand the marginalization/discrimination experienced by persons of color, my positionality has allowed me to benefit from both class and white privilege. Thus, it was particularly crucial that I explore my own implicit bias and the ways in which my background influenced the work. To that end, although I present this chapter through a personal narrative style that reflects my identification with this work and with environmental justice, I quote the participants as much as possible to weave the unfolding story of environmental justice and the changing dynamics of place and outdoor spaces in communities of color in the United States. My aim is to continually remind the reader of the centrality of the participants whose ideas this work presents and amplifies. I use the term "people of color" often and generally, simply for ease of writing, being fully cognizant of the vast variability contained in that term. This research, and any work I have done since, does not reflect the National Park Service's position and was carried out completely independently from it.

—Yonit Yogev, March 2019

In 1962, the Office of the Secretary of the Interior recruited Robert Stanton and appointed him into the ranks of the National Park Service (NPS) while he was a young college student attending an Historically Black University (HBU). His recruitment was a result of what Stanton referred to as the farsighted, thoughtful approach of high-level officials in government, namely President John F. Kennedy and Secretary of Interior Stuart Udall (Stanton, personal communication, June 2016). Stanton's seasonal work at Grand Teton National Park that summer launched an illustrious career with the NPS, culminating in his appointment as the first black park superintendent in the NPS in 1970, and later as its first black director. Federal agencies have been advised and required by the Civil Rights Act of 1964 and multiple executive memoranda to actively work on inclusion and equitable representation in their hiring and all aspects of their work. The most recent memorandum, issued by President Obama in January 2017, was the result of tireless grassroots organizing (next-100coalition, n.d.). Despite the legal imperative, neither federal agencies nor environmental organizations have succeeded in being fully accessible to many people in communities of color (Taylor 2015; Weber and Sultana 2013b). Moreover, millions of dollars are spent annually on programs that target under-represented youth, with little or no apparent change in the numbers of people of color working in or leading outdoor agencies (Fearn,[1] personal communication, November 2018; Taylor 2015). Stanton, Fearn, and many others continue to consult for organizations and agencies regarding steps they must take to become fully equitable and accessible, especially to people from underrepresented communities whose access is limited for a plethora of reasons.

This chapter presents the complexities and nuances of persistent structural racism that I contend surrounds our understanding of how people of color experience outdoor spaces, and the dynamics of how that understanding has been changing over the past few years. Terry Tempest Williams, author of *The Hour of Land: A Personal Topography of America's National Parks*, sums it up eloquently when she states,

> [O]ur national parks in all their particularity and peculiarity show us as much about ourselves as the landscapes they honor and protect. They can be seen as holograms of an America born of shadow and light; dimensional, full of contradictions and complexities. Our dreams, our generosities, our cruelties and crimes are absorbed into these parks like water. (Williams 2016, 12)

For this study, my research question was: *What multi-level approaches do people of color and national park staff or partners recommend to successfully increase diversity, equity, and inclusion in the park system, and what specific changes do they think need to occur in order for structural racism to be fully addressed?* Critical Race Theory (CRT) provided the theoretical framework, complemented by the concept of environmental justice (EJ), which provided a foundation and perspective for the study. Research focusing on EJ benefits from qualitative, participatory approaches in order to emphasize the centrality of personal lived experiences and narratives, and the deep collaboration needed for ensuring our public lands become equitable, just, all-inclusive spaces. Therefore, I employed a qualitative approach (Participatory Action Research or PAR), wherein forty research participants shared their lived experiences of a racialized outdoors, as well as their recommendations for steps our public lands agencies must take to dismantle the structural racism that lies deep within them (Byrne 2012; Taylor 2015). While I focused on the NPS when speaking with the participants, the results have clear implications for other federal agencies and the environmental movement as a whole (Taylor 2008; 2014).

In the following sections, I discuss the importance of structural racism at the root of these agencies' sluggish progress toward equity in staff compo- sition, hiring, visitation, and interpretation of history. I delve more deeply into CRT and EJ, after which I review the study context. Next, I explain the methodology, and finally, I relay the results, largely through the voices of participants. As is typical with PAR, the participants shared their stories, counternarratives, ideas, and recommendations for actions (Johnson 2017; Kindon 2003 in Hay 2010) that agencies and organizations must take in order to meet their missions and become fully accessible to all Americans.

STRUCTURAL RACISM: AT THE ROOT OF IT ALL

The nature of the research and my own positionality called for a critical explanatory framework such as CRT, which emerged out of "radical, criti- cal epistemologies which deconstruct the societal structures that create and perpetuate inequality, and the social relations and governmental policies that support continued inequality and injustice" (Yogev 2017, 30). CRT origi- nated in legal scholarship, and in time, the ideas spread into education and the social sciences. Its first underlying tenet states that the experience of rac- ism is the everyday experience of most people of color in the United States (Delgado and Stefancic 2012). The second tenet, "interest convergence," was developed by Derrick Bell, who asserted that gains in civil rights would not have occurred if those gains had not been in the interests of whites as well (Delgado and Stefancic 2012). Bell brought forward the example that World War II veterans of color did not return complacently to conditions of segre- gation after having fought side by side with their white fellow soldiers—at the same time the Cold War placed the (majority white) United States in the position of needing to appear socially progressive in order to win over uncommitted nations to their side, many of which were non-white majority nations (Delgado and Stefancic 2012).

The third tenet of CRT is that race is a social construction and the dominant population of whites racialize the different minority populations in different ways at different times according to the labor needs of a given time period (Delgado and Stefancic 2012). The fourth tenet emphasizes that those who experience racism are in the best position to write about it. This idea led to the importance of counter-storytelling and counternarratives—those that come from the lived experiences of people of color, who experience first-hand the insidious, sometimes subtle aspects of racism that whites do not experience, or worse, often perpetuate because of unexamined biases. Counternarratives led to the fifth tenet of CRT, which requires a reexamination of American history and its retelling from the standpoint of those whose voices have not been heard and whose histories have not been taught (Delgado and Stefancic 2012). As mentioned, the stories and counternarratives of the participants formed the essence of this research. Although CRT has been critiqued, reflected upon, and even reconceptualized abundantly, it remains a valuable perspective for understanding race and society (see Bonilla-Silva 2015; Crenshaw 2011).

Some of the first explanatory work on the institutional nature of racism goes back to the 1960s:

> [T]he process whereby, no matter whether the individual attitudes, motivations, and behaviour of ordinary white people were racist or not, all whites benefited from social structures and organizational patterns which continually disadvantaged blacks while allowing whites to stay well ahead in living standards, including housing, health and life span, neighbourhood amenities and safety, educational facilities and achievement, level of employment, and income and wealth. (Carmichael and Hamilton 1967 in Rattansi 2007, 132)

Further exploration of a systemic approach shows that "racism is not mere prejudice but, above all, institutional practices and mechanisms that form a system of racial domination" (Bonilla-Silva 2016, 27). Tied up in white privilege therefore, "racism exists today not as a remnant from the past or as the behavioral expression of prejudiced (bad) people as so many analysts believe. Instead racism remains in place because it benefits whites as a social group" (Bonilla-Silva 2016). The effects on people of color are usually invisible to those in the dominant race and culture, who often have no reason to question their position (Bonilla-Silva 2016).

The invisible nature of institutionalized racism for white people manifests in implicit bias, which DiAngelo describes as "unexamined beliefs that prop up our racial responses" (2018, 3). As humans we all have implicit biases, but if a white person is unaware of the barriers people of color face, there is no motivation to attempt to remove them (Delgado and Stefancic 2012; DiAngelo 2018). Because of the lack of exposure in our dominant white institutions, white people must consciously work on educating ourselves about it and bring our own individual implicit biases into everyday awareness (DiAngelo 2018). Textbooks, films, television, and other media have not traditionally included the stories of people of color (Finney 2014; Grossmann 2010). However, as people of color tell their stories and white people increasingly hear them, the dominant culture's versions are no longer the "only" truth, but rather "a" truth—one perspective among many, rather than history itself.

Racialized outdoor spaces are the complex result of institutionalized racism. The lack of access to the benefits of exposure to the outdoors is increasingly being viewed as an environmental *in*justice. The EJ movement has evolved over time to encompass various areas of focus including human environmental harm, unequal resource consumption across time and across groups, and discriminatory practices resulting in inequitable access to natural and human-made resources (Floyd and Johnson 2002). EJ trailblazers Dorceta Taylor and Robert Bullard and their colleagues have extensively researched the disconnect between the modern (white-dominated) environmental move-ment (generally focused on the physical environment and conservation) and the hugely detrimental effects of systemic environmental racism on commu-nities of color (Bullard, Johnson, and Torres 2011; Bullard and Wright 2009; Taylor 1992, 2000, 2008, 2014).

Both Taylor and Bullard expose the facts of environmental *in*justice rising from constrained access to outdoor spaces for underrepresented communities. They present the historically white-dominated environmental movement with the challenge of making the connections between the environment, social justice issues and environmental justice for the movement to remain relevant to a diverse populace and be more effective in the future.

EJ activists point out that environmentalism is directly connected to other social issues such as redlining and its institutionalized segregation of American cities and the subsequent lack of access to clean air, water, green spaces, or a decent education. With unequal access to the fundamental health benefits public lands and outdoor spaces provide, these communities experience yet another obstruction to achieving true equity in terms of how they can utilize those spaces and how or if they reap the benefits of basic health and well-being.

Societal and institutional change must occur in order to right past wrongs and sow seeds of justice. There has been huge momentum toward change on all fronts of social justice and human rights. However, in the absence of fundamental change at the level of structural racism, individual programs and policies can only go so far before the vagaries of cultural acceptance or rejection move the pendulum back and impede progress once again. In order to change institutions at the root, the participants in this research made abun-dantly clear that individual *and* system-wide policies and programs, as well as implicit bias, must be addressed simultaneously and from multiple angles.

CONTEXT: SITUATING THE STUDY

The concepts of structural and institutionalized racism and implicit bias discussed above draw our attention to the magnitude and all-pervasiveness of racialized spaces and their persistence through time. However, we cannot "understand modern forms of racism if we cannot or will not explore patterns of group behavior and their effects on individuals" (DiAngelo 2018, 12). The history of how our public lands came into being is one of the most egregious examples of environmental racism in U.S. history. Many of our national parks and forests were established on lands violently stolen from indigenous people who had been living on them for millennia (Finney 2014; Makopondo 2006; O'Brien and Njambi 2012). These are atrocities that must be included in our narratives about and interpretation of our national parks and their histories. Hearing the stories and counter-narratives we have not yet heard and retrieving those histories and stories that were effectively erased from our past is an inescapable and crucial way to begin to break down those barriers.

Academic as well as popular media sources complemented each other in my search for context and a greater understanding of equity and inclusion in outdoor spaces. The academic literature examines history and context; the popular media reveals stories that illustrate the theoretical in real time. Much of the academic literature about constraints to park visitation began to appear in the 1990s, including theoretical work related to race, ethnicity, and park use (Floyd 1999). Studies and surveys (some of which were contracted by the NPS) also focused on the demographics of visitors as well as employees (Taylor, Grandjean and Gramann 2011).

The early 2000s saw a growing critical approach (Shinew, Floyd, and Parry 2004), focusing on narratives that could complete the partial picture the demographics revealed (Byrne and Wolch 2009; Floyd and Johnson 2002; O'Brien and Njambi 2012; Weber and Sultana 2013a, 2013b). As the critical approach expanded (Taylor 2008, 2014), research focused more on constraints to park visitation as a direct result of structural racism and began with increasing frequency to use the terminology of EJ (Byrne 2012; O'Brien and Njambi 2012; Taylor 2008, 2014; Weber and Sultana 2013a, 2013b).

In recent years, geographers and others who study EJ have called for substantive changes to how public land agencies and environmental organizations operate (Finney 2014; Taylor 2008, 2014; Weber and Sultana 2013b). Increasing numbers of studies exposed individual stories of deficiencies and failures in NPS attempts to diversify and take the necessary steps toward becoming more equitable and inclusive (Makopondo 2006; Santucci et al 2014).

The mission of the NPS is to "preserve unimpaired the natural and cultural resources and values of the National Park System for the enjoyment, education, and inspiration of this and future generations" (National Park Service, n.d.). National parks are supposed to be for *all* Americans, an idea carved into the NPS's very existence. However, structural and institutionalized racism are key reasons why outdoor spaces have remained unwelcoming and exclusionary despite ongoing attempts to address this.

As discussed in the preceding section, structural racism not only stifles counternarratives but also renders people invisible, for example, through media representation, where the mostly white media portrayal of history shapes the narrative of who belongs where in outdoor spaces (Finney 2014). Whites see themselves enjoying the outdoors in a specific way, but blacks and other people of color come to see, in their own historical absence in media representation, that these spaces are not meant for them. Popular media I researched has burgeoned with newspaper articles, magazine feature stories, blogs, books, and films about the limits of access by communities of color to outdoor spaces and systemic racism in general (e.g., see DuVernay and Averick 2016; Finney 2014, 2016; Grossmann 2010; Nelson 2015, 2016a, 2016b; Peterman 2016a, 2016b, 2016c; Rowland-Shea 2016). Photos in magazines and books, television commercials, literature and film all inform us about our respective places in the outdoors (Finney 2014). If people of color do not feel they belong and do not feel welcome in such spaces, then public land agencies such as the NPS, whose stated mission is to serve all Americans, are fundamentally derelict in fulfilling that mission.

In the past few years, in short succession, several (now well-known) organizations such as Outdoor Afro and Latino Outdoors have sprung up from the grassroots, lighting the way for many others like them. These organizations formed out of people of color's unwillingness to wait for the dominant culture to invite them in (personal communications—Baker, November 2016; Gonzalez, May 2016; Participant #8, November 2016; Peterman, May 2016). Situating the research within its constantly changing societal context is analogous to the work that outdoors agencies and environmental organizations must themselves do to understand why things are the way they are and why they must change in order for a truly just and equitable society to emerge out of the turbulence.

METHODOLOGY

Participatory Action Research (PAR) is both an epistemological and a methodological approach (Hay 2010; Koirala-Azad and Fuentes 2009).

According to its fundamental components, it is community-based, oriented to the goal of changing a societal injustice, and an inherently democratic, dynamic, and iterative process. It challenges "old" ways of doing research and questions objectivity, and it emphasizes positionality (Johnson 2017). For this research project, the "community" of participants shared a passion for and worked toward increasing access to the outdoors for people from underrepresented communities. Since the research deals with structural racism "and how [it is] manifested through people's unequal access to and control over resources or their positions within inequitable social relationships" (Kindon 2003 in Hay 2010, 269), PAR was a logical choice for this type of research. Moreover, working towards EJ is an inherently democratic endeavor, requiring deep collaboration toward social change that will benefit the participants and society as a whole.

The Evergreen State College Human Subjects Review Board approved my proposal. All human subject interview protocols were followed, including obtaining written consent from participants. Snowball sampling through initial participant referrals led to a total of forty participants. I conducted in-depth, unstructured interviews that incorporated narrative and counter-storytelling with the participants who came from three "stakeholder" groups: people from communities of color with a stake in the outdoors, employees from the NPS, and people who work for partner organizations or environmental organizations with close ties to public lands (many of those in the latter two groups came from communities of color). The interviews took place over a period of seven months. Some were conducted in person and others by telephone. Included in the consent was permission to record the interviews (some participants requested anonymity and are identified here by randomly assigned numbers), as well as an offer for participants to become actively engaged in the research process. Many of them, already leaders in the movement for equity and justice in outdoor spaces, also helped guide the direction of this research. The integration of the forty interviews into a cohesive narrative resulted from regular consultation with them, in an iterative, highly reflexive process supported by the foundations of PAR.

To ensure data extraction quality, I assimilated the many stories, thoughts and ideas, by "sitting with" the material over time. Utilizing abundant notes from interviews, repeated listening to the audiotapes, and ongoing conversations with participants, I formulated diagrams which helped make sense of the material and identify themes and subthemes. Critical reflexivity, a crucial aspect of PAR, was central to realizing that the sense I made of the data, even with regular input from participants, still reflected my own lived experience, perspective, and privilege (Stoudt, Fox, and Fine 2012), and to guarding against my own unexamined biases.

FINDINGS AND DISCUSSION

Teasing out the salient themes and subthemes that flowed from participant interviews and follow-up conversations, the major themes emerged into absence and marginalization, barriers to access, and solution-oriented recommendations. This section is organized according to these three themes and their subthemes.

Absence and Marginalization

"Not seeing themselves" or absence was the first subtheme that emerged from participants' stories and counternarratives. While these stories are wide-ranging, they repeatedly recount not seeing "people who look like them" in the outdoors. An important aspect of this invisibility comes from how history is presented and interpreted. Many national park units are attempting to learn how best to interpret this "difficult" history. Their progress is constrained in part by the fact that there are stories they need to tell but sometimes choose not to. The following story poignantly illustrates this point.

Participant #2 began work at an NPS site that manages a cultural estate donated by the descendants of a historic figure. As part of the orientation, the employee was given a tour of the estate by a park guide. Although not normally part of public tours, the employee was taken to the attic where the employee noticed an enclosure-like structure. After asking about it, the employee was informed that the structure was used as a sort of holding pen for slaves, probably as punishment. The tour guide explained that at the request of the donor family, the park discouraged interpreting this particular history and the history of slaves on the estate in general when giving tours to the public. The guide seemed uncomfortable with this omission but probably feared the consequences of not following suit. The participant expressed strongly that "withholding stories like that is not helping us move forward in these conversations" (Participant #2, personal communication, November 2016). The NPS's selective interpretation of history greatly influences the lessons and impressions we all take away from these important places.

Other participants told stories of marginalization and how their families experienced the civil rights era and the years prior to its activism. Post–World War II America was an era of increasing prosperity in the United States, but also a time of increasing unrest. Typically left out of the post–World War II prosperity narrative of U.S. history is that not all segments of the population flourished. As interstate highways crisscrossed the nation and "America" took to the roads to see and enjoy the beauty of their land, national park visitation began to increase. "See the USA in your Chevrolet" was an advertisement of the day (Participant #1, personal communication, 2017). For most people of color, the narrative was quite different. *The Negro Motorist Green Book* (later popularly "The Green Book") by Victor Hugo Green was published between 1936 and 1966. It helped blacks navigate American highways, which were largely unfriendly and often dangerous to them. The same participant described the experience for an African American family traveling across the country in the following way: They would arrive at a hotel with a vacancy sign and the clerk or owner would say, "Oh, sorry, we just got a call. . . . [W]e're full." The "tone and energy of the proprietor [was] . . . you need to leave." (ibid.).

Some participants recounted their parents' humiliation as well as their own learned sense of not belonging, and the ever-lurking threats. "This was America's own apartheid," said Participant #1. "The areas that might cater to African Americans were islands. The ocean itself was hostile to their pres ence" (ibid.). The participant also described sundown towns, areas that blacks knew to avoid after dark because the townspeople could act with impunity. Sundown towns were still in existence well into the 1970s.

Participant #1 described this other side of post–World War II prosperity:

[T]he literal dark side of that story is who was NOT doing all of those things. It was easier and safer just to stay in your community. So, the internalized perception was that those places, "America's Best Idea"[2] were not for you. And because there isn't that cultural history, that's why it's been so difficult to jumpstart a new tradition. . . . [N]*o one goes on vacation to a place that fills them with fear and anxiety.* (Participant #1, emphasis added)

Parents and grandparents pass these stories down to their children and grand-children. The powerful effects of intergenerational trauma, especially as it relates to the African American community and other communities of color, are now better recognized (DuVernay 2016; Finney 2014).

The stories of marginalization and racial injustice from the distant past are difficult enough to hear. However, when those experiences and history mesh with the younger generation's own experiences of racism, they become intensely personal. Individual acts of racism and institutionalized racism are interwoven in highly complex and nuanced ways.

One activist shared stories that highlighted the reasons for her activism. She told me

there are places where we are not welcome. . . . [T]his black family a year and a half ago . . . went camping . . . north of Oakland, in a place where they've always camped. This . . . family . . . was totally experienced [in] camping. And in the middle of the night, someone in an adjacent camp was screaming racial epithets at them and chasing them with a shovel. (Participant #8, personal com-munication, November 2016)

She continued:

> [W]e had a "play in nature" event and I was working with this group that brings together . . . "found in nature" materials. . . . They were partnered with [us] . . . a well-meaning attempt to engage diverse audiences, they provided transportation, and had done all the engagement . . . and got these young kids and families. . . . And there was a woman who came by, a neighbor, and she was like, "what the heck is going on here? You have all these invasive species here." And she kept going on and on about "invasive species." Missing the fact that the kids were having this tactile, beautiful moment with their families in nature . . . but she kept going on and on about invasive species. And honey, she was not just talking about the plants.

The stories, then, are not just stories or history any longer. They are a person's current everyday reality writ large and super-imposed on the ever-present looming history of their people.

Barriers to Access

Another participant-identified theme overlapping "marginalization" was barriers to access due to current hiring practices, recruitment and retention, and lack of funding in public lands agencies. Positive change in hiring practices comes slowly in large federal bureaucracies like the NPS—until then, participants suggested that changes might entail rewriting position descriptions, using direct hiring authorities, and ensuring hiring managers are aware of the options available to them (personal communications—Beall, January 2017; Participant #6, November 2016, May 2017; Slaughter May 2016, March 2017; Thieda, October 2016). Regarding recruitment, the field data suggested NPS's internal work shows implicit bias. Regarding retention, again, unless the organization is actively working on implicit bias, people from marginalized communities hired into a majority white organization are likely to feel isolated, and are more apt to leave (personal communications—Participant #9, January 2017; Participant #7, January 2017). Another participant states, "[I]f you don't change the culture, none of the other solutions will stick" (Thieda, personal communication, October 2016).

Solution-oriented Recommendations

The participants made valuable recommendations for how the NPS and other agencies should address marginalization and reduce or remove the barriers to access. These themes are interconnected on many levels and all of them must be the *simultaneous focus* of outdoor and environmental agencies working toward becoming equitable and just organizations.

Role Models and Mentors

Many participants articulated the positive influence of mentors when they were younger or new to a job. They expressed how powerful those relationships were, especially when they continued over the long-term. The encouragement, support, and guidance they gained were invaluable and participants often described these relationships as changing the course of their lives. Moreover, the experience of being mentored had the effect not only of modeling mentoring, but also of engendering in the participants the desire to become mentors themselves. Another aspect of mentoring that participants spoke of was the importance of an organization or agency having a mentoring program or culture. Specifically, for people of color entering an organization or field that is white-dominated, in the absence of intentional mentoring, participants described feeling isolated.

Targeted Environmental Education (EE)

Robert Stanton, mentioned earlier in this chapter, emphasized the importance of courageous leadership at the top. For Director Stanton, a courageous leader possesses the farsightedness to see the need for long-range, strategic planning "to develop that kind of interest on the part of prospective candidates coming into the work force by engaging young people in conservation programs as far back as junior high or beyond that in terms of education programs" (Stanton, personal communication, June 2016). Many organizations focus on youth education since they are "the most influential in impacting the attitudes of their parents" (Fearn, personal communication, March 2019). Moreover, they are the future generations mentioned in the mission of the NPS. Latino Outdoors, for instance, actively engages Latinx families in outdoor excursions. This holistic strategy exemplifies a culturally relevant approach in which the employees and volunteers come from the same communities (Pinon, personal communication, January 2017). This organization found that if the parents are not on board, the youth will not participate. The strong family orientation in Latinx communities dictated a successful strategy for Latino Outdoors. This approach afforded the added benefit of reaching a larger adult population with previously limited access to the outdoors.

Youth Leadership Development

In the words of a passionate environmental educator of color,

> people need to put energy and resources . . . to engaging young people of color.
> . . . NPS conservation staff . . . often cite exposure to public lands and nature as

the key. For example, going on a camping trip, visiting Yosemite, will unlock a world young people will fall in love with and protect. I think this is a deeply false narrative that doesn't . . . explore the problems with the cultural norms of NPS and how it positions young people. . . . How young people are viewed and treated will have the largest impact on whether the park service will be heading in the right directions to increase DEI [Diversity, Equity, and Inclusion]. [The youth's] voices and their leadership should be transforming the park service to be reflective of their values, hopes, dreams, and the cultural and natural resources they want to protect. (Participant #3, November 2016)

This participant continued,

They have to care about themselves and their community before they can care about a national park 100 miles away. A lot of people miss that message—think they should be doing more restoration work or [be] more focused on climate change. It goes to this idea of relevancy. If it's a true relationship between a park and young people, we should be as open to a conversation that young people want to have, as we expect them to be open to a conversation we want to have. That's what youth development is—giving them a voice.

Diversity Training (Right Ways and Wrong Ways)

The prominent Oregon-based Center for Diversity and the Environment describes such work in this way: "Diversity and inclusion work is not swift: it is an iterative process of awareness building, information gathering, analysis, vision development, planning, and action. There is no magic short cut" (Center for Diversity and the Environment, n.d.). In the process of doing this research, I learned the importance of "doing" diversity trainings the "right way." Dobbin and Kalev (2016) and Morse (2016) argue that the environmental world has a lot to learn from the corporate world when it comes to analyzing what works and what does not, namely, so-called "diversity trainings." Most outdoor agencies have continued to use trainings or practices long since proven outmoded or outright ineffective. There are many potential reasons for this—from lack of funding to inertia to institutionalized racism.

For diversity trainings to succeed, an organization must be fully committed to equity and inclusion at all levels. The trainings must be done on a regular basis and must include a variety of learning types. These should include both formal sessions with a trained facilitator, as well as informal readings and discussions and *regular integration of concepts and conversations into the daily work-life of all the employees at all levels of the organization* (emphasis added) (Dobbin and Kalev 2016; Morse 2016).

One example of effective training came from a participant. Her work team regularly read an article or chapter about equity and justice and took a few minutes every day during their morning meetings to discuss how it related to their own implicit biases and where the implicit bias showed up in their everyday work, thinking, and actions. This type of activity makes it real and relevant for employees, while leadership must work to create a safe space for people to share. She continued, "[T]his isn't something you do once a year. It's always thinking about it in our work" (Participant #9, personal communication, January 2017). As one EE and diversity training veteran put it, "[W]hen you're looking at diversity, equity and inclusion, you're really looking at changing the culture of the organization and that the learning is going to take a decade or two or three. . . . [F]irst we have to understand what the biases are, then we have to un-learn them" (Thieda, personal communication, October 2016).

Relevancy

Making the outdoors relevant to younger generations as well as to underrepresented communities is the "spoke of the wheel" that brings all the other subthemes together. In 2013 the NPS established the Office of Relevancy, Diversity, and Inclusion (RDI), with the intention of addressing structural racism strategically throughout the service. The RDI website states that "relevancy is achieved when all Americans are able to establish a personal connection to the National Park Service parks and programs and find meaning and value in the mission of the National Park Service" (National Park Service, n.d.). One participant who was an NPS Urban Fellow (a program the agency instituted in 2015 in its attempt to connect the people in urban centers with national parks), suggested early in the research process that I add a sub-question regarding whether

> the NPS is telling the stories that are relevant to African Americans. . . . [I]t's not just a relationship with the outdoors that isn't being realized, but stories of national significance that the national parks should be telling. For example, the Black Panther party was founded 50 years ago, it had chapters in almost every state and . . . around the country and world that shaped the Civil Rights movement. Where can people interested in the Panthers see and experience this story? Currently, there is no national recognition. With so many hip-hop and R & B artists being the descendants of Panthers, and their music and culture shaped by it, wouldn't it be relevant to tell those stories also? That's one example of how the NPS can be more relevant to people of color and millennials, by making connections that they can identify with and providing an easy entry into the world of other NPS sites. (Slaughter, personal communication, September 2016)

Relevancy to the larger societal context is also essential. Around the time I was conducting interviews, there was growing unrest among people of color on American streets. Repeated headlines on police killings of unarmed black men brought to the forefront of cultural dialogue the fact that the murders were not isolated incidents; rather, they were the by-product of structural racism and implicit bias. A particularly potent story revealed such relevancy:

> The Black Lives Matter movement (BLM) is on my mind a lot. What is our role as an organization? The [partner organization] has been really silent about it. That's been difficult for me. I want to really believe in the place I work with. I also want to believe I'm not crazy in seeing an intersection. Wanting to make parks for all, and not acknowledging that there are some deadly serious injustices and inequity going on in our city, in our country. To feel like this organization, this park is playing neutral is painful for me. I am super privileged in that I have outlets in my work. And that the director . . . has not hesitated to let us engage in however we want to engage. . . . [I]ncreasingly it's felt like a big weight—the silence of the organization. (Participant #3, personal communication, November 2016)

The unrest in the streets was the most relevant thing for the youth in the participant's program. Some of the work in the Pacific Northwest demonstrates how the NPS can better communicate moving in the direction of engaging youth and local communities. Charles Beall, superintendent of the Seattle National Parks Units, asserted that they need to ask the questions that mattered to local communities. For example, "How can the NPS add value to people's lives?" (Beall, personal communication, January 2017). He described a meeting with a local community development association to illustrate his point. "Their questions are not, 'when do the trails open at Olympic National Park?' or 'what are the hours of your visitor center?' But it's . . . 'you know, we just finished this strategic plan about how to improve our community and number one on the list is we want more opportunities for physical activity—we don't have enough green space here. . . . Anything the Park Service can do to help there?' 'Oh yeah!!'" says Beall. "'Absolutely!' It's allowing the community to set what's important and meaningful and helping them be successful" (ibid.).

Partnerships and "Deep" Collaboration

The NPS has been partnering with community organizations for decades. However, "partnership" is not the same as "collaboration" (Makopondo 2006). The latter requires the most intense effort and attention. "Collaboration entails coming into a community, and asking what *they* need, being open to doing things differently, and listening" (Beall, personal communication, January 2017). Past practice in many agencies was to develop a plan and hope the community would buy in. However, for a community to genuinely support a plan, participants made it clear that the target communities must have an equal part in creating it. According to the participants, combining deep collaboration with mentoring programs, youth leadership development, targeted EE, and equity and inclusion training, all with a mind to increasing relevancy, are critical to the success of equity and inclusion efforts in these agencies.

CONCLUDING THOUGHTS

The process of change, especially social change, is inherently dynamic and difficult to pin down. Yet, in the brief time I have been involved in studying and working for equity in outdoor spaces, change has occurred rapidly both in the growing awareness and activism around equitable access to outdoor spaces, as well as in the language we use to think about and describe this movement. In a few years, Outdoor Afro and Latino Outdoors have grown exponentially, and brought blacks and Latinx respectively into outdoor spaces in numbers unprecedented prior to their existence. These organizations have created a sea change, allowing people of color to experiment with outdoor spaces in new ways and opening the doors for young people of color to find their place in outdoor-related careers. They have also paved the way for multiple organizations and individuals, creating a ground-swell of activity and a shift in the norms of who we now see in outdoor spaces. Such changes indicate that the NPS and other environmental organizations and agencies need to fundamentally change how they operate in order to be welcoming spaces to visitors and staff of color.

Participatory research is an inherently deeply collaborative and inclusive process, offering valuable lessons to the NPS and other agencies. Not only does it give voice to lesser-known aspects of our environmental history, but it embodies a key practice that outdoor agencies themselves can utilize in order to address inequity within their systems. Deep collaboration with underrepresented communities must be at the very heart of dismantling structural racism and implicit bias. In this research, the "counter-narratives [of forty people] weave a tapestry of moving stories of struggle and empowerment together with creative ideas for change. It is only when we begin to understand our own implicit bias that we can begin to chip away at the insidious way racism works within our society" (Yogev 2017, 172). Furthermore, the NPS and other outdoor agencies must heed the wave of grass-roots action that is dynamically changing the face of who is coming into the outdoors. For these agencies to stay relevant into the future requires deep collaboration, listening, finding out what communities need and want, and helping them achieve their goals. Listening to the stories and counternarratives of people from underrepresented communities is crucial to demonstrating genuine intent as well as to learning and interpreting the outdoors in a way that will be relevant for future generations.

Finally, outdoor agencies must take a multi-modal, multi-faceted approach—intentionally dismantling the old ways and creating new ones. Role models and mentoring, updated equity and implicit bias training, youth leadership development, targeted EE and outreach, and genuine, deep collaboration must all be part of the new system in order to keep the momentum moving and to continue to be relevant. This requires ongoing, integrated, and collaborative effort within and among the agencies and the people they include and represent, telling the stories that hold meaning, and serving *all* Americans more equitably and inclusively. In the words of Su Thieda (personal communication 2017), "I actually have this great hope that the environment can be the context for us unraveling racism faster. Because we share this, because we share the earth in common, we know we have to figure this out."

NOTES

1. Mickey Fearn served as deputy director of the NPS from 2012 to 2015. He was not one of the forty participants recruited for the study, but this work benefited from his input. Other named sources listed in this work as personal communication were participants who provided informed consent to share their words and identity.

2. The phrase "America's Best Idea" comes from the writings of historian Wallace Stegner: "National parks are the best idea we ever had. Absolutely American, absolutely democratic, they reflect us at our best rather than our worst." (Duncan and Burns 2010, xxii). While not as "absolutely democratic" as Stegner perceived them to be, it remains a vbgoal for many EJ proponents and various stakeholders given voice here.

REFERENCES

Bonilla-Silva, Eduardo. 2015. "More than Prejudice: Restatement, Reflections, and New Directions in Critical Race Theory." *Sociology of Race and Ethnicity* 1 (1): 73–87.

———. 2016. "Down the Rabbit Hole: Color-Blind Racism in *Obamerica*." In *The Myth of Racial Color Blindness: Manifestations, Dynamics, and Impact*, edited by Helen A. Neville, Miguel E. Gallardo and Derald Wing Sue, 25–38. Washington, DC: American Psychological Association.

Bullard, Robert D., Glenn S. Johnson, and Angel O. Torres. 2011. *Environmental Health and Racial Equity in The United States: Building Environmentally Just, Sustainable and Livable Communities*. Washington, DC: American Public Health Association.

Bullard, Robert D., and Beverly Wright, eds. 2009. *Race, Place, and Environmental Justice after Hurricane Katrina: Struggles to Reclaim, Rebuild, And Revitalize New Orleans and the Gulf Coast*. New York and London: Routledge.

Byrne, Jason. 2012. "When Green Is White: The Cultural Politics of Race, Nature and Social Exclusion in a Los Angeles Urban National Park." *Geoforum* 43 (3): 595–611. doi:10.1016/j.geoforum.2011.10.002

Byrne, Jason, and Jennifer Wolch. 2009. "Nature, Race, and Parks: Past Research and Future Directions for Geographic Research." *Progress in Human Geography* 33 (6): 743–65. doi:10.1177/0309132509103156

Byrne, Jason, Jennifer Wolch, and Jin Zhang. 2009. "Planning for Environmental Justice in an Urban National Park." *Journal of Environmental Planning & Management* 52 (3): 365–92. doi:10.1080/09640560802703256.

Center for Diversity and the Environment. n.d. *Building the Foundation: Exploring Diversity, Equity, and Inclusion*. Accessed April 4, 2017. http://cdeinspires.org/building-the-foundation-exploring-diversity-equity-inclusion.

Crenshaw, Kimberlé. W. 2011. "Twenty Years of Critical Race Theory: Looking Back to Move Forward." *Connecticut Law Review* 43 (5): 1253–354.

Delgado, Richard, and Jean Stefancic. 2012. *Critical Race Theory: An Introduction*. New York and London: New York University Press.

DiAngelo, Robin. 2018. *White Fragility: Why It's So Hard for White People to Talk about Racism*. Boston: Beacon Press.

Dobbin, Frank, and Alexandra Kalev. 2016. "Why Diversity Programs Fail." *Harvard Business Review* July-August: 52–60. Accessed April 4, 2017. https://hbr.org/2016/07/why-diversity-programs-fail.

Duncan, Dayton, and Ken Burns. 2010. *The National Parks: America's Best Idea*. New York: Alfred A. Knopf.

DuVernay, Ava, and Spencer Averick. 2016. *13th*. Netfix Original. Directed by Ava DuVernay. Los Gatos, CA: Netflix, October 7, 2016. http://www.netflix.com/title/80091741.

Finney, Carolyn. 2014. *Black Faces, White Spaces: Reimagining the Relationship of African Americans to the Great Outdoors*. Chapel Hill: The University of North Carolina Press.

———. 2016. "It Matter Who You See in Outdoor Media." *Outside Magazine*, August 8, 2016. https://www.outsideonline.com/2075586/it-matters-who-you-see-outdoor-media.

Floyd, Myron F. 1999. *Race, Ethnicity and Use of the National Park System*. Washington, DC: US Department of the Interior, National Park Service Social Science Program.

Floyd, Myron F., and Cassandra Y. Johnson. 2002. "Coming to Terms with Environmental Justice in Outdoor Recreation: A Conceptual Discussion with Research Implications." *Leisure Sciences* 24 (1): 59–77. doi:10.1080/01490400252772836.

Grossmann, James. 2010. "Expanding the Palette: As America's Population Become More Diverse, Will Its Changes Be Reflected in Park Visitors?" *National Parks* 84 (3): 1–14.

Hay, Iain. 2010. *Qualitative Research Methods in Human Geography*. 3rd ed. To-ronto, Canada: Oxford University Press.

Johnson, Laura R. 2017. *Community-Based Qualitative Research: Approaches for Education and the Social Sciences*. Thousand Oaks, CA: Sage Publications.

Koirala-Azad, Shabnam, and Emma Fuentes. 2009. "Introduction: Activist Schol-arship—Possibilities and Constraints of Participatory Action Research." *Social Justice* 36 (4): 1–5.

Makopondo, Richard O. B. 2006. "Creating Racially/Ethnically Inclusive Partner-ships in Natural Resource Management and Outdoor Recreation: The Challenges, Issues, And Strategies." *Journal of Park & Recreation Administration* 24 (1): 7–31.

Morse, Gardiner. 2016. "Designing a Bias-Free Organization: An Interview with Iris Bohnet." *Harvard Business Review* July-August: 63–67.

National Park Service. n.d. "About Us." Accessed on April 20, 2019. http://www.nps.gov/aboutus/index.htm.

Nelson, Glenn. 2015. "Why Are Our Parks So White?" *New York Times*, July 12, 2015. https://www.nytimes.com/2015/07/12/opinion/sunday/diversify-our-national-parks.html.

———. 2016a. "Why Has the National Park Service Gotten Whiter?" *High Country News,* April 8, 2016. https://www.hcn.org/issues/48.14/why-has-the-national-park-service-gotten-whiter.

———. 2016b. "As National Park Service Turns 100, Seattle Ranger Personifies Change." *Seattle Times,* August 21, 2016. https://www.seattletimes.com/life/outdoors/as-national-park-service-turns-100-seattle-ranger-personifies-change/.

Next 100 Coalition: Public Lands for All. http://next100coalition.org/. Accessed on April 20, 2019.

O'Brien, William E., and Wairimu Ngarũiya Njambi. 2012. "Marginal Voices in 'Wild' America: Race, Ethnicity, Gender, and 'Nature' in the National Parks." *Journal of American Culture* 35 (1): 15–25. doi:10.1111/j.1542-734X.2011.00794.x

Peterman, Audrey. 2016a "Needed: A National Conversation on the Future of Our Parks." *Huffington Post* (Blog), May 26, 2016. https://www.huffingtonpost.com/audrey-peterman.

———. 2016b. "Fears That 'Diverse and Qualified Are Mutually Exclusive Paralyze Change in Park Service." *Huffington Post* (Blog), August 9, 2016. https://www.huffingtonpost.com/audrey-peterman.

———. 2016c. "Vital Questions Must Be Answered on Eve of Park Service Centen-nial." *Huffington Post* (Blog). August 15, 2016. https://www.huffingtonpost.com/audrey-peterman.

Rattansi, Ali. 2007. *Racism: A Very Short Introduction*. Oxford and New York: Ox-ford University Press, Inc.

Rowland-Shea, Jenny. 2016. "The Rise to Power of the Congressional Anti-Parks Caucus." Center for American Progress. Accessed April 11, 2016. https://www.americanprogress.org/issues/green/reports/2016/04/11/135044/the-rise-to-power-of-the-congressional-anti-parks-caucus/.

Santucci, David C., Myron F. Floyd, Jason N. Bocarro, and Karla A. Henderson. 2014. "Visitor Services Staff Perceptions of Strategies to Encourage Diversity at Two Urban National Parks." *Journal of Park & Recreation Administration* 32 (3): 15–28.

Shinew, Kimberly J., Myron F. Floyd, and Diana Parry. 2004. "Understanding the Relationship between Race and Leisure Activities and Constraints: Exploring an Alternative Framework." *Leisure Sciences* 26 (2): 181–99. doi:10.1080/01490400490432109.

Stoudt, Brett G., Madeline Fox, and Michelle Fine. 2012. "Contesting Privilege with Critical Participatory Action Research." *Journal of Social Issues* 68 (1): 178–93.

Taylor, Dorceta E. 1992. "Can the Environmentalism Movement Attract and Maintain the Support of Minorities?" In *Race and the Incidence of Environmental Hazards*, edited by Bullard, R., 53–62. Boston, MA: South End Press.

———. 2000. "Meeting the Challenge of Wild Land Recreation Management: Demographic Shifts and Social Inequality." *Journal of Leisure Research* 32 (1): 171–79.

———. 2008. "Diversity and the Environment: Myth-Making and the Status of Minorities in the Field." *Research in Social Problems & Public Policy* 15: 89–147.

———. 2014. "The State of Diversity in Environmental Organizations: Mainstream NGO's, Foundations, and Government Agencies." Green 2.0 Working Group. Accessed December 20, 2015. https://www.diversegreen.org/wp-content/uploads/2015/10/FullReport_Green2.0_FINAL.pdf.

———. 2015. "Gender and Racial Diversity in Environmental Organizations: Uneven Accomplishments and Cause for Concern." *Environmental Justice* 8: 165–80.

Taylor, Patricia A., Burke D. Grandjean, and James H. Gramann. 2011. *National Park Service Comprehensive Survey of the American Public, 2008–2009: Racial and Ethnic Diversity of National Park System Visitors and Non-visitors*. National Resource Report NPS/NRSS/SSD/NRR—2011432. National Park Service, Fort Collins, Colorado.

Weber, Joe, and Selima Sultana. 2013a. "The Civil Rights Movement and the Future of the National Park System in a Racially Diverse America." *Tourism Geographies* 15 (3): 444–69. doi:10.1080/14616688.2012.675515.

———. 2013b. "Why Do So Few Minority People Visit National Parks? Visitation and the Accessibility of 'America's Best Idea.'" *Annals of the Association of American Geographers* 103 (3): 437–64. doi:10.1080/00045608.2012.689240.

Williams, Terry Tempest. 2016. *The Hour of Land: A Personal Topography of America's National Parks*. New York: Sarah Crichton Books, Farrar, Straus and Giroux.

Yogev, Yonit. 2017. "Diversity, Equity and Inclusion in the National Park Service: Narratives, Counter-Narratives and the Importance of Moving beyond Demographics." Master's thesis. Evergreen State College.

Chapter Three

Subversion of Gender Justice

Public Policy on Sri Lankan Migrant Housemaids

Vidyamali Samarasinghe

Currently an estimated 1.7 million Sri Lankans work overseas, most of them in the countries of the Gulf or Middle East region. An increasing flow of migrant workers from Sri Lanka, especially housemaids began in the early 1980s, and peaked in 1997, when it accounted for approximately 75 percent of total Sri Lankan migrant workers. At that time, along with female migrant workers from Indonesia and the Philippines, Sri Lankan female migrant workers outnumbered their male counterparts (Gamburd 2000, 35). By 2002, the proportion of female migrant workers had dropped to 65 percent of the total and then to 51.7 percent by 2009 (Sri Lanka Bureau of Foreign Employment [SLBFE] 2010). By 2016, the proportion of females to male migrant workers had declined to 34.7 percent of the total (Central Bank 2017). Despite these declines, more than eighty thousand Sri Lankan women migrated for overseas employment in 2017, 80 percent of whom were recruited for employment as housemaids in the Gulf region/Middle East (Central Bank 2017).

Sri Lanka has earned a reputation of a diaspora that has significant impact on many aspects of Sri Lanka. One such impact is on the Sri Lankan economy. Sri Lankan overseas housemaids account for the highest proportion of a single employment category among all transnational wageworkers from Sri Lanka. The remittances that overseas workers send back to their country, estimated at over $7 billion annually, is the largest foreign currency earner, surpassing the value of garment exports (Central Bank 2017). The earnings of the housemaids account for a significant proportion of such remittances. Though their earnings are low, Sri Lankan female domestic workers are known to be great savers among all fixed term Sri Lankan migrant workers, putting aside an estimated 92 to 96 percent of their earnings, almost all of which they reportedly remit home (Atukorale 1990). As Frantz has noted, as a single group sending remittances back to the county,

Sri Lankan migrant domestic workers have been one of Sri Lanka's most successful exports (Frantz 2013).

Over 75 percent of Sri Lankan migrant housemaids are married with children (Save the Children, Sri Lanka 2006), which also has a social impact on families and communities left behind. The Sri Lankan government has created national policy that aims to restrain women, especially mothers leaving children behind for domestic work overseas. This chapter focuses on examining gender justice, patriarchy, and masculine hegemony of such policies on the housemaid diaspora. The chapter organization follows the following sequence. First, I briefly analyze the theoretical bases of the discourse on social justice and its ramifications for understanding the prevalence of gender injustice. I argue that gender injustice in policy is a manifestation of patriarchy, intersected by class, created by the power of hegemonic masculinity. Second, I present the methods and multiple sources of published literature and textual data. Third, I analyze the prevalence of gendered injustice in public policy on female migrant domestic workers, drawing critical attention to the impact of the Family Background Report Circular (FBRC) of 2013 mandated by the Government of Sri Lanka (GOSL). Fourth, I showcase the highly contradictory scenario where the GOSL extracts the comparative advantage of cheap female labor to earn needed foreign currency via remittances, while it also entrenches gender injustice by imposing restrictions based on the perception of the sanctity of the mother-child relationship for women seeking such jobs. Fifth, I show how women, desperate to seek wage-earning opportunities overseas embark on risky strategies in order to achieve their goal of migrating overseas for employment. Finally, I briefly highlight possible ways to limit/reverse the gender injustices perpetrated by the GOSL on migrant housemaids.

GENDER JUSTICE, PATRIARCHY, AND MASCULINE HEGEMONY

Justice as fairness, a theory articulated by John Rawls, a political philosopher in his seminal book *Justice as Fairness* (Rawls 1971) and restated in 2001 provides the principles of justice identified as a fundamental premise for the development of modern social order. More specifically, his theory of social justice views "just" economic distribution as a result of fairness and equality of opportunity. Thus, as the main drivers of economic opportunity, modern nation states are assumed to have free and fair access to equal opportunities. It is also assumed that a community of citizens would put in place cooperative arrangements that would benefit all. However, in practice, equality and fairness is not the norm of social practices and in modern states a plethora of socioeconomic and political factors intersect to subvert Rawls's articulation of universal principles of justice and fairness (see Sen 1991, 2009). One such subversion comes in the form of gendered social injustices. Based on the premise that people are situated differently according to their gender, feminist theorists have identified both overt and covert forms of institutional gender injustice demonstrated over a range of issues ranging from gendered dimensions of war, human rights, global governance, political freedom, migration, indebtedness, poverty, and climate change (Jagger 2009).

Gender injustice in modern societies is attributed mainly to the prevalence of patriarchal practices in society. As Lerner (1986) argues, organizational principles of society, such as ethnicity, caste, race, and religion have invariably brought out different faces of patriarchy over time and place, aiding in numerous ways to weave its norms tightly into the fabric of society. Patriarchy, in its modern usage, captures the overall gendered relations of subordination and power. A powerful driving force that entrenches patriarchy in modern society is hegemonic masculinity. Masculinities, just like femininities, structured by gender relations are pluralistic and framed by multiple social and geographic interstices (Cornwall, Karioris, and Lindisfarne 2016) that facilitate hierarchies of power. Hegemonic masculinity blends this pluralistic nature of masculinity with the Gramscian concept of hegemony and is about men winning and holding power over other men who do not conform to heteronormativity or other perceptions of masculinity, as well as over women, who by the very definition of being female are perceived to lack the power of maleness (Connell 1987; Connell and Messerschmidt 2005).

Furthermore, as Donaldson has noted, an essential part of the process of establishing masculine hegemony in society is in its ability to "impose a definition of the situation, to set the terms in which events are understood and issues discussed, to formulate ideals and define morality" (Donaldson 1993, 644). Masculine hegemony entrenches patterns and practice, not merely roles, which allow men's domination over women to continue (Connell and Messerschmidt 2005; Donaldson 1993). While patriarchy explains the overarching system of the dominance of the male agenda over the female agenda, masculine hegemony captures the dominant practices of males over females *at all levels and hierarchies* from individual to group behavior.

Males in patriarchal societies have jealously guarded their supremacy in the public sphere of political decision making as a male preserve by exercising hegemonic control over the political agenda on women's lives in three ways: first, by enacting laws and statutes that control women's role in the reproductive sphere; second, by the failure to enact public provisions that would create enabling conditions for women to successfully straddle the private sphere of reproduction and public sphere of production; and third, by using their position in the public sphere to articulate the importance and indeed, the sanctity of traditions, conventions and beliefs that are orchestrated to confirm that a woman's place is in the home (Samarasinghe 2015).

The most fundamental way in which patriarchy is embedded in society is the demarcation of the primary role for women in the reproductive/domestic sphere, physically separate from the sphere of production in the public sphere inhabited by men. While gender construction frames the main narrative of women's role in household caregiving, class within gender adds a decisive dimension of machinations of public policy. While women who are better educated and in positions of leadership in the public sphere of production still have to juggle demands of motherhood and childcare (Sandberg 2013), they enjoy the financial advantage of hiring another woman as nanny or housekeeper. Poorer women who become housemaids run the higher social risk of being targets of criticism of neglecting their so called primary social responsibility of caring for the children when compelled by economic necessity to work away from home.

METHODOLOGY

My methodology entailed undertaking an interpretive analysis of multiply-sourced textual data and generating and applying a theoretical framework under which they could be cohesively understood, using Sri Lankan state policy as a case in point. The data collection of Sri Lankan material for the study included four sets of mutually supportive literature. First, I undertook an extensive perusal and analysis of GOSL reports on migration of its citizens for employment, in particular as housemaids. This included a large number of reports and circulars produced by the SLBFE and reports commissioned by the Ministry of Foreign Employment on Sri Lankan migrant housemaids and in particular on the implementing processes of the FBRC.

Second, I was able to obtain and peruse the publicly available reports and documents maintained by five officially registered foreign employment agencies located in Colombo. This was an important resource since the SLBFE has left the entire responsibility of pre-departure certification of housemaids in the hands of the foreign employment agencies and their subagents. Aspiring migrant housemaids are required to provide the officially authenticated certification to the privately owned foreign employment agencies.

Third, I undertook an extensive literature survey on reports compiled by local as well as foreign NGOs on migrant housemaids. These included surveys undertaken by the Sri Lanka Women's Media Collective; Center for Women's Research (CENWOR) Caritas, Luxembourg; Women's Development Center,

Kandy; Human Rights Watch, New York; Human Rights Commission, Asia; ILO, Sri Lanka and the UN office in Sri Lanka. The data in this dataset were based on field survey results undertaken by the different institutions. This dataset also included local media reports on the migrant housemaids.

Fourth, I accessed published data from the early 1990s to 2018 compiled by the SLBFE, the Central Bank of Ceylon, and the Sri Lanka Department of Census and Statistics. The SLBFE kept records of registered migrants, disaggregated by sex and age, their destinations and departure data from airport records. Central Bank reports provided data on remittances.

STUDY CONTEXT: GOSL POLICIES AND STANCES REGARDING WOMEN AND WORK

Overseas Migrant Labor Policy of Sri Lanka: 1985–2010

This subsection provides an overview of policies relevant to migrant labor as well as women's rights, particularly as related to work and work opportunities. The 1978 Constitution of the Republic of Sri Lanka explicitly enshrines gender equality. Sri Lanka is a signatory to the Convention for the Elimination of All Forms of Discrimination Against Women (CEDAW) of 1981. The Sri Lanka Bureau of Foreign Employment Act of 1985 was enacted by parliament to establish the Sri Lanka Bureau of Foreign Employment (SLBFE), which was charged with the task of regulating and streamlining the processes of labor migration.

Sri Lanka also enacted a Women's Charter (1993), which recognizes a woman's right to employment. In 1996, the GOSL ratified the 1990 UN Convention of the Protection of Rights of All Migrant Workers and Their Families, which went into force in 2003 when it received the requisite twenty signatories. However, most of the labor receiving countries are not signatories of the Conventions, which makes mockery of the efficacy of the conventions since, by definition, at least two parties are involved in labor migratory processes, and both have to adhere to the principles laid down. Sri Lanka has not ratified the International Labor Organization (ILO) Convention no. 189 on Decent Work for Domestic Workers adopted by the ILO in 2011 and ratified in 2013. The Gulf States have not ratified this Convention either, although they voted to adopt it at the 100th Session of the ILO in 2011.

Since the mid-1990s, when female overseas domestic workers accounted for the bulk of Sri Lankans seeking fixed-term foreign employment, there was a growing concern that the mothers' absence will lead to the creation of dysfunctional family units and, more importantly, that it will have adverse effects on the children left behind (Perera and Ratnayake 2013; Hettige et al. 2012; Save the Children Sri Lanka 2006). In 2007, new legislation was proposed in parliament to completely prohibit women with children less than five years of age to migrate for work as domestic workers, and to allow women with children over the age of five years to leave for domestic work overseas only if they had made adequate childcare arrangements. However, this legislation was abandoned since it was believed to be unworkable due to a plethora of reasons.

However, in 2009, a newly appointed presidential task force was charged with proposing measures to redress the negative issues related to migrant workers, especially females. The task force invited a variety of stakeholders including migrant workers, trade unions, and civil society organizations in a consultative process to draft the new policy. Consequently in 2009, the GOSL adopted the Sri Lanka National Migration Policy, which recognized the need to develop a long-term vision for the role of labor migration, enhance the benefits of labor migration for the economy, the migrant, and the families, while reducing its negative effects and continuing to work toward the fulfillment and protection of human and labor rights (Abeyasekera and Jayasundere 2015).

Changing Motives of the GOSL

In the early 1980s, there was widespread acknowledgement of the important contributions of migrant housemaids who were bringing in a large proportion of foreign remittances to Sri Lanka to bolster the flagging economy. However, by the first decade of the new millennium, the government seemed to experience an increasing sense of discomfort and, possibly a sense of shame as well at the globally visible "image" of Sri Lanka as a labor exporter of housemaids. For instance, the Ministry of Foreign Employment Promotion and Welfare (MFEPW) categorically stated, "Even though a large outflow of unskilled male and domestic female workers contributed to earn the much needed foreign exchange for the country, this *also had the negative impact on the broad image of Sri Lanka as a country sending mostly housemaids and unskilled workers*" (MFEPW 2011, 8, emphasis added). Highlighting the housemaid as the source of a negative image of the country, the GOSL clearly shows the class and gender issue embedded in policy deliberations. Men in high bureaucratic positions who make these policy pronouncements often enjoy the servitude of maids in their own homes, and they obviously nurture a class distinction in terms of dignity of labor between their own work and that of the maids.

New Policy Initiative: The Family Background Circular 2013

In 2005, Rizana Nafeek, a seventeen-year-old Sri Lankan girl, used a local employment agency to obtain employment as a housemaid in Saudi Arabia.

It is against the law in Sri Lanka for a seventeen-year-old female to travel unaccompanied overseas to work as a housemaid. However, a fraudulent employment agency was able to obtain the necessary travel and employment documentation. In 2007 Rizana was sentenced to death for the alleged murder of an infant in her care in her employer's household. In 2010, despite appeals for clemency by human rights organizations and the government of Sri Lanka, including the president of Sri Lanka, Rizana was beheaded by the Saudi government (BBC News Asia 2013). It is noteworthy that the Asian Human Rights Watch reported its dissatisfaction with the representatives of the GOSL in not moving expeditiously in seeking clemency for Rizana (Asian Human Rights Watch 2011).

Rizana Nafeek's case was not about migrant mothers in the maid trade. However, it led to a renewed frenzy of activity in parliament about the migrant housemaid issue. The politicians' knee-jerk reaction to the incident was to issue a set of mandatory actions in the form of government circulars, which effectively laid out rules limiting the overseas employment opportunities as housemaids for Sri Lankan mothers. The Family Background Report Circular (FBRC)[1] enacted in 2013 sets strict age limits (twenty-one/twenty-five to maximum of fifty-five) on women seeking employment abroad as housemaids, bans the migration of mothers with children under the age of five years for such work, and requires women with children over the age of five years to show "guarantees" for the protection of their children by nominating a substitute caregiver. A "clearance certificate"[2] is issued only when the migrant hopefully obtains written permission of a "guardian," (i.e., the husband, or father if unmarried, or an alternative caregiver, another adult relative), a signed declaration by the caregiver consenting to fulfill the primary caregiver's role for the entire duration of the mother's absence, attested by the signatures of several government officials, that is, (1) *Grama Niladhari* (government officer at the community level); (2) the family health worker; (3) the migration development officer (MDO); and (4) the Divisional Secretary (the top-ranking civil servant for each of the twenty-six administrative districts) (Abeyasekera and Jayasundere 2015). This initiative did not adhere to any consultative process with stakeholders.

ANALYSIS AND DISCUSSION

Policy-Mandated Gender Injustice

The FBRC clearly targets poor non-professional women. It is applied only to women who aspire to work as housemaids and explicitly exempts women who are designated as "skilled," such as seamstresses, design makers, embroiderers, accountants, beauticians, clerks, computer operators, nurses, teachers, doctors, and managers. All of them can claim professional/educational and/or trade-related formal skills.[3]

The FBRC gives the "guardianship" of an adult Sri Lankan woman to a man (husband/father) and reduces her to a status of a juvenile. Its specific requirement of the husband or father's consent to seek foreign employment puts a woman in a dependent, submissive position that violates the principles and norms of nondiscrimination guaranteed in the constitution of Sri Lanka. If a married woman with children wants to escape an abusive husband, she still must obtain his permission since she will be identified as a married woman.

Since the decision to seek foreign employment for the category of house-maids is based primarily on economic reasons to uplift the socioeconomic status of the family, research demonstrates that the decision to seek overseas employment is primarily a joint family decision (Kottegoda et al. 2013; Abey-asekera and Jayasundera 2015). The FBRC requirement of a male guardian's attested approval is an acknowledgement of the mother's subordinate position within her immediate household. Furthermore, in the certification process, a hierarchy of mainly male bureaucrats are given the power to ascertain from the bureaucrat's perspective, whether the "guarantees" given for childcare in the mother's absence are adequate or appropriate. This situation resonates clearly with Hartman's analysis of patriarchal control of men over women across masculine hierarchical ordering in support of one another to maintain control over women (Hartman 2003).

Studies in Sri Lanka clearly show that the male stakeholders who were tasked with the certification process were reluctant to endorse the childcare guarantees, especially when the household had girls, particularly teenage girls (Jayasundere, Abeyasekera, and Idemegama 2015). Media reports were also known to sensationalize the allegations that teenage and adolescent girls left behind by their migrant worker mothers were routinely sexually abused by close male relatives (see also Hettige et al. 2011; Abeysekera and Jaysundera 2015; Perera and Ratnayake 2013). An internal study undertaken by the Women's Development Center (WDC), Kandy, Sri Lanka, had indicated that the sexual abuse of young girls by male relatives was much less, at 8 percent among the families where the mother was an overseas housemaid, compared to the national average of over 50 percent where both parents were present in a household (Pearl Stevens, director, WDC, and, Perni Thevarapperuma, deputy director, WDC, personal communication, April 21, 2012).

Research studies on households in Sri Lanka where the mother has mi-grated overseas to work as a housemaid yield mixed results on the issue of neglect of the children left behind. Hettige et al. (2012) noted that the separation from the mother could have negative social and psychological effects on families and children left behind. However, Gamburd's ethnographic survey in Naeagama, a coastal village in the southwest segment of Sri Lanka, which is a popular source village for recruitment of migrant housemaids, does not "support media claims that children suffer abuse and neglect in their mothers' absence." It does, however "support in part, survey information on reduced education, shifting marriage patterns and alcoholism" (Gamburd 2008, 1). It is evident that families of migrant housemaids weigh the pros and cons of mother's physical absence in the child's life over the mother's desperate need to earn the highest income possible for the survival of the household (Kottegoda et al. 2013). The women's employment is only for a fixed term. The comparative advantage of earning a higher income, which they can never expect to earn locally, seems to outweigh the psychosocial distress of separation of the mother from her children.

Women migrants assume the responsibility of "mothering from a distance" seriously and they are known to make different arrangements for the welfare of the children left behind (Kottegoda et al. 2013; Peng and Wong 2015). The migrant housemaids while working overseas continued to maintain communications with the husbands, caregivers, and children on a regular basis through social media, regular telephone calls, and by writing letters, and 95 percent of the sample participant mothers believed that they had made adequate caregiving provisions for the children left behind (Hugo and Ukwatte 2010). While problems of childcare remain a major issue for the migrant mothers and the families, the women are driven to seek wage employment overseas due to their overriding rationale that money earned by the mothers is critical since it goes to "fill hungry bellies, clothe and educate children, provide health care, and generally improve living standards for loved ones left behind" (UNFPA 2010 as quoted in Hugo and Ukwatta 2010, 257).

The stipulation of age in the FBRC of twenty-one/twenty-five years to fifty-five years for women aspiring to work as migrant housemaids explicitly targets women of reproductive age cohorts and invariably, mothers with young children become the majority stakeholders. At the same time, the upper age limit of fifty-five years imposes strict limits on active older women from seeking overseas domestic employment as well. The life expectancy of women in Sri Lanka at seventy-eight years is higher than that for men at seventy-two years (2016 data, WHO 2019). This not only highlights age discrimination but also gender discrimination since there are no such restrictions on men. The age limitation on women as stipulated in the FBRC moves beyond the issues of mothers and children left behind. This rule effectively declares that women over fifty-five years of age are "too old" to work as housemaids, while men fifty-five years and above who seek unskilled work overseas, for example, in physically taxing construction work, are not subjected to government strictures on age. Since the FBRC is only for the category of Sri Lankan women who seek employment as housemaids overseas, the upper age limit does not affect women in other professions seeking overseas employment either. While this age rule could be circumvented with fraudulent documentation, it is a deterrent since local foreign employment agencies run the risk of facing penalties by the SLBFE if they violate this rule. The age limitation on migrant housemaids may be imposed by the labor-receiving country, certainly; however, by implementing the FBRC, the GOSL violates the gender equality and nondiscrimination clauses of the Sri Lankan constitution.

The FBRC spells out an explicit class/gender discriminatory outlook in that poor families with absent mothers are highlighted as a cause of child neglect, marital dysfunction, and indeed, alcoholism as well. Most professional women who are mothers who migrate for work overseas are not subjected to a policy stipulation that requires them to provide guarantees that their children are adequately looked after if they leave. A report commissioned by UN Sri Lanka on the impact of Sri Lankan policies on Sri Lankan migrant workers, finds that the FBRC is clearly discriminatory against Sri Lankan women's right to migrate for work and that motherhood should not be used by the GOSL to violate that right (United Nations Sri Lanka 2015).

In a media interview, G. S. Withanage, the secretary of the Ministry for Foreign Employment was asked why the FBRC restricts a mother's right to choose employment that would lead to her economic empowerment. He insisted that the sole aim of restricting the migration of mothers for domestic work is to protect the children and safeguard the family unit (Yatawara 2017). Obviously, the right of the mother as a worker was not considered important. Mr. Withanage is the top official in the Ministry of Foreign Affairs and his response illustrates the masculine hegemonic rhetoric of the male leadership in framing public policy that affects a poorer class of Sri Lankan women.

The FBRC does not restrict fathers among poorer classes from obtaining wage work overseas and leaving behind their children. The secretary of the Ministry of Foreign Employment in the same interview cited above observed, "We have taken a decision to *request* from fathers having children younger than five years of age and planning to migrate for work, a statement ascertaining the safety and welfare of his children. He should indicate in writing about who will take care of the children, how will their welfare measures get fulfilled etc., *though this will not be as strict as the family background report,* we plan to implement it in the near future" (Yatawara 2017, emphasis added). This illustrates that male policy makers strictly adhere to the gendered binary of production and reproduction. Furthermore, as noted by the UN commissioned report on the FBRC, "More fundamentally, by regulating women, and not men, the policy places the responsibility of childcare in particular and the wellbeing of the family squarely on the women's shoulders and disregards the role of the father and the consequences the absence of the father has on the wellbeing of the children" (United Nations Sri Lanka 2015, 24).

Contradictions in Policy Goals of GOSL

The policy initiatives proposed by the legislators clearly demonstrate the conflicts in dealing with the necessity to maintain a flow of revenue from a specific cohort of workers, while imposing gendered limitations on the women's rights as individuals. A female migrant domestic worker is at the same time a "cash cow" and a "necessary evil." The refusal of the male dominant political narrative to accept the many roles of a woman as an individual, mother, and a wageworker is exemplified by the attitude and utterances of Mahinda Rajapaksa, president of Sri Lanka (2005–2015) himself. In one section of his political manifesto, *Mahinda Chintanaya* (Vision of Mahinda), he extols the primacy of the mother in Sri Lankan family and society in keeping the family unit together (Ministry of Planning 2010, 22). Then, when he goes on to acknowledge the contributions of female migrant workers to the economy and promises to protect them from economic and sexual exploitation (ibid., 23), he cannot be unaware that a migrant working mother will not be in a position to fulfill the traditional mothering role with her physical presence. Contradicting these statements in the election manifesto and in public statements, Mahinda Rajapaksa has accused migrant mothers of increasing school dropout rates, juvenile delinquency, increasing the vulnerability of children to abuse, and for the increase in alcoholism in men who are left at home (Kodikara 2014). The migrant housemaid cannot be in two physically separate places at the same time and yet, she often becomes the unfortunate victim of politically driven, impossible expectations (Hondagneu-Sotelo and Avila 1997). The social perception that Sri Lankan women's central role as mother and caregiver located in the reproductive sphere is not by any means a new creation. Women were celebrated primarily for their role as mothers in the nationalistic rhetoric nurtured during the late colonial period ending with independence from British colonial rule in 1948 (Jayawardena 1986), and again during the latter part of the thirty-year civil war (de Alwis 2004), which ended in 2009. It has continued into the current post–civil war political rhetoric in Sri Lanka.

According to official reports of the Sri Lanka Foreign Employment Bureau and the Central Bank of Sri Lanka, there has been a notable drop in total migrant labor since 2014, with a sharper drop in the category of migrant housemaids. The drop-in housemaid migration has seen a steady downward trend since 2009 from 46 percent to 37 percent in 2014. From 2014 to 2015 the departures for housemaids dropped by 17.9 percent, while the drop for males for the same period was only 9.2 percent (SLBFE 2016; Central Bank 2016). While these decreases are by and large attributed to the slump in oil prices in the host countries leading to a contraction of the recruitment market, the Sri Lanka Central Bank Report of 2016 also notes with concern that the drop in female departures was "due to the restrain in the departures of female workers from Sri Lanka for low skilled employment categories" (Central Bank 2016, 128). Indeed, if the motive was for the Sri Lanka government to slow down women seeking employment as housemaids overseas, it has succeeded.

Financial institutions are nervous about the drop in corresponding remittances. The Central Bank notes "worker remittances are the largest sources of foreign exchange earnings in the country and any set back in the remittances flow would adversely affect the external current account" (Central Bank 2017, 140). While overseas migration of Sri Lankan workers declined for all categories of unskilled workers since 2011, as of 2017 nearly 60 percent of migrants were in the unskilled category. Among them, migrant housemaids still remain the single largest category.

Circumventing the Restrictions: Risky Manipulations

As discussed earlier, despite the restrictions on women imposed by the implementation of the FBRC, the percentage of women who seek foreign employment as housemaids remains very high at over 80 percent of all female labor migrants (SLBFE 2016). Hence, it is not surprising that those women who aspire to seek employment overseas as housemaids often seek to circumvent policy restrictions imposed by the GOSL in order to achieve their goal of migrating for work as housemaids. Given the continuing demand for housemaids not only from the Gulf/Middle East region but also from countries of South East Asia, gendered limitations imposed by the FBRC may bring unintended consequences of women becoming more vulnerable to machinations of employment agencies, both local and in receiving countries.

There are no overt foreign travel restrictions for ordinary citizens of Sri Lanka, adult female or male. Passports are issued for a standard fee. However, prospective Sri Lankan overseas travelers need a valid visa from the destination country. Visa entries are routinely checked for validity at the immigration counter at the sole international airport in Colombo, Sri Lanka. Employment agencies that recruit women for employment overseas, even those that are officially registered with SLBFE, are known to assist potential migrant housemaids navigate the process, resorting to both legal as well as illegal means to obtain visas, sometimes as visitors, since lower recruitment levels would mean loss of revenue for them as well. While the SLBFE requires a registration process for all housemaid recruitment agencies in an effort to control unscrupulous recruitment procedures of such agencies, foreign employment agencies in Sri Lanka are known to collaborate with foreign housemaid recruitment agencies in the receiving countries to circumvent the FBRC regulations on recruitment of housemaids who are mothers. As noted earlier, by circumventing the FBRC and the registration requirement of the SLBFE, migrant housemaids will lose even the limited protection offered by the SLBFE, not to mention the additional expenses they will undoubtedly have to incur by dealing with unscrupulous local and foreign employment agencies.

Any aspiring migrant housemaid was required to furnish the clearance certification to the recruiting agent, which would be the foreign employment agency for the purpose of officially registering as a housemaid seeking foreign employment. At the same time, it is in the financial interest of such agencies to "help" aspiring migrant housemaids to obtain the certification. The foreign employment agencies and their subagents are known to use fraudulent recruitment methods to deceive and coerce potential workers into exploitative employment. They were charged exorbitantly high fees by the recruiting agencies (Caritas 2012; Human Rights Watch 2007). This was before the implementation of the FBRC. Thus, the process of obtaining foreign employment was already expensive for a category or class of people who can least afford such initial financial outlays. Desperate to seek a possible new space to climb out of poverty, the woman and her family are very likely to incur further debts to get additional funds to obtain fraudulent certifications of the type now required under the FBRC. Furthermore, even for an individual who would want to follow the rules, the certification process often involves traveling to different locations to obtain copies of marriage and birth certificates and to meet with the relevant authorities. All these activities incur expenses and time, which the economically strapped migrant housemaid hopefuls can ill afford.

It is also noteworthy that the stipulations of the FBRC on the restriction of migration of housemaids who are mothers and older females over the age of fifty-five years, if strictly observed, would further reduce the pool of potential overseas housemaids. Despite the policy-induced limitations, the fact that there remains a steady push of low-income women seeking overseas employment as housemaids leads us to speculate that women, their families and recruitment agencies actively seek illegal and often risky ways to circumvent the strictures imposed by the FBRC.

CONCLUSIONS

Reversing Gender Injustice? Suggesting Strategies

Every research study on the situation of migrant Sri Lankan housemaids cited in this paper invariably points out the failure of successive Sri Lankan governments in implementing and monitoring facilities mandated by the state for migrant workers, especially women and the children left behind. These include failure to monitor the practices of recruiters who often abuse prospective migrant domestic workers, lethargy in implementing child welfare facilities, and failure to provide information on documentation for travel and expected work situations. While the lack of resources is often cited as an excuse for these failures, it raises the question as to why the state cannot initiate programs to funnel a small part of the revenue it extracts from remittances exclusively for such purposes.

Stories are widely circulated, both factual and fictional, that by and large fathers are not able to take proper care of the children (Kottegoda et al. 2013). To be sure, the presence of both parents in a household is known to be the best option for the well-being of a child (Hettige et al. 2012). However, when circumstances make it necessary for the mother to be the absent parent, fathers/husbands in Sri Lanka have taken the responsibility of being the main caregivers of the children left behind. One survey noted that among transnational households with school age children where the mother is a migrant housemaid, 25.9 percent of fathers had stepped up to assume the full responsibility of being the primary caregiver (Save the Children, Sri Lanka 2006). The SLBFE has made no attempts to reach out and support the left-behind fathers in their new role of primary caregiver.

It is also important that the SLBFE sets up mechanisms at different local levels to talk with returnee migrants and prospective migrants together so that problems and prospects of mothers migrating for domestic work could be aired openly and discussed. As one of the studies notes, the dominant voice in the discourse advocating the restriction on mothers to migrate for domestic work comes from outside the real migration process, that is, male policy makers and male and female upper-middle-class Sri Lankans who have taken the tone of moral gate keepers of society (Jayasundere et al. 2015).

Rescinding the FBRC is a prerequisite for the restoration of gender justice for migrant mothers seeking employment as housemaids. The FBRC is a document that clearly articulates the dominant hand of masculine hegemony in entrenching the patriarchal norm that a woman's place is only in the home and if she chooses to move for work it is her sole responsibility to make arrangements for childcare. The explicit intersectionality of class with gender bias in the FBRC has no place in a just society. As guaranteed in the constitution of Sri Lanka, adult women in Sri Lanka, married or single, have a right to work. Following that guarantee would entail the recognition that providing a supportive structure for both mothers and children left behind is not a favor granted by the male politicians to a set of poor women, but the responsibility of a democratically elected government to ensure gender justice to a set of productive workers.

It is often said that politics is a man's game and government a men's club. What is remarkable about the migrant housemaids of Sri Lanka is the extent of political control exercised over their work and livelihoods. The prevalence of hegemonic masculine control is clearly demonstrated in how the FBRC policy is instrumental in subjecting mothers of poorer classes to layers of patriarchal controls.

Sri Lanka may be one of the very few countries in the world where the burden of earning foreign currency rests on the shoulders of three different cohorts of Sri Lankan women: migrant housemaids, garment workers, and plantation workers, all drawn from the poorer, less-educated segments of Sri Lankan society (Samarasinghe 1998). They bring money to the state but do not set socioeconomic or political policy agendas. In particular, in the case of migrant housemaids, the structure and location of employment and the desperate need for employment for individual women are not conducive to success in collective action and resistance. When the so-called "breadwinners" are males it is well known that they have the opportunity to set the agenda for society's collective socioeconomic and political behavior. But when the "breadwinners" for the country are women, the roles are certainly not reversed. That, in itself, is a clear manifestation of gender injustice.

NOTES

1. The first circular was issued by the SLBFE on June 7, 2013 (No. 13, 2013) to all foreign employment agencies. The second circular issued in December 2013 was addressed to all divisional secretaries as well. The third was issued on January 15, 2014. The third circular, in addition to the provisions in the first two circulars, set higher minimum age requirement of eighteen years and a maximum age limit of fifty-five years for Sri Lankan females planning to migrate overseas as paid housemaids. The FBRC also stipulated minimum age requirements for specific destination regions (Saudi Arabia, twenty-five years, all other countries including Middle East and Gulf countries, twenty-one years).

2. The clearance certificate requires that a Sri Lankan mother aspiring to obtain employment as a housemaid overseas should furnish proof of the following: (1) declaration of marital status; (2) declaration of the number of children with dates of birth; (3) the name and signature of a "guardian"; (4) nomination of a caregiver, with his or her name and address; (5) nominated caregiver's kinship relationship to the migrant; (6) status of caregiver's health; and (7) proof of nominated caregiver's attendance on "family day" and declaration of the person's consent to fulfill the primary caregiver's role for the entire duration of the mother's absence.

3. The FBRC policy was extended in 2017 to incorporate all mothers who leave their children behind for work overseas. However this rule is not enforced since women, other than those leaving for overseas employment as housemaids, do not need

to register with any agency prior to leaving the country. Furthermore, family visas are issued for many categories of professional women seeking employment overseas.

REFERENCES

Abeyasekera, Asha, and Ramani Jayasundere. 2015. "Migrant Mothers, Family Breakdown, and the Modern State: An Analysis of State Policies Regulating Women Migrating Overseas for Domestic Work in Sri Lanka." *The South Asianist* 4, no. 1: 1–24.

Asian Human Rights Commission. 2011. "Sri Lanka/Saudi Arabia: New Revelations on the Case of Rizana Nafeek Who Is Facing the Death Sentence in Saudi Arabia—GOSL Should Initiate an Inquiry into the Scandalous Conduct of the Ministry of Foreign Affairs and the Embassy Staff in Saudi Arabia." June 16, 2011. http://www.humanrights.asia.

Atukorale, Premachandra. 1990. "International Contract Migration and the Reintegration of Return Migrants: The Experience of Sri Lanka." *International Migration Review* 24 (Summer 1990): 323–46.

BBC News Asia. 2013. "Sri Lankan maid Rizana Nafeek Beheaded in Saudi Arabia." January 9, 2013. http://www.bbc.com/news/world-asia-20959228. Accessed June 14, 2017.

Caritas. 2012. *Migration of Sri Lanka Women: Analysis of Causes and Post-Arrival Assistance.* Luxembourg: Caritas.

Central Bank. 2009. *Central Bank Report 2009.* Colombo: Central Bank. Accessed May 23, 2019. https://www.cbsl.gov.lk/.

———. 2015. *Central Bank Report 2015.* Colombo: Central Bank. Accessed May 23, 2019. https://www.cbsl.gov.lk/.

———. 2016. *Central Bank Report 2016.* Colombo: Central Bank. Accessed May 23, 2019. https://www.cbsl.gov.lk/.

———. 2017. *Central Bank Report 2017.* Colombo: Central Bank, Accessed May 23, 2019. https://www.cbsl.gov.lk/.

Connell, Raewyn W. 1987. *Gender and Power: Society, the Person and Sexual Politics.* Cambridge: Polity Press.

Connell, R. W., and James W. Messerschmidt. 2005. "Hegemonic Masculinity: Rethinking the Concept." *Gender and Society* 19 (2005): 829–59.

Cornwall, Andrea, Frank J. Karioris, and Nancy Lindisfarne, eds. 2016. *Masculinities under Neoliberalism.* London: Zed Books.

Daily Mirror. 2013. "Rizana Rafeek Executed." January 9, 2013. http://www.dailymirror.lk/article/rizana-nafeek-executed—24864.html. Accessed June 14, 2017.

De Alwis, Malathi. 2004. "The Moral Mother Syndrome." *Indian Journal of Gender Studies* 11, no. 1 (2004): 65–73.

Donaldson, M. 1993. "What Is Hegemonic Masculinity?" *Theory and Society, Special Issue: Masculinities* 22, no. 5 (October 1993): 643–57.

Frantz, Elizabeth. 2013. "Jordan's Unfree Workforce: State-Sponsored Bonded Labor in the Arab Region." *Journal of Development Studies* 49, no. 8: 1072–75.

Gamburd, Michelle. 2000. *The Kitchen Spoon's Handle.* Cornell University Press.

Gamburd, Michelle. 2008. "Milk Teeth and Jet Planes: Kin Relations in Families of Sri Lanka's Transitional Domestic Servants." *Anthropology Faculty Publications and Presentations.* Paper 42. Portland State University, 2008. Accessed June 16, 2016. http://pdxscholar.library.pdx.edu/anth_fac/42.

Hartman, Heidi. 2003. "The Unhappy Marriage of Marxism and Feminism: Towards a More Progressive Union." In *Feminist Theory Reader,* edited by Carol R. McCann and Seung-Kyung Kim, 206–21. London, New York City: Routledge.

Hettige, S. T., Evangeline Ekanayake, Ramani Jayasundere, Anula Ratnayake, and Pushparani Figurado. 2012. *Understanding the Psychosocial Issues Faced by Migrant Workers and Their Families.* Colombo: The Ministry of Foreign Employment and Promotion.

Hondagneu-Sotelo, Pierrette, and Ernestine Avila. 1997. "I'm Here, but I'm There: The Meanings of Latina Transnational Motherhood." *Gender and Society* 11, no. 5: 548–71.

Hugo, Graeme, and Swarna Ukwatta. 2010. "Sri Lankan Female Domestic Workers Overseas—The Impact on Their Children." *Asian and Pacific Migration Journal* 19, no. 2: 237–63.

Human Rights Watch. November 2007. *Exported and Exposed: Abuses against Sri Lankan Domestic Workers in Saudi Arabia, Kuwait, Lebanon and the United Arab Emirates.* Volume 19, No.6 C. New York. Human Rights Watch.

Jagger, Allison. 2009. "The Philosophical Challenge of Global Gender Justice." *Philosophical Topics* 37, no. 2: 1–15.

Jayasundere, Ramani, Asha L. Abeyasekera, and Kumari Idemegama. 2015. "Deciding for Sri Lanka Women Migrant Workers: Protection and Denial of Rights?" http://www.academia.edu/13567250/Deciding_for_Srilanka_S_Women_Workers_Protection_Or_Denial_Of_Rights. Accessed September 10, 2016.

Jayawardena, Kumari. 1986. *Feminism and Nationalism in the Third World.* London: Zed Books.

Kodikara, Chulani. 2014. "Good Women and Bad Women of the Post-War Nation." *Groundviews.* Last modified May 22, 2014. https://groundviews.org/2014/05/22/good-women-and-bad-women-of-the-post-war-nation. Accessed September 10, 2016.

Kottegoda, Sepalika, Ramani Jayasundere, Sumikā Perera, and Padma Atapattu. 2013. *Transforming Lives: Listening to Sri Lankan Returnee Women Migrant Workers.* Colombo: Women and Media Collective.

Lerner, Gerda. 1986. *The Creation of Patriarchy.* Oxford: Oxford University Press.

MFEPW. 2011. *Annual Performance Report—2011.* Colombo: Ministry of Foreign Employment.

Ministry of Foreign Employment and Welfare (MFEW). 2013. *Migration Profile Sri Lanka.* Colombo.

Ministry of Planning/Ministry of Finance and Planning. 2010. *Sri Lanka: The Emerging Wonder of Asia. Mahinda Chintanaya: Vision for the Future.* Colombo: Department of National Planning.

Parreñas, Rhacel Salazar. 2005. *Children of Global Migration: Transnational Families and Gendered Woes.* Stanford: Stanford University Press.

———. 2001. "Mothering from a Distance: Emotions, Gender and Intergenerational Relations in Filipino Transnational Families." *Feminist Studies* 27, no. 2 (Summer 2001): 361–90.

———. 2015. *Servants of Globalization: Women and Domestic Work.* Stanford: Stanford University Press.

———. 2010. "Transnational Mothering: A Source of Gender Conflicts in the Family." *North Carolina Law Review* 88, no. 5: 1825–56.

Peng, Yinni, and Odalia M. H. Wong. 2015. "Who Takes Care of My Left-Behind Children? Migrant Mothers and Caregivers in Transnational Child Care." *Journal of Family Issues* 37, no. 14: 1–24.

Perera, Nirasha, and Madhubhashini R. Ratnayake. 2013. *Sri Lanka's Missing Mothers: A Working Paper on the Effects of Mother Migration on Children.* Colombo: Save the Children.

Rawls, John. 1971. *A Theory of Justice.* Cambridge: Harvard University Press.

———. 2001. *Justice as Fairness: A Restatement.* Cambridge: Harvard University Press.

Samarasinghe, Vidyamali. 1998. "Feminization of Foreign Currency Earnings: Women's Labor in Sri Lanka." *Developing Areas* 32 (Spring 1998): 301–26.

———.2015. "Impact of Corruption on Women's Political Participation at the Local Government Level: The Case of Sri Lanka." *South Asian Journal of Policy and Governance* 37, no. 2 (December 19): 19–36.

Sandberg, Sheryl. 2013. *Lean In: Women, Work and the Will to Lead.* New York City: Alfred A. Knopf.

Save the Children, Sri Lanka. 2006. *Left Behind, Left Out: The Impact on Children and Families of Mothers Migrating for Work Abroad. Summary Report* Colombo, Save the Children.

Sen, Amartya. 1999. *Development as Freedom.* New York City: Alfred A Knopf. Random House.

———. 2009. *The Idea of Justice.* New York City: Alfred A. Knopf, 2011. Random House.

Sri Lanka Bureau of Foreign Employment (SLBFE). 2010. *Annual Statistical Report of Foreign Employment.* Colombo: Sri Lanka Bureau of Foreign Employment.

———. 2016. *Annual Statistical Report of Foreign Employment.* Colombo: Sri Lanka Bureau of Foreign Employment.

United Nations Sri Lanka. 2015. *Sri Lanka Domestic Workers: The Impact of Sri Lankan Policies on Workers' Right to Freely Access Employment.* A Study for the United Nations Country Team in Sri Lanka. Colombo.

WHO. 2019. Sri Lanka: Country Profile. Accessed May 26, 2019. https://www.who.int/countries/lka/en/.

Yatawara, Dhaneshi. "Illegal Migrants Mainly Face Issues." *Daily Mirror*, June 14, 2017. http://www.dailymirror.lk/.

Chapter Four

Territorialization of Violence: Temporality and Scale

The HIV/AIDS Epidemic in Mumbai, India, in the Mid-1990s

Emmanuel Eliot

FRAMING VIOLENCE AND TERRITORIALIZATION

There is a growing interest in the forms and effects of violence on societies. Among this literature, Nixon (2013, 2–3) distinguishes structural violence "as an event of action that is immediate in time, explosive and spectacular in space" from slow violence "that occurs gradually and out of sight, a violence of delayed destruction that is dispersed across time and space." Causation and agency are central issues in understanding structural violence whereas slow violence is described as a set of complex categories "enacted slowly over time" (Nixon 2013, 11). Time is a central element that is necessary for capturing the different temporalities or different rates of progression of violence that reconfigure places. As Massey (2002) noted, places are part of complex spatial networks. Places are always in a process of transformation, shaped by interactions through which "networked mobilities of capital, objects, signs and information" (Urry 2006, ix in Cresswell and Merriman 2011) are brought together. "Places," therefore, are dynamic space-time constructs of actions and interactions.

This chapter focuses on the violence used for territorializing actions. Territoriality refers to the "attempts by an individual or a group to affect, influence, or control people, phenomena, and relationships by delimiting and asserting control over a geographic area" (Sachs 1986, 387–88). Claiming space operationalizes the exclusion of specific groups or monopolizes benefits to a specific group, resulting in the creation of a new place. Local and global forces are not in opposition in this process since global forces reinforce the process. The interaction of global and local is a core mechanism in globalization.

One expression of the link between violence and globalization is found in the description of globalization as the "speed and intensity with which both material and ideological elements now circulate across national boundaries [and which] have created a new order of uncertainty in social life" (Appadurai 2005, 5). This new order is rooted in new relationships between the "majority" and the "minority." In his essay, "Fear of Small Numbers," Appadurai (2005, 8) states, "Numerical majorities can become predatory and ethnocidal with regard to small numbers precisely when some minorities (and their small numbers) remind the majorities of the small gap which lay between their condition as majorities and the horizon of a unsullied national whole, a pure and untainted national ethos." These relationships produce new "incentives for cultural purifications" and for exorcizing the "new, the emergent, and the uncertain, one name for which is globalization" (Appadurai 2005, 48). Power is a central issue in understanding violence. It questions the individual and the collective, the "us" and "them," the "I" and the "Other," and is embedded within a matrix where sovereignty, governmentality (Foucault 2004), and life are interwoven and interrelated.

In the 1980s, the emergence of the HIV/AIDS pandemic contributed to the production of new spaces. In this chapter, I examine the dynamics of the HIV/AIDS epidemic in Mumbai during the 1990s by analyzing the relations between actors and scales that led to the emergence and spread of the epidemic in this city. This time frame spanning the as-yet early years of the epidemic is particularly valuable for such an analysis since it best encapsulates and captures the actions and reactions of local and regional actors in creating new places through territorialization. There is little research on the geography of HIV/AIDS transmission in India despite some notable contributions (Asthana1996; Godwin 1998; Ghosh 2002; Verma and Roy 2002; Ghosh, Wadhwa, and Kalipeni 2009; Wadhwa 2012). However, more than thirty years after the first reports of HIV/AIDS cases by Indian health authorities in 1986, there are only a few micro studies that generate in-depth understanding, since most of the official epidemic data are generally aggregated or produced from an epidemiological perspective. There is even less research that examines the connecting patterns of scales in producing spaces. Focusing on territorialization is important in understanding that epidemics are not only made of epicenters and carriers but are social constructions of disease and identity (Brown 1995). In the mid-1990s, a political strategy founded on fear and an ideology of purification contributed to the buildup of insecurity in specific areas and some communities of Mumbai. Violence played a major role in the dynamic of the epidemic by creating local nodes of transmission that relayed the global dynamic of the epidemic's course.

In the first part of this chapter, I present the study context, including the state of the epidemic in India in general and in Mumbai in particular. I also briefly touch upon the geopolitical and socioeconomic makeup of Mumbai, which facilitated the spread of the epidemic. Next, I address the methodology along with a critique of the data. In the third part, I analyze the evolution of HIV/ AIDS mortality patterns with an emphasis on the networks that underlay the emergence and the progress of the epidemic in Mumbai and present the ways some places acted as sources for new spatialities. Finally, I return to the debate on HIV/ AIDS, globalization, and an analysis of the violence that contributed to the reorganization of spatialities in central Mumbai in the mid-1990s.

CONTEXT: HIV/AIDS IN INDIA IN THE 1990s

South Asia and the Pacific is the second most affected region by the HIV/ AIDS pandemic with 5.1 million people living with HIV in 2018, although far below Sub-Saharan Africa's 22 million. In India, between 2 million and 3.1 million people were living with the virus (UNAIDS 2018). Data furnished by the National Aids Control Organization of India (NACO) indicate that HIV prevalence among Sexually Transmitted Diseases (STD) and Ante Natal Clinic (ANC) patients from the North-Eastern and the Southern States is higher than in other parts of the country. Since the launch of the National AIDS Control Programme (NACP) in 1986, these regions and especially the six states of Manipur, Nagaland (North-East India), Maharahstra, Karnataka, Andhra Pradesh, and Tamil Nadu (Western and Southern States) have reported higher HIV-prevalence rates than other states in India (NACO 2017).

Despite improvements in the national surveillance system since 1999 (Kadri and Kumar 2012), the data are difficult to analyze since disease surveillance activity and the policies of each screening center may vary. By the mid-1990s, nearly a decade after the first HIV/AIDS cases were identified, data were still scarce. Indian authorities denied the full extent of the epidemic in its early years. National disparities in HIV/AIDS screening were maintained or reinforced because of the difficulties involved in setting up screening and prevention programs linked to shortcomings in the health system, and the diversion of funds for fighting the epidemic (Rammasubban 1998; Wadhwa 2012).

Mumbai Case Study: A Spot for Exploring HIV/AIDS in the Mid-1990s

The conurbation of Chennai received a significant proportion of investment from the Indian government and international donors since the late 1980s due to its status as the place where the first HIV cases were identified. However, the western Indian State of Maharashtra and its capital, Bombay (officially renamed Mumbai in 1995), soon became a special case when HIV cases began to be diagnosed and identified there. National and international funders subsequently focused their attention on Mumbai, viewing it as a potential "laboratory" in which this epidemic could be studied (Ramachandran 2012; Sehgal 2014).

Mumbai is divided into wards that reflect the city's history and socioeconomic and political growth and change. They are the essential units at which life is played out in the city. Of these wards, the central wards of Mumbai include several areas located in the center of Mumbai's peninsula. They were first created by the British at the beginning of the twentieth century. The first settlements in central Mumbai date back to the late nineteenth century and major expansions began in the early twentieth century. In the colonial urban space, they filled the gap between the native town and the industrial textile colonies (Patel and Thorner 1996). Throughout the centuries, the central wards have been the passage and transit areas for different populations where there existed a "network of social relationships out of which the working-class experience was formed. . . . The neighborhoods, integral to the relationships of the workplace, became an important base for industrial and political actions" (Chandavarkar 1981, 647).

The textile crisis of the 1970–1980s led to the "great strike" of 1981–1983 and was the final step in the collapse of the textile industry, which was established during the era of the Bombay Presidency (1843–1936). The 1981–1983 strike had a major impact on several generations in these working-class wards. They became spaces of the poorest populations, forming a rear base for Mumbai's underworld. They were located close to the business centers of the southern parts of Mumbai's peninsula and were targeted by public and private investors who were interested in these centrally located and, therefore, attractive places for the developing land market. In the 1970s, changes in the labor market plunged most of the working populations in these central wards into a crisis, consequently strengthening the activities of the underworld in the trafficking of goods, prostitution, and racketeering. This also led to the take-over of traditional trade-union organizations by a Mumbai-based Hindu nationalist movement, the *Shiv Sena*[1] (Army of Shiv; Heuzé 1992; Banerjee 1996).

These central wards were significant in the city for several reasons that are worth underscoring. They were central places of urban planning policies, nodes in terms of localities, foci of Mumbai's identity, cores of social movements, and symbols of the culture of "made in Mumbai." As discussed later in this chapter, at all scales, these areas played a central role in the emergence and expansion of the epidemic.

METHODS AND DATA ISSUES

The study methodology comprised triangulation of data and methods within a case study approach. Descriptive analyses (trend lines and cross-tabulation) and mapping of statistical and survey data were integrated with content analysis of media reports, literature and interview data to provide a fuller picture of unfolding events and to characterize actor interactions.

Research approval for various portions of the study came from a co-investigator's institution (see note 2), and permission from Mumbai Municipality officers. Further, all surveys and interviews adhered to existing guidelines for human subject research prescribed by the Indian Council for Medical Research (ICMR 1980), including obtaining informed consent, anonymization of findings, and minimal risk to participants. Data for the first three datasets detailed below were aggregated by wards, preventing individual identification. Further, all information from interviews and surveys is folded into the analysis, without identifying any participants.

The Need for Cross-Data for Understanding the Epidemic in Mumbai

In Mumbai, there was a significant lack of medical records on AIDS mortality before the early 2000s. Therefore, it was necessary to use multiple data sets for cross-referencing. Three such data sets were used for this study, even though each had its flaws. These were supplemented by literature, reports, media coverage, and key interviews. The first dataset was collected from 1986 to 1994 from the largest HIV/AIDS screening centers of the city. Only cases confirmed by a Western blot test or Elisa tests were included. Data included gender, age, place of the residence, type of transmission, and occupation of the HIV-positive individuals.[2] The samples cover thirteen of the twenty centers that conducted HIV tests during the 1990s; a total of 10,209 cases were recorded where almost 90 percent were residents of Mumbai (Bharat 1996). While this information refers only to detected cases and the sample does not cover all the screening facilities of the city, this was the only dataset available, however, to study the HIV/AIDS epidemic in the twenty-three wards of Mumbai even by the end of 1990s. The limitations of these data are obvious in that they are biased: a high proportion of the data comes from public establishments and some private screening centers were not included in the collection because the collections were not authorized; a disproportionately large percentage of the HIV infection was reported among men than among women that may reveal the poor access of women to health facilities; the records mainly came from blood banks and sexually transmitted diseases (STD) departments and were based only on in-patient data. However, this dataset provides a valuable overview of Mumbai's HIV/AIDS epidemic in the mid-1990s. It does not depend only on the screening of the so-called "high risk groups" defined by Mumbai's health authorities and also offers a basis for an intra-urban analysis, especially in the central parts of the city where almost all of the screening facilities were located. Lastly, it provided the opportunity to overcome the major problem of data underreporting that occurred at national, state, and municipal levels.

The second dataset used to supplement the HIV data contained mortality data from the Mumbai Municipal Corporation for the years 1986, 1989, 1991, and 1994 from the annual reports of the executive health officer. Mumbai's death registration system is unique in India, requiring a death certificate for each cremation and burial, and the death is declared at the place of residence. Like other systems, it has its flaws, nonetheless, any changes in death rates were unlikely to be the result of improved reporting by municipal health authorities because it was already thorough, and most likely to be from changes of mortality patterns. Moreover, previous robust analyses have also been based on this dataset (e.g., Ramasubban and Crook 1985, 1996). Combined with the AIDS mortality dataset, these previous works provided a sound basis for a long-term analysis of the mortality patterns in Mumbai.

A third dataset was collected to enable the mix-method approach to studying the HIV/AIDS epidemic in Mumbai. A survey of 280 families was conducted in Mumbai's central wards between July and October 1997. This provided the social and cultural contexts of these wards, and helped to direct the search for the actors who might have played a role in the dynamic of the epidemic. In addition, relevant literature and English-language Indian national, regional, and local newspaper articles were analyzed to trace the events that might have affected the dynamic of the epidemic. Finally, health officers, nongovernmental organization (NGO) officials, community leaders, police officers, and local gang leaders were interviewed. These data provided indices and tools for explaining how networks and actors are connected and how they formed a system for the circulation of the epidemic in some parts of the city. All analysis and observations made in the following sections are based on the multiple data sources described above, unless otherwise noted.

ANALYSIS OF MUMBAI'S HIV/AIDS EPIDEMIC: TEMPORALITY, SCALES AND ACTORS

The Long-Standing Circulation of Diseases in Mumbai's Central Wards

As mentioned in the context, Mumbai's central wards were a significant scalar unit of the epidemic. Figure 4.1 shows mortality data trends between 1986 and 1994, revealing a decrease in youth mortality rates and mortality rates of people over fifty years of age but a significant rise in mortality rates among young adults. The overall number of deaths by groups of pathologies

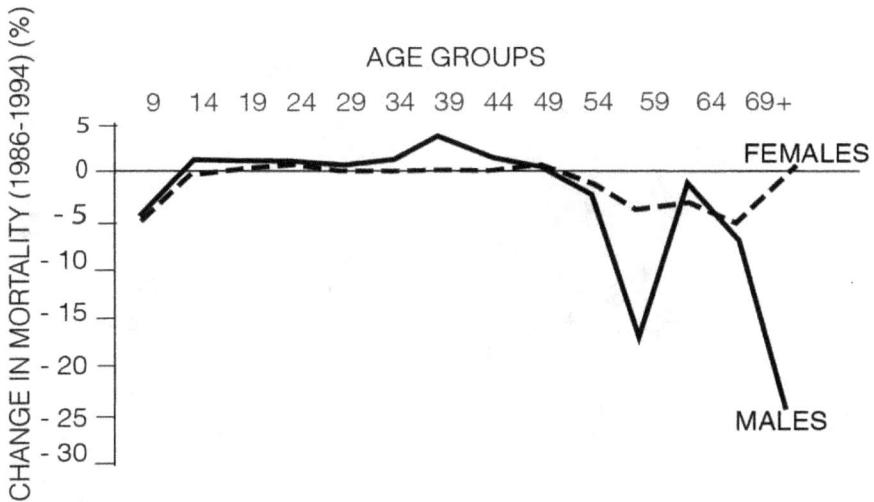

Figure 4.1.   Change in age-specific mortality rates by sex between 1986 and 1994 in Greater Mumbai.

Data collected from the Reports of the Executive Health Officer (1986-1994), Mumbai Municipal Corporation

revealed a higher rate of degenerative diseases, especially increases in cancers (6.8 percent increase), cardiovascular diseases (5.9 percent increase), and certain infectious diseases, for example, tuberculosis (31.7 percent increase) and hepatitis B (24.7 percent increase). The strong link between these last two infectious diseases and HIV/AIDS, the increase in mortality rates among young adults and a decrease in mortality rates in the youngest and older age groups, all point to the emergence of new epidemiological patterns over the period. As shown in figure 4.2, these changes were highly concentrated in certain areas of Mumbai. To put these trends into context, it is important to note that since India's independence in 1947, mortality rates in the central wards, especially ward E, have remained higher than in any other ward in the municipality (Klein 1986; Ramasubban and Crook 1985, 1996; Arnold 1993). However, there were some notable differences from typical mortality trends that were visible in the mortality data from 1986 to 1994. Figure 4.1 shows that the southern and central wards showed a greater increase in mortality among young adult men than for women. These shifts are paralleled by changes in the causes of death, most notably HIV/AIDS-related "opportunistic infections" of tuberculosis, hepatitis B, and pulmonary pathologies in the central wards. Among these, Ward E provides the most striking example. Figure 4.2 shows that these pathologies accounted for 18.4 percent of deaths in 1986 but rose sharply to 42.2 percent in 1994. This ward also had a high concentration of HIV/AIDS cases for this period.

1986   1994

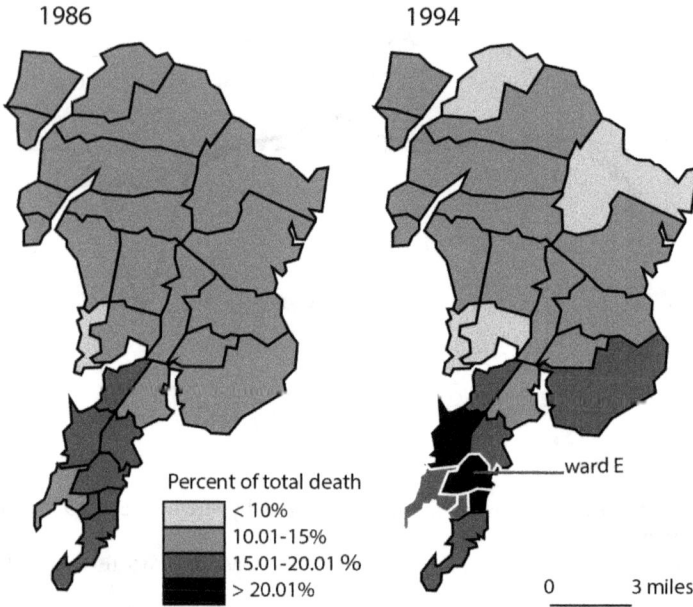

Figure 4.2.   **Change in Mortality from Infectious Diseases between 1986 and 1994 in the 23 Greater Mumbai Wards.**
Data collected from the Reports of the Executive Health office (198601994), Mumbai Municipal Corporation

The early 1990s mark a clear turning point in the spread of the epidemic in the city with HIV/AIDS clustered in the central parts of Mumbai's peninsula. After the early 1990s, the epidemic expanded to other parts of the city (Mudur 1997; Hira, Srinivasa, and Thanekar 1999). The higher number of deaths were likely the result of the opportunistic diseases associated with HIV. While the data do not show any direct connection between mortality and HIV, it strongly suggests that the increase in mortality among young adults, the shift in the causes of deaths, and the spatial patterns of the mortality data were likely the result of the emergence of HIV/AIDS in the 1980s and 1990s. The central wards, notably Ward E, presented a critical situation. This change in the dynamic of the epidemic may be explained by understanding how actors created high-risk spaces in Mumbai's central wards. These spaces were neither delimited by fixed boundaries nor by properties of continuity. They resulted from specific actor spatialities moving through global spatial configurations.

These central wards were interstitial places (Trasher 1963) through which the HIV/AIDS virus circulated. The collapse of the socioeconomic structure was associated with the rise of extremist nationalist Hindu movements produced places of trafficking. In this political-underworld system, flows of people circulated throughout these highly connected places, creating local hubs that relayed and redistributed regional and global activities of the underworld. Because of their position in the urban network, these central wards of poverty, trafficking and violence constituted spaces of risk for the circulation of the virus. Previous studies show that conflicts are associated with risk factors such as gender violence, behavioral changes, and reduction in resources and services, which have consequences on the spread of HIV (Iqbal and Zorn 2010; Smallmann-Raynor and Cliff 1991).

High-Risk Spaces in Motion: The Role of the 1992–1993 Mumbai Communal Riots

In the mid-1990s, the Indian government's AIDS policy was very limited. It only focused on the screening of sex workers, STD patients, drug users, and on the distribution of condoms among these "high-risk" groups, especially truck drivers (who often acted as "bridge" populations of the infection) and sex workers. Despite this, Mumbai was an attractive place for international funds, though some places within the city remained isolated from policy actions. Indian officials did not formally recognize the epidemic in the early 1990s, and there were only two policies in place regarding people affected by HIV/AIDS: people with HIV were either isolated or relocated to another location. This was especially true for sex workers. These measures merely reduced the visibility of the disease.

Added to this lack of effective policy was the reign of the Shiv Sena that gave rise to an atmosphere of suspicion and conflict in the 1990s. The leaders of the Shiv Sena instilled among the poor and middle classes an image of a fortress to defend against enemies. This divided the population into "them," the "impures" (non-Hindu and of non-Maharashtrian origins) and "us," the "pures" (Hindu and of Maharashtrian origins). With the emergence of the HIV/AIDS epidemic and the fear associated with this new disease, the division between the "pures" and "impures" went further with new divisions of "infected" and "non-infected." Some communities were thought to contain "HIV/AIDS infected deviants" who needed to be either isolated or relocated.

Figure 4.3 shows the assemblages of actors, scales of actions, and their consequences that likely influenced the epidemic course in central Mumbai. The diagram illustrates how the bonds that tie actions to one another consequently reorganized into new spatial configurations. Because causation and agency are central issues in understanding violence, this figure aims to generate an understanding of the interactions between actors at different levels that fueled the territorialization process in the central wards. It shows the particular articulations in the networks of social, political and economic rela-

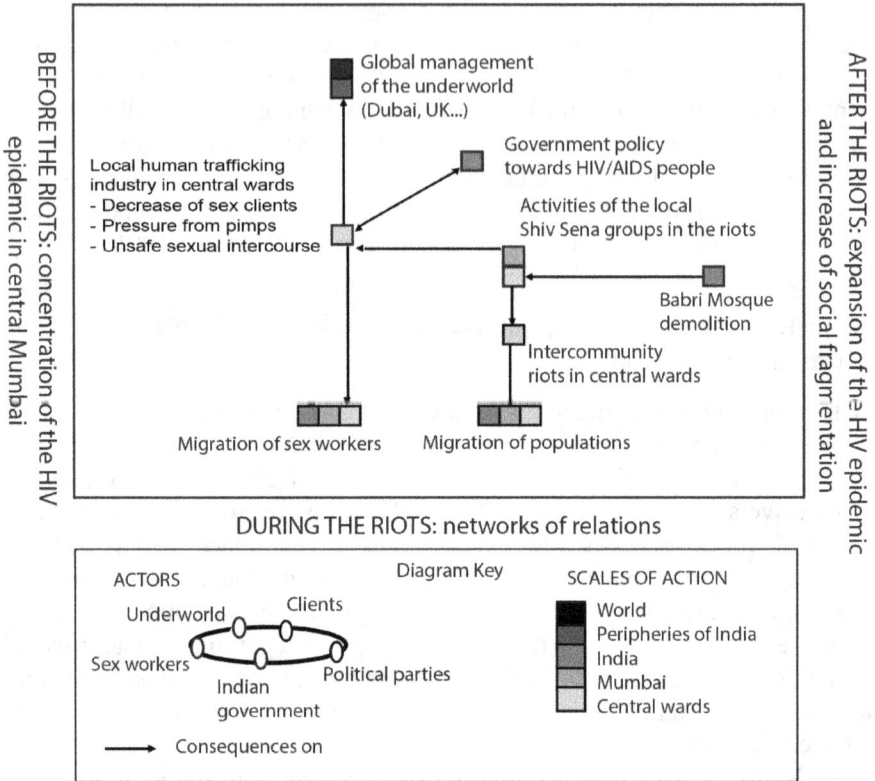

Figure 4.3. Mumbai riots (1992–1993) and their consequences on the HIV epidemic.
Created by Emmanuel Eliot, June 4, 2019

tions that led to increased HIV diffusion and social fragmentation within the city after the riots. These actors and their interactions and networks depicted in figure 4.3 are explained at length below.

The central wards in Mumbai catalyzed the riots as an echo of the immediately preceding event of destruction of the Babri Masjid (Babri Mosque) in Ayodhya, North India.[3] The 1992–1993 riots can be considered a major contributor to the spread of HIV/AIDS to other parts of the city. By integrating several spaces of action in the central wards, by creating a rupture in the temporality of the epidemic, by reorganizing and changing the spatiality of the epidemic combined with the intercommunity riots, these wards became local relays in the dynamic of the epidemic. The riots created a rupture in the dynamic of the epidemic and reshaped its course.

During the riots, the concentration of the main centers of prostitution (in Kamathipura in the central wards) and their proximity to the main circulation corridors of Mumbai made these wards important hubs of interaction with the rest of the city. The absence of care facilities for patients, the lack of prevention programs, and the stigmatization of certain populations (especially sex workers) contributed to the creation of high-risk spaces and the epidemic's spread. Specific populations such as sex workers or the Muslim minorities were particularly vulnerable, and they moved to other areas of the city where they became less visible to doctors, screeners, and the police. These relocations were also a result of repressive actions led by the local police forces and municipal authorities formed and/or controlled by the Shiv Sena. The sex workers driven out of the central wards became more isolated from effective health measures yet more likely to expand the epidemic throughout the city as explained below.

In central Mumbai's red-light district of Kamathipura, violent massacres, lack of food, and blackmail by pimps, together with police pressure supported by the Shiv Sena during the riots, all affected the spread of the epidemic. Both during the riots and in the period following them, customers began staying away from these districts. A study of fifty brothels in the area (Gilada 1994) showed that there had been a 25 percent to 30 percent decrease in customers, which increased the rate of unprotected sex and the movement of sex workers in search of work to other parts of the city.

By instilling a permanent feeling of fear within the Muslim populations in the central wards both before and after the riots, the actions of Shiv Sena led to the migration of Muslims to peripheral wards where communities grouped together for greater safety (Sharma 1996). The fear of violence and stigmatization resulted in reinforcing the communal nature of certain parts of the central and peripheral wards of Mumbai resulting in a partial redesign of the city's community map.

Regarding the HIV dynamic, community riots contributed to the spread of HIV all over the city. During the turning point in the early 1990s, the expansion of the epidemic in Mumbai was not random. It took this trigger to place various actors in interaction with one another for the epidemic to emerge in wards beyond its initial source. In short, it required an apparatus to act as the facilitator of a new spatial organization of the epidemic, which was provided in the combined form of the riots, and the actions of the Shiv Sena and the political underworld.

THE TERRITORIALIZATION PROCESS
OF VIOLENCE: A DISCUSSION

The territorialization process within the central wards helped activate the spread of the epidemic, even though it was polarized toward certain communities. This process, while aiming to control and isolate certain parts of the urban space, also uncovered a sociospatial ideology, a collective and local-ized galvanization of violence, and an identity-forming spatial rhetoric that helped to propagate the development of risk.

Spatial Purification and Biopolitics

The old central wards and especially ward E were sites more generally of the supposed first inhabitants of Bombay and specifically of its working class. It was the heart of the city even under the British Raj, and it was to be defended. Ancestral connections, origins, and purity became major slogans in the cre-ation of a *Mumbaikar*'s (Mumbai resident's) city. In the central wards, mem-ories were tied up with the construction of an identity that shaped the urban landscape (Heuzé 1999). In this context, the HIV epidemic was considered a source of "pollution" for this identity/memory space. Some communities were thus identified as impure and labeled as bodily carriers of HIV/AIDS because of their religion or their occupations. The visibility of the epidemic and the carriers required greater controls and actions, so spatial purification based on a network of forces became a key feature in the organization of space. Both the control of the epidemic and these supposedly affected communities were associated together and supported by forms of social hierarchies. The actors stigmatized certain groups as the enemies of national or local unity and also as the disease bearers that endangered the integrity of the community. The central wards, conceived as territorial sources of the identity, needed to be defended and governed. The control of the epidemic by the police forces and health authorities, including *cordons sanitaires*, and the organization of a new society based on pro-nationalist precepts was associated with economic and social developments.

These strategies reached a critical point with the communal riots. Indeed, after the riots, new spatialities came into being, which redefined the bound-aries between the communities and which led to new patterns of HIV/AIDS diffusion. The defense of these so-labeled "pure" places met resistance from some minority communities. Various actions launched by the Shiv Sena contributed in isolating and excluding such people. Marginalized, these communities converted this situation of relocation and isolation into a form of defense and a mode of survival for their community. For instance, the interviews showed that among the Muslim populations of the central wards, some people reinforced the identity barriers, strengthened the Islamic tenets and social control, especially among young adults, in order to protect their community from the "others" and to maintain their presence in the central wards. In contrast, after the riots, some families moved from these central wards to Mumbai's northern suburbs in order to find more peaceful and more homogenous residential areas. Both polarities of biopolitics (power on life and the resistance against power) were embedded in local withdrawals based on ethno-fundamentalist drifts. Both contributed in redefining the boundaries between individuals and communities on a foundation of powerful purification principles. The safety and the security of one required the exclusion of the others, but at the same time, the excluded required a greater inclusion inside the community. Finally, as Sibley (1988, 417) noted, the key issue is "the desire to homogenize space and to erect boundaries which secure the interiority of purified spaces." Place is an important element in understanding and answering this question and needs a deeper analysis that questions the spatialities of globalization and violence.

Immunization and Places

As Esposito (2006) pointed out, the immunization paradigm is a fundamental framework for the analysis of contemporary societies. The immunization paradigm extends Foucault's debates on biopolitics by focusing on the intersections of biology and politics and by emphasizing the importance of survival issues for the citizen. Immunization refers to the protection from a risk to which a community or a body is exposed. Societies and individuals are concerned with assuring their survival with respect to the risk of environmental or interhuman relationships. As Esposito explains, "[No] society can exist without a defensive apparatus, however rudimentary it might be, that is capable of protecting itself" (2006, 30). However, if protection is pushed beyond a certain limit, it constrains the community and may have potentially lethal effects. Indeed, excess of defense and exclusion may turn against the community itself and then to autoimmunizing itself.

In this work, the nexus of violence is found in three interwoven loops: the construction of an identity based on memories that were reinterpreted and recycled, the mechanism of defense by the claiming of "purity" against the supposed-HIV bearers and vectors, and the development of social techniques of security based on fear and anger. Rooted in sociospatial imaginaries, the identity is the frame within which violence takes off; the purity norms strengthened this identity by adding secular, religious, and sacred conceptions, and the need of security in a context of a crisis called for action: destroying "them" to save "us" (Sémelin 2005). HIV/AIDS became a mediator in the governing of these central wards because it refers to life and death and thus questions the ways communities take care of themselves and of the others. When deaths increased within some communities and when the protection of life became a criterion that legitimatized the use of power, security defenses increased.

These immunization techniques took root in an apparatus that was external to the State, different from it, but was also strongly linked. In fact, ambivalent relationships seem to be a central issue in the way regulations, actions, and reactions took place. For instance, these techniques refer to the State ideology of protection and care of the populations but were rooted in xenophobic considerations, or, the role of the Shiv Sena that was presented as an emanation of the Indian pluralistic model of the State but was also an actor of contestation of the latter's sovereignty.

The role of numbers in organizing exclusionary policies and procedures (Appadurai 2005) toward HIV positive people, and the construction of micropolitics based on purity introduce ambivalences in the analysis. They highlight the "preoccupations of life and survival at the heart of the political action" (Abélès 2006, 12). This anxiety feeds actions and determines the relationships between the individuals and the communities. By the end of the 1980s the visibility of the HIV/AIDS epidemic became evident. It constituted a step in the process of disjunction that finally transformed into new spatialities in central Mumbai. This entire process requires considering places neither as stationary nor as containers for action, but as new fluid structures for the transformations of spaces.

De-territorializing and Re-territorializing

Under some conditions, epidemics reach a threshold where they spread and change the stable patterns of the process (Watts 2003). Likewise, spatiotemporal micro-constructions may constitute a tipping point for the emergence of new spatial patterns and for the creation of new spaces. By connecting the processes of de- and re-territorialization, places contribute to redefining connections, relations, and pathways inside and between the spaces of the communities.

Therefore, places can be considered as mediators because they capture the complexity of regimes of practices of space (Legg 2011) within which they are extended. They help to understand the significance and values associated with the governing of spaces. Places are thus sites that integrate, fix, and embody the various spatialities of actors. By redefining the borders between *and* within communities through the exclusion of "impure polluters," places function both as a release mechanism and as a source for the creation of new spaces.

CONCLUSION

In the late twentieth century, in central wards of Mumbai, economics, politics, cultures, and the HIV/AIDS epidemic were intertwined. Together, they produced spaces of insecurity and resistance that helped to intensify population movements, especially after the 1992–1993 communal riots. This major event was *the* moment for past and memories, present and action, future and potentialities to mix together, becoming both interdependent and strongly exclusive. Based on this case study, place highlights the creation of spaces by individuals and groups, operating both as a temporal and spatial disjunction between situations, that is, operating through the before-and-after as well as transitioning from an old spatial organization to a new one. Place functions as more than simply a physical site as it includes many spatially oriented social productions. The territorialization process identifies the systems of entry and closure, or isolation, and controlled interactions that contribute to spatial change. In this process, the epidemic was propagated through a set of interactions that included individual and collective temporalities as well as specific scales. These points of mobility, coexistence, and interaction by different actors in different times, scales and metric properties form new territoriality. Social techniques based on purification established a frontier between human beings and their environments. Distances define what or who is close, in contact, or far and rejected. Politics organizes and structures ways of seeing, governing, and representing the environment and operationalizes a displacement. This process of de- and re-territorialization requires a spatiotemporal event or a "place" (see Massey 2002) that channels, connects, and contextualizes the course of the epidemic.

In sum, both structural and slow violence are connected to a variety of factors including economy, policy, norms, actor resources, and ideologies. All these factors are unequally distributed in space and are not connected at the same level or at the same time. All these factors have their own temporalities that can aggregate and cumulate themselves in order to effect or bring about major transformation in space.

NOTES

1. Shiv refers to Shivaji Bosle, commonly known as Chhatrapati Shivaji Maharaj, who is considered the founder of the Maratha Confederacy (1674–1818). He became a mythical hero for the nationalist Hindu wing as the one who routed out of the Moghul Rule before the advent of the British Raj.

2. A major part of the HIV data collection was conducted by Dr Shalini Bharat, Tata Institute of Social Sciences. See S. Bharat, 1996. *Facing the Challenge: Household and Community Response to HIV/AIDS in Mumbai, India*, Global Programme on AIDS.WHO, Geneva.

3. Since the end of the nineteenth century, Ayodhya's Babri mosque has been at the core of contestations and clashes between Hindus and Muslims. The mosque

was built at the beginning of the sixteenth century during the Moghul rule. It was widely considered as having replaced a temple dedicated to the Hindu god Rama. With the rise of "pan-Hindu" political movements since the 1970–1980s, Ayodhya became a symbol for the "anti-Muslim rule" sentiments of the Hindu nationalist movements. For them, the mosque was a symbol of the "threatened" Hindu majority. In December 1992 and January 1993, the tensions culminated with the destruction of the mosque by groups of Hindu activists and consequently led to communal riots throughout Indian metropolises.

REFERENCES

Abélès, Marc. 2006. "Globalization, Power and Survival: An Anthropological Perspective." *Anthropological Quarterly* 79, no. 3: 483–508.

Appadurai, Arjun. 2005. *Fear of Small Numbers: An Essay on the Geography of Anger*. Durham and London: Duke University Press.

Arnold, David. 1993. *Colonizing the Body: State Medicine and Epidemic Disease in 19th Century India*. New Delhi: Oxford University Press.

Asthana, Sheena. 1996. "The Relevance of Place in HIV Transmission and Prevention: Geographical Perspectives on the Commercial Sex Industry in Madras." In *Putting Health into Place: Landscape, Identity and Well-Being*, edited by Robin A. Kearns and Wilbert. M Gesler, 168–90. New York: Syracuse University Press.

Banerjee, Sikata.1996. "The Feminization of Violence in Bombay: Women in the Politics of the Shiv Sena." *Asian Survey* 36, no. 12: 1213–25.

Bharat, Shalini. 1996. *Facing the Challenge: Household and Community Response to HIV/ AIDS in Mumbai, India*. Geneva. Global Programme on AIDS, WHO.

Brown, Michael. 1995. "Ironies of Distance: An Ongoing Critique of the Geographies of AIDS." *Environment and Planning D: Society and Space* 13, no. 2: 159–83.

Chandavarkar, Rajnarayan. 1981. "Workers' Politics and the Mill Districts in Bombay between the Wars." *Modern Asian Studies* 15, no. 3: 603–47.

Craddock, Susan. 2000. "Disease, Social Identity and Risk: Rethinking the Geography of AIDS." *Transactions of the Institute of British Geographers* 25, no. 2: 153–68.

Cresswell, Tim, and Peter Merriman. 2011. *Geographies of Mobilities: Practices, Spaces, Subjects.* London: Ashgate.

Esposito, Roberto. 2006. "The Immunization Paradigm." *Diacritic* 36, no. 2: 23–48.

Foucault, Michel. 2004. *Sécurité, Territoire, Population.* Paris: Seuil.

Ghosh, Jayati. 2002. "A Geographical Perspective on HIV/ AIDS in India." *Geographical Review* 92, no. 1: 114–26.

Ghosh, Jayati, Vandana Wadhwa, and Ezekiel Kalipeni. 2009. "Vulnerability to HIV/ AIDS among Women of Reproductive Age in the Slums of Delhi and Hyderabad, India." *Social Science & Medicine* 68, no. 4: 638–42.

Gilada, Ishwar. 1994. "The IHO Relief Story." *AIDS Asia*. February 2, 1994.

Godwin, Peter. 1998. The Looming Epidemic: The Impact of HIV and Aids in India. London: Hurst & Company, 1998. 190 p.

Heuzé, Gérard. 1992. "Shiv Sena and 'National' Hinduism." *Economic and Political Weekly* 27, no. 41: 2253–63.

Heuzé, Gérard. 1999. "Populism and the Workers Movement: Shiv Sena and Labor in Mumbai." *South Asia: Journal of South Asian Studies* 22, no. 2: 119–48.

Hira, Subbash, Rao Srinivasa, and Thanekar Jairaj. 1999. "Evidence of AIDS-Related Mortality in Mumbai, India." *The Lancet* 354, no. 9185: 1175–76.

ICMR (Indian Council of Medical Research).1980. "Policy Statement on Ethical Considerations Involved in Research on Human Subjects." New Delhi: ICMR.

Iqbal, Zaryab, and Christopher Zorn. 2010. "Violent Conflict and the Spread of HIV/ AIDs in Africa." *The Journal of Politics* 72, no. 1: 149–62.

Kadri, A. M., and Pradeep Kumar . 2012. "Institutionalization of the NACP and Way Ahead." *Indian Journal of Community Medicine* 37, no. 2: 83–88.

Klein, Ira. 1986. "Urban Development and Death: Bombay City, 1970–1914." *Modern Asian Studies* 20, no. 4: 725–54.

Legg, Stephen. 2011. "Assemblage/Apparatus: Using Deleuze and Foucault." *Area* 43, no. 2: 128–33.

Massey, Doreen. 2002. *For Space.* London: Sage Publications.

Mudur, Ganapati.1997. "Death Rate from HIV Infection Rise in Bombay." *British Medical Journal* 315, no. 7120: 1400.

National Aids Control Organization. 2017. "NACO Annual Report 2016–17, Chapter 24." Accessed May 3, 2019. http://naco.gov.in/sites/default/files/NACO%20AN NUAL%20REPORT%202016-17.pdf.

Nixon, Rob. 2013. *Slow Violence and the Environmentalism of the Poor.* Cambridge: Harvard University Press.

Patel, Sujata, and Alice Thorner.1996. *Bombay: Metaphor for Modern India.* New Delhi: Oxford University Press.

Ramachandran, Prema. 2012. "ICMR's Tryst with HIV Epidemic in India: 1986– 1991." *Indian Journal of Medical Research* 136, no. 1: 13–21.

Ramasubban, Radika. 1998. "HIV/AIDS in India: Gulf between Rhetoric and Reality." *Economic and Political Weekly* 33, no. 45: 2865–72.

Ramasubban, Radika, and Nigel Crook. 1985. "Mortality Toll of Cities: Emerging Patterns of Disease in Bombay." *Economic and Political Weekly* 20, no. 8: 999–1005.

Ramasubban, Radika, and Nigel Crook. 1996. "Spatial Patterns of Health and Mortality." In *Bombay: Metaphor for Modern India*, edited by Sujata Patel and Alice Thorner, 143–69. New Delhi: Oxford University Press.

Sachs, Robert. 1986. *Human Territoriality: Its Theory and History.* Cambridge: Cambridge University Press.

Sehgal, Shobha. 2014. "Unfolding of HIV Epidemic and Spectrum of AIDS in North India." *World Journal of AIDS* 4, no. 1: 52–61.

Sémelin, Jacques. 2005. *Purifier et détruire: Usages politiques des massacres et génocides.* Paris: Seuil.

Sharma, Kalpana.1996. "Chronicle of a Riot Foretold." In *Bombay: Metaphor for Modern India*, edited by Sujata Patel and Alice Thorner, 268–86. New Delhi: Oxford University Press.

Sibley, David.1988. "Purification of Space." *Environment and Planning D: Society and Space* 6, no. 4: 409–21.

Smallman-Raynor, Matthew R. and Andrew David Cliff. 1991. "Acquired Immune Deficiency Syndrome (AIDS): Literature, Geographical Origins and Global Patterns." *Progress in Human Geography* 14, no. 2: 157–213. https://doi.org/10.1177/030913259001400201

Trasher, Frederik. 1963. *The Gang: A Study of 1313 Gangs in Chicago.* Chicago: Phoenix Books, the University of Chicago Press (original 1927) abridged version, 1963.

UNAIDS. "UNAIDS Data 2018." Accessed May 1, 2019. https://www.unaids.org/sites/default/files/media_asset/unaids-data-2018_en.pdf.

Verma, Ravi K., and Tarun Kumar Roy. 2002. HIV Risk Behaviour and the Socio-cultural Environemnt in India. In *Living with the AIDS Virtue: The Epidemic and the Response In India*, edited by Panda S., A. Chatterjee and A. S. Abdul Quader. New Delhi: SAGE Publication.

Wadhwa, Vandana. 2012. "Structural Violence and Women's Vulnerability to HIV/AIDS in India: Understanding through a 'grief model' Framework." *Annals of the Association of American Geographers* 102, no. 5: 1200–1208.

Watts, Duncan. 2003. *Six Degrees: The Science of a Connected Age.* New York, London: W.W. Norton & Company.

Chapter Five

A Woman's Place

Examining Perceptions of
Urban Social Space in India

Vandana Wadhwa and Jennifer Y. Pomeroy

On December 16, 2012, Jyoti Singh Pandey, a twenty-three-year old female physiology student was beaten and gang raped by six men in a private bus in Delhi. She was accompanied by a male friend, who was also severely beaten. Thirteen days later, Jyoti died from her injuries at a hospital in Singapore where she had been transferred for specialty care for acute injuries. In keeping with Indian laws prohibiting naming of rape victims to protect against stigma, and for her fight against her attackers, for her life and for justice, Jyoti was dubbed "*Nirbhaya*" (fearless one). Three years later, her mother pushed against norms of stigma and shame and publicly named her daughter (Mandhana and Trivedi 2012; Bresnehan, Udas, and Ramgopal 2013; *Times of India* [TOI] 2015).

The sheer brutality of this incident shook the nation awake from its seeming apathy toward crimes against women, triggering extensive national and international media coverage, demonstrations, and subsequently, several socioeconomic, legal, and urban planning changes (Himabindu, Arora, and Prashanth 2014; Bhattacharya 2015; Phillips et al. 2015). The heavy impact of this incident is why we chose to treat it as the launching point of our analysis. From scholarly understandings as discussed in the context and theoretical framework, this incident points to the presence of social injustice arising from deep-rooted unequal gendered power relations, or structural violence. For this study, we chose to analyze the state and perceptions of social justice not merely from the perspectives and understandings of scholars and experts in the field, immensely valuable as they are, but primarily from the perspectives of those who actually inhabit India's urban spaces. Therefore, our overarching research question was "What does this incident tell us about social perceptions of women's place in Indian society and its urban areas?"

To do this, the "Nirbhaya" incident and surrounding events were used as the grounding for a critical case study and analysis. We used a wide sample of media coverage surrounding the December 16 incident because such coverage provided perspectives of the women who navigate Indian urban space, urban policy decision makers and related professionals, activists and groups, and those entrusted with security of this space and its inhabitants. We used a mixed methodology, wherein we supplemented the above textual data with statistical crime data to contextualize spatiotemporal trends and patterns of crimes against women in India. Further, we used scholarly literature to provide understandings of violence with a broad yet elemental definition of social injustice, to which we added a social theory of space and a feminist geography framework to understand the relationships between society and space. The scope of this work is limited to the analysis of violence that occurs in India's public urban spaces.

The significance of this work is twofold. First, it spotlights social justice issues in Indian cities, where highly hierarchical, patriarchal social structures reflect in the exclusionary nature of its urban built environments, and which in turn reify the very same structures. Second, it allows for taking one step back from existing theories of space as a social construct to conceptualizing society as a space itself, expanding on and examining how one's occupation of urban space may be affected by one's claimed or denied place in society, based on one's social position or characteristics within that social context. Inferred from this conceptualization is the understanding of how viewing "society as a space" provides an accurate lens for capturing its hierarchical power structures that promote and perpetuate social injustices.

CONTEXTUALIZING GENDER INEQUALITY IN URBAN INDIA

India's sociocultural milieu is highly patriarchal, characterized by strong son-preference, traditional gender norms, and differential gender power relations that favor males. The undervaluing and devaluing of women manifest in practices such as early marriage and dowry, worse health outcomes, low education attainment, low workforce participation, and low autonomy in decision making. Unsurprisingly, India ranks very low on international gender equality scales. Such gender imbalances both signal and reinforce situations leading to high rates of domestic violence and other emotional and physical abuses against women that occur across social interstices of class, caste, and age (Johnson and Johnson 2001; Kishor and Gupta 2009; Banerjee 2014; Bhattacharya 2015; Jejeebhoy et al. 2015; Joy, Belk, and Bhardwaj 2015;

Pande 2015). Bhattacharya (2015) convincingly makes the case that the patriarchal sociocultural perceptions responsible for high rates of domestic violence spill over into public spaces, resulting in sexual assaults against women outside the home; women largely internalize these patriarchal notions, accepting such treatment as justified or unavoidable (Gupta, Arnold, and Lhungdim 2009; Himabindu, Arora, and Prashanth 2014).

The last couple decades have seen rapid urbanization in India. Particularly, 2011 was a watershed year where urban absolute population growth exceeded that of rural areas since Independence in 1947. It is the first time India's urban areas had an absolute increase in population while its rural population declined by 4 percent. India's fifteenth census since 1872 reports that its urban population accounted for 31 percent of its total population in 2011, compared to 28 percent in 2001 (Census of India 2011).

Such a high rate of urbanization is projected to continue, which is primarily caused by the large influx of rural migrants to Indian cities. Many of these new urban migrants live in poor conditions or in urban slums that have partly resulted from urban sprawl, where semi-rural and rural surrounds are embraced by city boundaries. The interior slums and those resulting from the incorporation of the semi-rural and rural fringes and their populations have contributed to the changing characteristics of Indian cities. These areas are at once modern and progressive, as reflected in higher educational and income attributes as well as greater opportunities for women's participation in urban life, while also displaying splintering social kinships and retaining of regressive characteristics reminiscent of their patriarchal and feudal histories. These are terrains of diversity, yet of great income and socioeconomic inequality and disparities (Census of India 2011; Thapan 2001; Gupta, Arnold, and Lhungdim 2009).

An overview of urban crime geography from the 1970s to early 2000s revealed higher crime rates in cities with higher rates of urbanization and urban growth. It also found positive correlations of violent crime with low income and unemployment and highly negative correlations with general socioeconomic variables. Clustering of certain types of crime revealed the existence of a "subculture of violent crime" in north-central India (Wadhwa and Dutt 2012; also see Pomeroy, Dutt, and Wadhwa 1999). Dreze and Khera (2000) claim a significant negative relationship between violent crimes (including crimes against women) with literacy and high female-to-male sex ratios. They also found that gender relations had a "crucial bearing on criminal violence." However, Iyer and Topalova (2014) found a significant negative effect of income channels on violent crimes, but not on crimes against women, perhaps pointing toward the greater importance of social factors over economic ones. These separate, varied findings warrant a different research lens investigating the rapidly urbanizing cities as complex social spaces.

Urban inequities and its "clash of cultures," meaning progressive and regressive tensions, produce landscapes of exclusion and insecurity for women in urban India, where they experience high rates of sexual harassment, and domestic and other violence (Paul 2011; McIlwaine 2013; Bhardwaj 2014; Himabindu, Arora, and Prashanth 2014; NCRB 2014; Bhattacharyya 2015). Rates of increase in such crimes are lowest in states with low Gender Inequality Index (GII) and highest in states with moderate and high indexes; however, states with both low and high GII showed similar rates of gender-based crimes (Sharma 2015), perhaps pointing to the pervasiveness of the phenomena regardless of formal measures of gender inequality. Two studies that surveyed urban men and women just around the timeframe of the December 2012 incident found that an overwhelming majority of women (95 percent) felt insecure and/or are harassed, whether in streets, markets, transit nodes and modes, or their own neighborhoods; one in five women opted out of participating in public life for fear of violence. This is startling, but not surprising, given that just over half the men admitted to sexual aggressions and many laid the blame for such aggressions on women's dress and behavior (Kambou 2014; Bhattacharya 2015). Moreover, the policing and legal system inhibit women's access to recourse in the face of domestic and other violence, including through sexual harassment and violence from its own members, calling into question "state tolerance" of such crimes and contributing to the gross underreporting of such crimes (Prasad 1999; Patel 2014; Bhattacharya 2015).

THEORETICAL FRAMEWORK:
OF SOCIAL SPACE AND SOCIAL JUSTICE

In this section, we present the understandings of social justice/injustice, violence, society, and space that underpin this particular work. We place the current analysis in conceptualizations of violence and injustice, understandings from social theory, and critical and feminist conceptualizations of space and society and the inequities therein. One of the distinctions and categorizations Galtung (1969) makes is between direct and indirect violence, based on whether an agent of violence can or cannot be identified, referring to the latter as "structural violence," wherein violence is embedded in social structures and practices. For our purposes of understanding violence in urban contexts, we require a framework that can encompass both forms of violence and thus turn to other conceptualizations. However, we adopt here Galtung's (1969) basic understanding of the "absence of violence" as "social justice" and the "condition of structural violence" as referring to "social injustice." Whilst elemental, this definition is broad enough in its simplicity to embrace the ideas of social justice/injustice we refer to in this chapter.

Without delving further in the many nuanced conceptualizations of violence (see Scheper-Hughes and Bourgois 2004), we use a conceptualization of "violence as operating along a continuum from direct physical assault to symbolic violence [that wrought by dominant power] and routinized everyday violence, including the chronic, historically embedded structural violence" (Bourgois and Scheper-Hughes in Farmer 2004, 318). This concept accurately captures the violence women and marginalized others face in India's urban spaces: direct physical assaults, "symbolic violence" born of patriarchal hierarchies within the "everyday violence" of socioeconomic, political, and institutional/legal structures of society.

The term "social space" was seemingly first used by Emile Durkheim in the sense of "an area inhabited by a group" (Claval 1984, 105). The Marxist School used it in its evolved sense to convey *space as the product of human and social practices*, structures, and relationships, including its iniquitous forms in the face of social injustices (Lefebvre [1974] 1991; Harvey [1973] 2009). In this chapter, we use two conceptualizations of social space. The first conceptualization is the above interpretation of "social space" as (built) space that is a social construct. So far, we understand that society is responsible for the character of its built form, that is, that urban spaces reflect society and social practices It becomes incumbent on us, therefore, to then understand the nature of society itself. This understanding can be greatly facilitated by regarding society itself as a geographic space. In other words, for this work, we forward a *dual* understanding of "social space:" (a) built spaces as the product of social processes, but also, (b) expanding this idea by taking one step back to further understand *society itself* as an abstract geographic space, where one's position (place) in that space is what determines one's access to, use, and experience of physical built space.

The latter conceptualization of social space is best expressed by Durkheim's contemporary, Georg Simmel, whose writings on space are well distilled and encapsulated by Škorić, Kišjuhas, and Škorić (2013). According to them, in Simmel's view,

The human experience of social surroundings is similar to the experience of spatial form—they are something that people can be included in or excluded from, something they are "trapped in" or they wish to escape to etc. From this it can be concluded that man [*sic*] has experience of *society as space*. (Škorić, Kišjuhas, and Škorić 2013, 595; emphasis added)

To further clarify this conceptualization, we refer to social space as understood by Campbell (Campbell and Oliver 1996, 184–85) who recounts how discriminatory and bigoted attitudes (in the context of disability) frequently hinder "claim" to space in society, where space here refers to "abstract" or "virtual" social space rather than physical (Wadhwa 2012). Treating society as a space itself provides the benefit of viewing more clearly its (built) structures, vertical hierarchies, and horizontal segregations (see Wadhwa, "Conclusion," this book).

At this juncture, where one needs to better understand the complexities and structures of this "society as space," a feminist lens can shed better light on our particular concerns of women's marginalization and oppression in the Indian context. This is where we rely on the valuable work by feminist scholars that both demonstrates and explains women's occupation of restricted and lower hierarchical place in virtual social space. The preceding section highlighted how Indian sociocultural, socioeconomic, law enforcement, and legal milieus together contribute toward violence against women, often manifesting in psychological and/or physical violence against women or their everyday marginalization in the routine processes of life (Bhattacharya 2015; Gupta, Arnold, and Lhungdim 2009; Himabindu, Arora, and Prashanth 2014; Patel 2014). Additionally, Das (2008) provides an insightfully useful review of gender violence and its normalization at multiple scales in multiple contexts. Similarly, Datta (2016) highlights the continued ascribing of gender-based violence to external spatialities rather than its embeddedness in unequal power relations across diverse scales and spaces traversing the public/private spheres.

It is also important to point out that "society as a space" does not simply exist as the "progenitor" to "city as a social construct"; the relationship between the two types of social spaces is not static, or one sided. Simmel's viewpoint as presented by Škorić, Kišjuhas, and Škorić (2013) above, continues, "The city in particular was a "sociological entity formed spatially," yet cities, and space in general, were more than mere social constructs due to the complex and dynamic relationships within societies and between society and space." (Škorić, Kišjuhas, and Škorić 2013, 594). Further, we add to it Massey's assertion that while space is socially constructed, "the social is spatially constructed too" (Massey 1994, 254). Thus, society and social space (physical space as a social construct per Lefebvre and Harvey) are highly interactive. That is, physical built social space is the product of society's practices and structural characteristics, but in turn also reinforces those same social practices and structures.

The latter idea of experiencing and understanding the above conceptualization of social space through its spatial expressions is better understood through feminist urban geography that examines social (re)constructions and the gendered nature of marginalization and social injustice in urban space (Gilbert 1997; Bondi and Rose 2003; Raju and Lahiri-Dutt 2011; Narayanan

2012; Peake 2015). Such crimes are not only inherently spatial, but also occur at the nexus of the "private-public," involving space, place, and gender. Such involvements naturally allow an important avenue for feminist geographic research on crime patterns and processes that benefits both feminist analyses and crime research (Pain 1991). One final understanding of social space utilized in this chapter is a feminist perspective of "paradoxical space" (Rose 1993), where women occupy both center and margin, and along with experiencing "confinement" in space and other tensions and paradoxes, can also exercise resistance in these very same spaces of marginalization.

METHODOLOGY, DATA, AND SCOPE

This work uses a mixed-method, case study approach to facilitate investigating a complex phenomenon within its context and answering *how* and *why* questions (Baxter and Jack 2008). It offsets limitations of a single data source and single analyses through triangulation of both, permitting cross-checking for data quality and analysis verification (Creswell 2009; Hussein 2009). We combined statistical analysis and geographic information systems (GIS) mapping with text analysis for intensive and extensive information gathering and analysis for a broad as well as nuanced understanding of the experience of women in India's urban spaces.

Statistical data was sourced from the National Crime Records Bureau (NCRB). However, definitions and categorizations of the various crimes have shifted over time, thus we restricted our data gathering to the three most consistent categorizations of crimes against women (rape, dowry[1] deaths, and sexual harassment), available from 1998 to 2015. At the time of analysis, spatial data for these crimes types were only available until 2012, but not for Delhi, thus our mapping reflects 2012 data, but Delhi data appears in the text instead.

Descriptive statistics and geographical information system (GIS) mapping were used to discern and highlight spatiotemporal patterns and trends and buttress content analysis. For mapping, Z-scores (measures of the distance in standard deviations of a sample from the mean, calculated by subtracting the sample mean from the data and dividing by the standard deviation) were used to facilitate comparability. All fifty-one cities appearing in NCRB 2012 crime records were included in this study. Together, they accounted for a population of 126 million, and after including Delhi, accounting for 35.2 percent of India's urban population (NCRB 2012; World Bank 2016).

The textual data was gathered from national and international news media coverage of the Nirbhaya incident and subsequent similar incidents across urban India. We used a combination of search terms including variations of woman/girl, urban/city, crime/violence, India, and "Nirbhaya" to comb through the most comprehensive search engine for media resources, Lexis-Nexis Academic. The time frame spanned from December 15, 2012, (a day before the incident) to June 30, 2015, to provide a couple of years' worth of data to accommodate for changing perspectives before analysis was performed. All items not directly referencing urban violence against women were excluded, resulting in just over one thousand unduplicated items. The textual data was subject to a content analysis to identify and enumerate emerging themes (Creswell 2009). Both authors reviewed the raw data, noting major and/or recurrent themes, then compared notes to arrive at a mutually satisfactory thematic schema.

Study Limitations

Textual data is limited to English-language media coverage due to the authors' language constraints. However, since coverage in English-language media was extensive and English is widely used internationally, we believed limitations emanating from single-language sources could be off-set by their extensiveness. Additionally, study scope was restricted to a general overview of violence in public urban areas despite its occurrence in public/private spheres and at every urban spatial scale, from the most elemental unit of home, to schools, hospitals, and workplaces. Examinations of violence at each of these scales and spaces would require a depth that is near impossible to achieve in one paper. Additionally, neither textual nor statistical data yielded any substantial/detailed data on the role of other social axes of class, caste, and other socio-demographic factors in violence against women in urban India, thus any in-depth analysis of these also had to be eschewed—any available information is mentioned in the analysis.

RESULTS AND DISCUSSION

Two other studies that expressly looked into media coverage surrounding the Jyoti Singh gang rape. Kaur (2013) found that overall, after "horror," media coverage focused on "optimism" for the victim, but the study's female respondents focused on "struggle" and "fight" in context of both the victim and women in general. Phillips et al. (2015) found that 56 percent of stories lauded Jyoti Singh's courage, 40 percent highlighted social outrage, while 11 percent discussed victim blaming. Much of this is reflected in our analysis as well. The current work extends beyond the above studies in its analysis.

Apart from responses and attitudes toward the incident and women (including Jyoti Singh), the present analysis also provides a window into the perceptions of the women who navigate these urban spaces, and into the ways in which other urban residents, civil society, and decision makers deal with issues of women's safety. The presented themes reflect these aspects, beginning with responses and attitudes, moving on to women's own experiences and perceptions of urban space and culminating with cited causes of and prescriptions for safeguarding against urban violence against women. Findings from our statistical analyses and GIS mapping are woven into these themes.

Social Attitudes and Responses

Media coverage at the time of the December 16 incident reported immediate outrage and disgust, which was reflected in protests, marches, and vigils. Coverage also underscored Jyoti Singh's courage as well as the extension of well wishes while she was simultaneously fighting for her life and for justice. However, media coverage also revealed heavy critique by the public and civil society for the initial police reaction of quelling their demonstrations and the slow response of top national leaders. The heavy attendance of young men at the demonstrations was reported as an encouraging sign of changing social attitudes, as captured in the following excerpt from Jayashree Nandi in her December 23, 2012, article in *Times of India* (*TOI*), quoting a young, male demonstrator:

> "We are fighting the character of this city [Delhi] which stinks of feudalism. Of course, we demand justice for the girl, but it's also time the police and government change their ways. Girls [should] go out whenever they like," said Rahul, an engineer.

However, our textual analysis suggests that gender discrimination is deeply rooted in Indian society and belies the enduring influence of gender discrimination and traditional norms both then and later. One symptom of such deeply rooted patriarchal cultural attitudes is victim blaming, which was evident from the content analysis. At the time of the incident, some social and political "leaders" blamed the victim or women in general and favored restrictive measures for women. As reported by Mahendra Ved in *New Straits Times* (Malaysia), dated January 14, 2013,

> [The words of] Asaram Bapu, a spiritual preacher, himself facing criminal charges. As per his wisdom, the girl, who had gone to see a movie with her "boyfriend," was "equally guilty." Rather than resist her attackers, she should have called them "brothers" and with folded hands should have begged for mercy.

The same article continued with this report: "Minister Mohammed Azam Khan said: 'Girls should not be out late at night with boyfriends. A system is needed to keep such behavior in check.'"

Parents of girls and women responded with an abundance of caution or even similarly restrictive coping mechanisms. In an article titled "Nirbhaya Shadow over New Year's Eve," Aparna Nair wrote in the December 31, 2012, edition of *TOI*, "Parents too have become extra cautious for their girls' safety. 'Till now I used to celebrate New Year's eve with my friends on my own. This year, my parents have told me to stick with my brother and not go to any party without him,' said Swati Gupta, a student." Similarly, an article by *PNG-Post Courier* (Australia) on February 28, 2013, reported,

> [A] common strategy against harassment was to simply keep girls and women at home. One girl explained: "If we tell our parents about boys harassing us, they would blame us only and say that it is our fault. Our parents might even stop us going out of the house."

Such attitudes restricting women is not surprising, given the results of an urban youth survey conducted little more than a year later, found within the media coverage. The survey reported that more than half of fifteen- to nineteen-year-olds agree that women's dress and behavior provoke men and that women's main role is taking care of household chores and raising children. Approximately 40 percent felt that women should accept that dowry is a community practice and that a degree of violence against women is inevitable (*Yuva Nagarik* [Youth Citizen] Metre, 2014/2015 in Dipti Singh, "55% Students Feel Attire and Behaviour of Women Provoke Men," *Indian Express*, January 22, 2015, Mumbai).

Women's Own Perceptions and Experiences

The content analysis revealed that in general, the recurrent theme regarding urban spaces was that women considered them as unsafe, insecure, dangerous, and requiring constant vigilance on their own part. Lack of safety and fear were apparent in women's statements such as those reported by Suman Chakraborty in her December 30, 2012, article in *TOI:* "We live in a free country yet can't move about freely. We [women] are afraid and feel unsafe." A survey found within the textual data of media coverage reported that 92 percent of women aged eighteen to forty-five years feel insecure in urban spaces, with Delhi ranking as the most unsafe by its female residents, followed by Bangalore and Kolkata (ASSOCHAM survey in T. Dutta, "In India, One Rape Every 40 Mins: Study," *Indian Express*, December 19, 2012).

These perceptions of danger are supported by numerous incidents and statistics reported within the textual data, and by data from the NCRB. An example of the former was reported by Mitchel, Ahmed, and Dhar in *The Guelph Mercury* (Canada) on August 23, 2013, "Last week, an 11-year-old girl in Kolkata (Calcutta) succumbed to her injuries after resisting her attacker, while a seven-year-old was assaulted then dumped from a train travelling through Chhattisgarh." Accounts of incidents seemed to span all ages, however, and references to caste were often included in incident accounts from rural areas. The acknowledged presumption was that "lower caste" women possibly faced higher violence in urban areas as well. The high numbers of incidents reported in the media was congruent with NCRB data revealing steady rises in violent crimes against women since 1998. By 2014, crimes against women constituted 11.4 percent of all crimes in the country (NCRB 2014). Some of this increase is certainly due to higher reporting of such crimes, particularly since 2012 (McDougal et al. 2018) but nevertheless, such crimes are not only frequent and common, but also go severely underreported (NCRB 2014; Pande 2015). The year 2015 was the first time a decline in such crime rates was seen, which dipped to 9.17 percent (NCRB 2015).

Other recurrent subthemes in the survey and in general textual data included constant and pervasive sexual harassment ranging from lewd remarks and stares to groping, touching, and molesting. Higher incidence of such practices was reported in public transport modes, which worsened limited mobility and opportunities. Other areas cited as unsafe were communal water sources, public toilets, and narrow alleys. The spatial pervasiveness of such harassment is well exemplified by this quote taken from Afrin Humayon's February 28, 2013, article in *TOI*: "Safety is something that cannot be taken for granted anymore. . . . I had to deal with eve-teasers right outside my house." Women were often hesitant to talk about these rampant issues, as they feared that they themselves might have to pay the price through their own loss of freedom, as exemplified by this report from *The Pioneer*, dated August 7, 2014, about the central Indian city of Bhopal,

> The girl students [reported] that they do not ask for help at the time when someone teases them [nor do they] even discuss it with their parents [and] instead they talk the issue [over] with friends with the fear that parents could stop sending them to college.

Figures 5.1, 5.2, and 5.3 as a group show the spatial distribution of three types of the most prevalent gender-based crimes. These three types of crimes are rape, dowry death, and sexual harassment. The raw data was processed into standard Z-scores enabling comparisons across Indian cities. Higher Z-scores indicate a greater departure from the mean, therefore higher positive Z-scores indicate higher concentration crime incidence. Figure 5.1 shows the cluster of highest rape Z-scores in the northcentral region of India. This

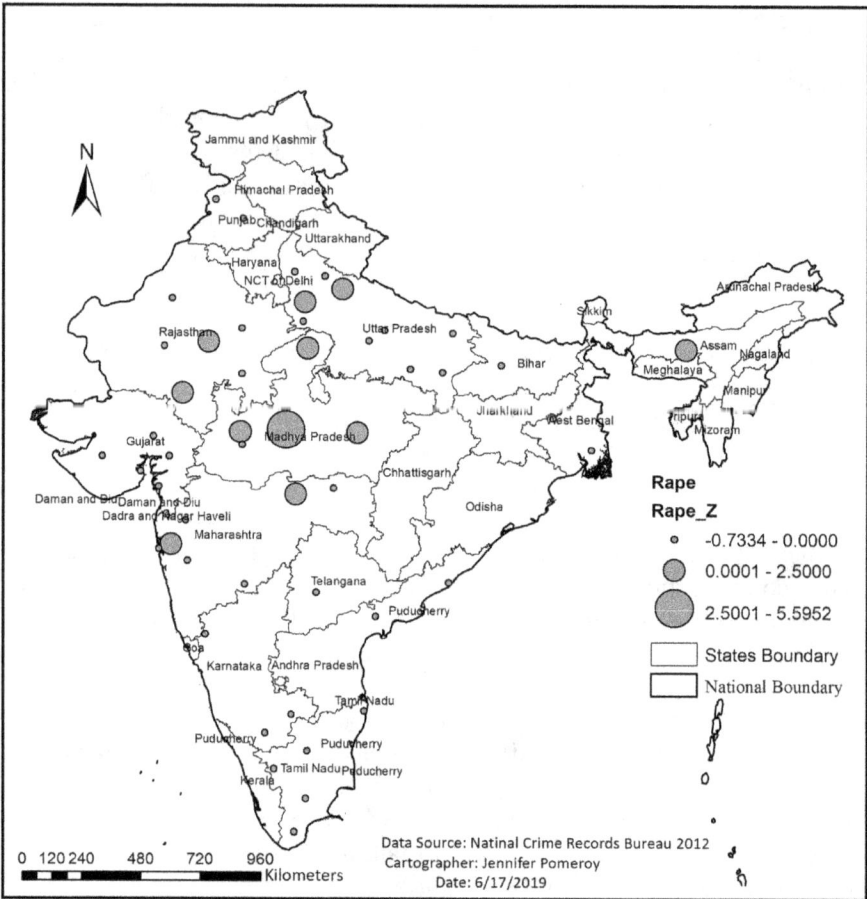

Figure 5.1.   Z-Scores Distribution for Incidence of Rape in Indian Cities, 2012.
National Crime Records Bureau, India, 2012. Cartographer: Jennifer Pomeroy. June 5, 2019

hot-spot region encompasses the cities of Bhopal (5.595) in Madhya Pradesh, Ajmer (2.143) in Rajasthan, Jabalpur (1.643) in Madhya Pradesh, and Bareilly (1.041) in Uttar Pradesh state. A separate stand-alone hot spot, which is Guwahati with a Z-score of 1.092, is located in the eastern state of Assam between the Brahmaputra River and the Shilong plateau.

Figure 5.2 displays the distribution pattern of dowry death Z-scores that are similarly concentrated in the northcentral region but with somewhat different member cities. These cities' Z-scores from highest to lowest are Bhopal (4.985) in Madhya Pradesh, Bareilly (1.943) in Uttar Pradesh, Asansol (1.754) in West Bengal, Kanpur (1.428) in Uttar Pradesh, and Agra (1.176) in Uttar Pradesh. Other than Asansol, which is located away from

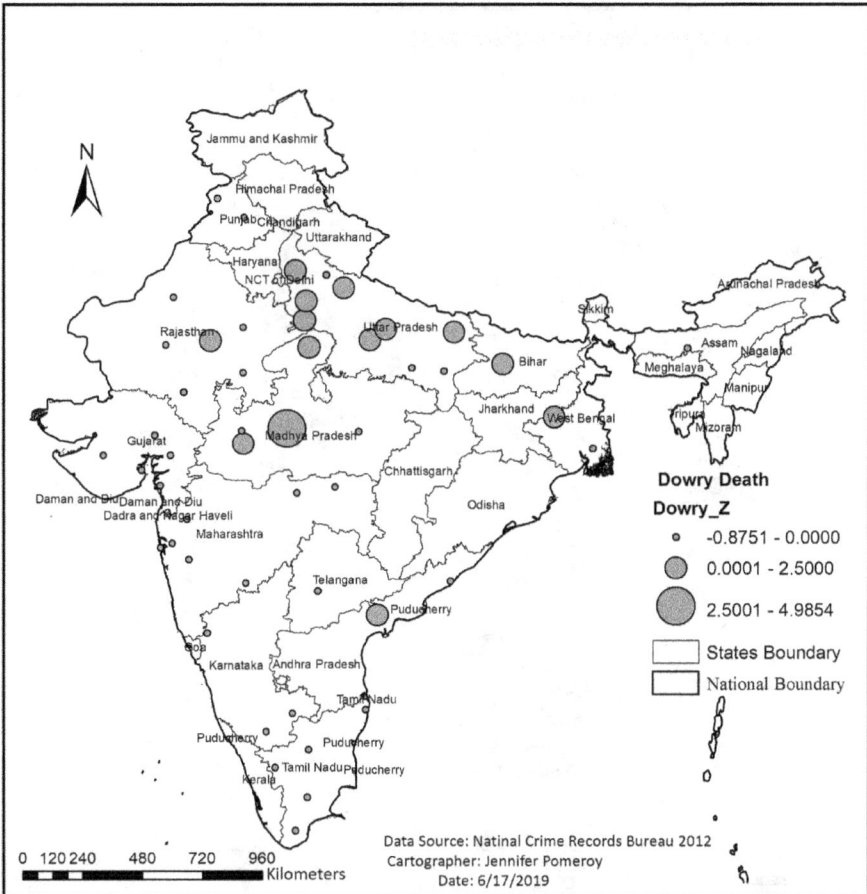

Figure 5.2.   Z-Scores Distribution for Incidence of Dowry Death in India Cities, 2012.
National Crime Records Bureau, India, 2012. Cartographer: Jennifer Pomeroy. June 5, 2019

the primary northcentral hot-spot region, the other four cities are located in two northcentral Indian states of Madhya Pradesh and Uttar Pradesh. Asansol is the second largest and most populated urban place in the Indian state of West Bengal.

Figure 5.3 demonstrates the spatial distribution of Z-score for sexual harassment. Vijayawada is the city with the highest Z-score for sexual harassment, which is 4.998. The city is located on the banks of Krishna River in southern Andhra Pradesh. Cities with Z-scores from highest to lowest are Bareilly (1.888), Lucknow (1.873), Kanpur (1.591), and Meerut (1.146). All four cities are located in one state: Uttar Pradesh, forming a large extent of the sexual harassment hot-spot region.

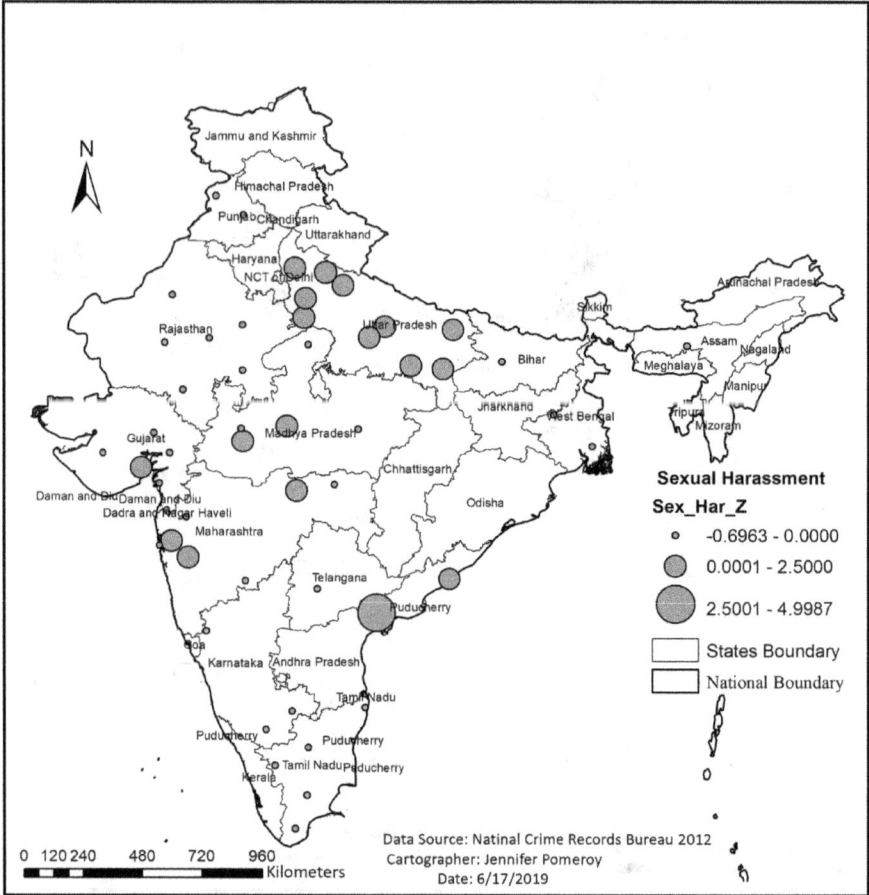

Figure 5.3.   Z-Scores Distribution of Incidence of Sexual Harassment in Indian Cities, 2012.

National Crime Records Bureau, India, 2012. Cartographer: Jennifer Pomeroy. June 5, 2019

Collectively examining all three figures, the distribution pattern of the three main crimes against women—rape, dowry deaths, and sexual harassment—are concentrated in the northcentral region, forming a regional hot spot that encompasses Madhya Pradesh and Uttar Pradesh; such findings are consistent with the "subculture of violence" theorization (Pomeroy, Dutt, and Wadhwa 1999; Wadhwa and Dutt 2012). Also part of these hot-spot regions are Rajasthan and West Bengal. Interestingly, Vijayawada, in the southern part of country, has the highest Z-score in sexual harassment. Southern states and their urban areas have typically seen lower levels of reported crimes against women (Pomeroy, Dutt, and Wadhwa 1999), but increasingly, these metropolises are also perceived as largely unsafe for women, as is also apparent in this account from interviews of women in urban areas as reported in the *New Indian Express* on June 16, 2014:

> A lot of my friends tell me that they can't join me after 9 pm as they are either afraid to come out or their parents don't let them. There are plenty of girls who feel really scared and unprotected late in the night even in some of the busiest roads in the city [Hyderabad, Andhra Pradesh, Southern India].

Despite increase in crime, the same article as above reports that many women look at these unsafe urban spaces as spaces of resistance, akin to Rose's (1993) concept of paradoxical space:

> Whether it is travelling alone or with a group, girls in urban India are certainly not averse to going out at night, which is a highly encouraging sign, feel some. . . . "I strongly feel that we girls are capable of taking care of ourselves together and I often hang out at night with my girlfriends. All of us carry a pepper spray can with us."

Causes and Prescriptions

This theme and the first two have one thread of overlap. Women are made to take the responsibility for both the commission of violence against them (victim blaming) as well as their own safety by restricting themselves and their behavior. This theme echoed more of the same sentiment.

Released some months after the Delhi gang-rape incident, the documentary "India's Daughter" received praise for evoking self-examination but also critique for giving voice to, and thus "normalizing" sexist/misogynistic attitudes, as in this telling and horrifying quote from the movie by Mukesh Singh, one of Jyoti Singh's rapists: "A girl is far more responsible for rape than a boy. When being raped, she shouldn't fight back. She should just be silent and allow the rape" (in "Ostrich. Head. Sand," *Tangerine*, March 6, 2015). Likewise, Mithila Phadke reported in an article for *Times City*, dated June 16, 2013, that a range of people were interviewed by documentary filmmaker Padmalatha Ravi regarding perceptions about women: "The answers were a revelation . . . especially when people were asked who they would hold responsible in case of a rape. Only a handful said 'rapist.' A majority blamed society and women."

Women are thus seen to be culpable and themselves the cause of violence against them. Some of the media coverage, however, did reveal that some sections of society recognized the role of patriarchy as a causative factor. The direct implication of the patriarchal nature of Indian society and related social aspects encompassed society in general but also how related attitudes bleed into it. Francis Elliott's December 22, 2012, article in the *Weekend Australian* reported,

> Ratna Kapur, a law professor, said the attack showed a crisis of male identity in India, where boys are often more valued than girls. "The grooming of young men to have a feeling of entitlement by Indian parents breeds a sense of masculinity and male privilege." . . . Hindol Sengupta, a Delhi-based social activist, said: "Female empowerment is totally unsettling to many men. It has shaken up their sense of entitlement and their response is violent and volatile."

Pop culture is typically indicative of and an expression of the mainstream of a society. The effect of patriarchal norms on everyday life by way of popular life through violent video games and Bollywood films (made in Bombay [Mumbai]) was frequently mentioned as a cause, as were the insensitive attitudes of police and the extremely low conviction rates of accused perpetrators. For example, as reported by Isha Jain in a *TOI* article dated December 21, 2012, quoting social activist Roop Rekha Verma, "Insensitive and callous attitude of the police towards such complaints is demoralizing. To top it all, the judiciary takes whole life[time] in providing justice."

The patriarchy subtheme, however, was relatively short-lived. Direct implication of society's gender norms was largely restricted to about a month or so after the December 16 incident, then replaced by a large corpus of coverage and discussions on governance failures and the design and form of urban areas that made them unsafe for women. Recurrent subthemes in the latter were lack of sanitation and water, inadequate transportation systems, and unlit or underlit streets. Some discussion of the role of the changing nature of urban areas was also found as an ascribed cause of increasing rates of crimes against women, such as rapid city growth, socioeconomic and demographic inequities (including skewed sex ratios), urban anonymity, and weakening of social structures.

Prescriptions for addressing the complex and pervasive issue of violence against women went largely the same way as causes. Some prescriptions themselves reflected patriarchal attitudes, for example, as seen in the following excerpt from Vinita Chaturvedi's April 10, 2013, article in *TOI*: "Haryana's former Chief Minister Omprakash Chautala gave his own analysis of how the increasing crime of rape can be handled in India, saying: 'Marry off girls early to prevent rape.'" Policy makers, urban planners, and the police initially made similar public announcements regarding safety measures against gender-based crimes that were either non-productive or still held women responsible in a manner. For example, wearing "appropriate" clothing, not going out late, and preferably being accompanied by a trusted male relative or friend. However, many media stories also pointed out that such announcements only reinforced stereotypes and did not account for the occurrence of violence against women regardless of times of day, dress style, or being accompanied by a male. These statements elucidate that, despite its rapid growth and urbanization, Indian urban society as a space itself has little place for women or their concerns as elucidated in this interview by Aparna Nair in her December 31, 2012, article for *TOI*:

> "Our society is male dominated. And even if we say otherwise many families unconsciously ask the girls to behave in a 'proper' way while boys are allowed to roam in a care free manner," said Kavita Rattan, a lecturer. Small actions like not asking boys where they are going while putting restrictions on the movement of girls give the former a sense of power over the latter. "Boys must also be taught how to behave with a woman. They should also be made responsible for their behaviour like it is with the girls. Our social fabric is such that it does not do anything to give women safety and dignity and that is why we have to resort to being cautious for our own safety," she said.

Media coverage also discussed federal, state, and local initiatives and changes resulting from public and media pressure. The social and institutional responses below highlight the short-term vision of most policy makers and how physical social space (city as a construct of society) is inherently problematic for women. Various city/state administrations undertook measures to improve roads and lighting, increase sanitation infrastructures, and increase the operation of segregated buses and railway compartments. Media coverage also included opinions that pointed out that such measures were ineffective and rather reinforced a damaging inequality.

Police departments across the country promised increased police presence, incorporating more women into their ranks, and gender-sensitization workshops. The federal government set up a committee chaired by Chief Justice J. S. Verma to recommend necessary enforcement and legal reforms, resulting in the creation of fast-track courts, criminalization of new offenses against women, and modifications to existing sentencing guidelines. The "Nirbhaya Fund" was set up to improve urban safety. However, the fund went unused for its entire first year.

Almost all of the above measures largely address issues of physical social space, not society itself, or place the onus of safety either squarely on a woman's shoulders or at least require removing herself from situations/spaces where she might encounter violence. There were, however, a few exceptions that were productive. Civil society organizations encouraged bottom-up female empowerment campaigns such as "Respect for Women" and *"Bell Bajao"* ("ring the bell," indicating boarding the bus to reclaim public transit for women). The organization Jagori stepped up city safety audits and launched a crowd-sourced app, Safetipin, that evaluates safety in Indian cities and acts as a tracker for personal safety. Media coverage also mentioned launches of several self-defense programs. Another initiative was the participation of Indian cities in the global "safe city" initiative funded by USAID, which apart from women-centered infrastructural and safety improvements includes partnering with educational institutions. The latter initiative includes a critically important component: to engage males into programs that raise gender awareness and promote safer cities for women.

CONCLUSION

As illustrated in the preceding sections, Fenster's observation, "the denial of the right to the city is a daily practice for many women" (2005, 218), rings true in the Indian urban context. The Indian urban setting, viewed as virtual geographic space, even in its more progressive urbanization and growth era, affords little place to women. This is reflected in its construct or physical urban social space, which manifests continuing low regard, often blindness to women's specific needs and desires regarding their access to and use of urban space, and frequently presents unsafe environments and situations of precarious security. Thus, violence, and therefore social injustice (Galtung 1969) takes place at both levels of social space in the Indian city, within its social structures, and within the resulting physical constructions of space.

Jyoti Singh's brutal gang rape highlights both the above. The horror of the incident forced several changes, but our study also highlights that Indian society largely missed the chance for deep introspection regarding the place it affords women (and other marginalized gender/sexual identities) by not engaging in sustained discourse related to its entrenched patriarchy that spills over into social, political, and legal institutions (Patel 2014). While some political leaders and policy makers responded to public pressure and took some action, much of it sought to treat the *symptoms* of patriarchal and unequal gender power relations. Some adopted short-term solutions such as gender-segregated transport only reify entrenched ideologies of difference and are not likely to lead to long-term change without addressing social attitudes themselves. Even the few empowerment programs (e.g., self-defense classes) put the onus of safety on women—other, more robust programs continue to be funded by civil society, as always. It is also telling that a majority of the media coverage that included articles written by women and opinions expressed by women themselves, still refer to women as "girls," reflecting that the patriarchal practice of infantilizing women (Richardson 1981) is often subconsciously internalized by the very women who protest patriarchy's stifling norms.

Legal reforms typically possess the power to create lasting change. However, they also do not amount to much unless buttressed by a change in attitudes. Crimes against women in urban India have continued to climb, and the Criminal Law (Amendment) Bill of 2013 (legal reforms triggered by the December 16 incident) still does not provide women safety in their own homes since it does not recognize marital rape as a criminal offence—the inclusion of that provision was blocked by several legislators (Himabindu, Arora, and Prashanth 2014; Patel 2014; Bhattacharya 2015). The much-needed Nirbhaya Fund had not been put to much use as of the end of the data analysis period, although various educators did propose its use for gender-sensitizing curricula in schools. No surprise then, that the second anniversary of the incident witnessed Jyoti Singh's father lamenting that all reforms and talk of reforms had come to nothing (*TOI* 2014). The Nirbhaya Fund has been used since then to carry on the "safe cities" project (*TOI* 2018), but most funded activities still treat the social space of "city as social construct." Since these spaces do influence the experience of "society as space," they are likely to wield some impact on social justice. However, while the above actions for safe and inclusive urban planning and legal reforms are critical to addressing social justice, unless the social aspect of equity and equality is addressed in tandem with its physical manifestation in the city, and women given full access to their right to social space, the virtual and constructed social spaces of the Indian city will continue to be contested, oppressive, and exclusionary for women and other marginalized identities. Aparna Nair's interviewee for the *TOI* article dated December 31, 2012, puts it best: "Girls [*sic*] have been teased or raped despite following safety directions. What is needed is a change in the mentality of people themselves."

NOTE

1. Dowry refers to wealth/property transferred from to the bride's family to the groom's, akin to a dower. Dowry deaths often result when the groom's family regard such wealth as inadequate—these crimes are typically indicative of domestic violence, but we opted to include it in our analysis since it also serves as a contextual proxy indicator of women's status in a particular society.

REFERENCES

Banerjee, Priya. R. 2014. "Dowry in 21st-Century India: The Sociocultural Face of Exploitation." *Trauma Violence & Abuse* 15, no. 1: 34–40. doi: 10.1177/1524838013496334.

Baxter, Pamela, and Susan Jack. 2008. "Qualitative Case Study Methodology: Study Design and Implementation for Novice Researchers." *The Qualitative Report* 13, no. 4: 544–59.

Bhardwaj, Bhawana. 2014. "Molestation, Sexual, Abuse and Violence against Women in India: An Overview of Crime Cases in Himachal Pradesh." *Journal of Business Management & Social Science Research* 3, no. 9: 44–46.

Bhattacharyya, Rituparna. 2015. "Understanding the Spatialities of Sexual Assault against Indian Women in India." *Gender, Place & Culture* 22, no. 9: 1340–56.

Bondi, Liz, and Damaris Rose. 2003. "Constructing Gender, Constructing the Urban: A Review of Anglo-American Feminist Urban Geography." *Gender, Place & Culture* 10, no. 3: 229–45. http://dx.doi.org/10.1080/0966369032000114000.

Bresnehan, Samantha, Sumnima Udas, and Ram Ramgopal. 2013. "'Nirbhaya,' Victim of India Gang Rape Fought for Justice." CNN. December 15, 2013. Accessed November 7, 2016. http://www.cnn.com/2013/12/04/world/asia/nirbhaya -india-rape/.

Campbell, Jane, and Mike Oliver. 1996. *Disability Politics: Understanding Our Past, Changing Our Future*. London and New York: Routledge.

Census of India. 2011. Accessed November 8, 2016. http://censusindia.gov.in/

Claval, Paul. 1984. The Concept of Social Space and the Nature of Social Geography. *New Zealand Geographer* 40, no. 2: 105–09. doi:10.1111/j.1745-7939.1984 .tb01046.

Creswell, John W. 2009. *Research Design: Qualitative, Quantitative and Mixed Methods Approaches.* Thousand Oaks, CA: Sage.

Das, Veena. 2008. "Violence, Gender, and Subjectivity." *Annual Review of Anthropology* 37: 283–99.

Datta, Anindita. 2016. "The Genderscapes of Hate: On Violence Against Women in India." *Dialogues in Human Geography* 6, no. 2: 178–81.

Datta, Ayona. 2016. "Another Rape? Persistence of Public/Private Divisions in Sexual Violence Debates in India." *Dialogues in Human Geography* 6, no. 2: 173–77.

Dreze, Jean, and Reetika Khera. 2000. "Crime, Gender, and Society in India: Insights from Homicide Data." *Population and Development Review* 26, no. 2: 335–52. https://www.jstor.org/stable/172520.

Farmer, Paul. 2004. "An Anthropology of Structural Violence," with comments by Philippe Bourgois and Nancy Scheper-Hughes, D. Fassin, Linda Green, H. K. Heggenhouen, Laurence Kirmayer, and Loic Wacquant. *Current Anthropology* 45, no. 3: 305–25. Accessed January 18, 2014. http://www.jstor.org/stable/10.1086/38 2250?origin=JSTOR-pdf.

Fenster, Tovi. 2005. "The Right to the Gendered City: Different Formations of Belonging in Everyday Life." *Journal of Gender Studies* 14, no. 3: 217–31. http:// dx.doi.org/10.1080/09589230500264109.

Galtung, Johan. 1969. "Violence, Peace, and Peace Research." *Journal of Peace Research* 6, no. 3: 167–91.

Gilbert, Melissa. R. 1997. "Feminism and Difference in Urban Geography." *Urban Geography* 18, no. 2:166–79. http://dx.doi.org/10.2747/0272-3638.18.2.166.

Gupta, Kamla, Fred Arnold, and H. Lhungdim. 2009. *Health and Living Conditions in Eight Indian Cities, National Family Health Survey (NFHS-3), India, 2005–6.* Mumbai/Calverton Maryland: International Institute for Population Sciences/ICF Macro. http://www.measuredhs.com/pubs/pdf/OD58/OD58.pdf.

Harvey, David. [1973] 2009. *Social Justice and the City. Revised Edition.* Athens & London: University of Georgia Press.

Himabindu, B. L., Radhika Arora, and Nuggehalli Srinivas Prashanth. 2014. "Whose Problems Is It Anyway? Crimes against Women in India." *Global Health Action.* Accessed December 26, 2017. http://dx.doi.org/10.3402/gha.v7.23718.

Hussein, Ashatu. 2009. "The Use of Triangulation in Social Sciences Research: Can Qualitative and Quantitative Methods be Combined?" *Journal of Comparative Social Work* 1: 1–11.

Iyer, Lakshmi, and Petia B. Topalova. September 2, 2014. "Poverty and Crime: Evidence from Rainfall and Trade Shocks in India." *Harvard Business School BGIE Unit Working Paper No. 14-067.* http://dx.doi.org/10.2139/ssrn.2419522.

Jejeebhoy, Shireen J., Sharmistha Basu, Rajib Acharya, and A. J. Francis Zavier. 2015. *Gender-Biased Sex Selection in India: A Review of the Situation and Interventions to Counter the Practice.* New Delhi: Population Council. https://assets.publishing.service.gov.uk/media/57a0897eed915d3cfd000284/61192_India_Lit_Review_Sex_Selection.pdf.

Johnson, Pamela S., and Jennifer Johnson. 2001. "The Oppression of Women in India." *Violence against Women* 7, no. 9: 1051–68. doi:10.1177/10778010122182893.

Joy, Annamma, Russell Belk, and Rishi Bhardwaj. 2015. "Judith Butler on Performativity and Precarity: Exploratory Thoughts on Gender and Violence in India." *Journal of Marketing Management* 31, no. 15-16: 1739–45. http://dx.doi.org/10.1080/0267257X.2015.1076873.

Kambou, Sarah D. 2014. "Are India's Cities Any More Safe Today for Women and Girls?" *The Huffington Post*, June 9, 2014. Accessed November 8, 2016. http://www.huffingtonpost.com/sarah-degnan-kambou/are-indias-cities-any-mor_b_5474459.html.

Kaur, Reetinder. 2013. "Representation of Crime against Women in Print Media: A Case Study of Delhi Gang Rape." *Anthropol* 2: 115. http://www.omicsonline.org/representation-of-crime-against-women-in-print-media-a-case-study-of-delhi-gang-rape-2332-0915.1000115.php?aid=21911doi: 10.4172/2332-0915.1000115.

Kishor, Sunita, and Kamla Gupta. 2009. *Gender Equality and Women's Empowerment in India.* National Family Health Survey (NFHS—3), India, 2005–06. Mumbai: International Institute for Population Sciences; Calverton, Maryland, USA: ICF Macro.

Lefebvre, Henry. [1974] 1991. *The Production of Space.* Oxford: Blackwell Publishers.

Mandhana, Niharika, and Anjani Trivedi. 2012. "Indians Outraged by Account of Gang Rape on Bus." *The New York Times,* December 18, 2012. Accessed November 8, 2016. http://india.blogs.nytimes.com/2012/12/18/outrage-in-delhi-after-latest-gang-rape-case/. Retrieved on December 26, 2015.

Massey, Doreen.1994. *Space, Place and Gender.* Minneapolis: University of Minnesota Press.

McDougal, Lotus, Samuel Krumholz, Nandita Bhan, Prashant Bharadwaj, and Anita Raj. 2018. "Releasing the Tide: How Has a Shock to the Acceptability of Gender-Based Sexual Violence Affected Rape Reporting to Police in India?" *Journal of Interpersonal Violence*, 1–23. doi:10.1177/0886260518811421.

McIlwaine, Cathy. 2013. "Urbanisation and Gender-based Violence: Exploring the Paradoxes in the Global South." *Environment and Urbanization* 25, no. 1: 65–79. doi:10.1177/0956247813477359.

Narayanan, Yamini. 2012. "Violence against Women in Delhi: A Sustainability Problematic." *Journal of South Asian Development* April 7 no. 1: 1-2. doi:10 .1177/097317411200700101

National Crime Records Bureau (NCRB). 2012. *Crimes in India*. http://ncrb.nic.in/StatPublications/CII/CII2012/Statistics2012.pdf.

———. 2014. *Crimes in India*. http://ncrb.nic.in/StatPublications/CII/CII2014/Statistics2014.pdf.

———. 2015. *Crimes in India 2015 Statistics*. http://ncrb.gov.in/StatPublications/CII/CII2015/FILES/CrimeInIndia2015.pdf . Accessed on December 20, 2017.

Nigam, Shalu. 2014. "Violence, Protest and Change: A Socio-Legal Analysis of Extraordinary Mobilization after the 2012 Delhi Gang Rape Case." *International Journal of Gender and Women's Studies* 2, no. 2: 197–221.

Pain, Rachel. 1991. "Space, Sexual Violence and Social Control: Integrating Geographical and Feminist Analyses of Women's Fear of Crime." *Progress in Human Geography* 15, no. 4: 415–31.

Pande, Rohini. 2015. "Keeping Women Safe: Addressing the Root Causes of Violence against Women in South Asia." *Harvard Magazine* November 28, 2015. Accessed on November 8, 2016. http://www.tinyurl.com/z2blc8r.

Patel, Vibhuti. 2014. "Campaign against Rape by Women's Movement in India." *DEP. Deportate, Esuli, Profughe.* http://www.unive.it/media/allegato/dep/n24-2014/Ricerche/03_Patel.pdf.

Paul, Tanusree. 2011. "Space, Gender, and Fear of Crime: Some Explorations from Kolkata." *Gender Technology and Development* November 2011 15, no. 3: 411–35. doi:10.1177/097185241101500305.

Peake, Linda. 2015. "The Twenty-First Century Quest for Feminism and the Global Urban." *International Journal of Urban and Regional Research* 40, no. 1: 219–27.

Phillips, Mark, Fargol Mostofian, Rajeev Jetly, Nazar Puthukudy, Kim Madden, and Mohit Bhandari. 2015. "Media Coverage of Violence against Women in India: A Systematic Study of a High-Profile Rape Case." *BMC Women's Health* 15:3 http://bmcwomenshealth.biomedcentral.com/articles/10.1186/s12905-015-0161-x. Accessed November 8, 2016. doi: 10.1186/s12905-015-0161-x.

Piedalue, Amy. 2017. "'Beyond Culture' as an Explanation for Intimate Violence: The Politics and Policies of Plural Resistance." *Gender, Place & Culture*, 24, no. 4: 563–74.

Pomeroy, George M., Ashok Kumar Dutt, and Vandana Wadhwa. 1999. "Spatial Patterns of Crime in Indian Cities." In *Urban Growth and Development in Asia: Living in Cities, vol. II*, edited by Graham Chapman, Robert Bradnock, and Ashok Kumar Dutt, 292–312. Aldershot, Hants, England: Ashgate Publishers Ltd.

Prasad, Shally. May 1999. "Medicolegal Response to Violence against Women in India." *Violence against Women* 5, no. 5: 478–506.

Raju, Saraswati, and Kuntala Lahiri-Dutt. 2011. *Doing Gender, Doing Geography.* New Delhi: Routledge.

Richardson, Laurel. 1981. *Feminist Frontiers: Gender Stereotyping in the English Language.* New York: McGraw-Hill.

Rose, Gillian. 1993. *Feminism and Geography: The Limits of Geographical Knowledge.* Cambridge, UK: Polity Press.

Scheper-Hughes, Nancy, and Philippe Bourgois. 2004. "Introduction: Making Sense of Violence." In *Violence in War and Peace: An Anthology*, 1–27. Oxford: Blackwell.

Sharma, Paribhasha. 2015. "A Subnational Analysis: Gender-Based Crime and Gender Inequality in India." *Economic & Political Weekly* 50, no. 45: 48–55.

Škorić, Marko, Aleksej Kišjuhas, and Jovana Škorić. 2013. "'Excursus on the Stranger' in the Context of Simmel's Sociology of Space." *Sociologia* 45, no. 6: 589–602.

Thapan, Meenakshi. 2001. "Adolescence, Embodiment and Gender Identity in Contemporary India: Elite Women in a Changing Society." *Women's Studies International Forum* 24, no. 3-4: 359–71. http://dx.doi.org/10.1016/S0277-5395(01)00181-9.

Times of India. 2014. "Nothing Has Changed Since December 16: Nirbhaya's Dad." PTI, December 15, 2014. Accessed November 8, 2016. http://timesofindia.indiatimes.com/india/Nothing-has-changed-since-Dec-16- Nirbhayas-dad/articleshow/45524232.cms.

———. 2015. "My Daughter's Name Was Jyoti Singh. Not Ashamed to Name Her: Nirbhaya's Mother." December 16, 2015. Accessed on March 25, 2016. http://timesofindia.indiatimes.com/india/My-daughters-name-was-Jyoti-Singh-Not-ashamed-to-name-her-Nirbhayas-mother/articleshow/50206977.cms

———. 2018. "Government Okays Rs 2,919cr Nirbhaya Fund for Creating 'Safe Cities.'" March 1, 2018. Accessed June 6, 2019. http://timesofindia.indiatimes.com/articleshow/63132242.cms?utm_source=contentofinterest&utm_medium=text&utm_campaign=cppst.

Wadhwa, Vandana. 2012. "Geographies of Disability: An Emergent Theme in Social Geography." In *Facets of Social Geography: International and Indian Perspectives*, edited by Ashok K. Dutt, Vandana Wadhwa, Baleshwar Thakur, and Frank Costa, 94–118. New Delhi: Cambridge University Press. http://dx.doi.org/10.1017/UPO9788175969360.008.

Wadhwa, Vandana, and Ashok K. Dutt. 2012. Spatial Patterns of Crime in India. In *Facets of Social Geography: International and Indian Perspectives*, edited by Ashok K. Dutt, Vandana Wadhwa, Baleshwar Thakur, and Frank Costa, 416–36. New Delhi: Cambridge University Press. doi: http://dx.doi.org/10.1017/UPO9788175969360.024

World Bank. 2016. *The World Bank Data.* Accessed November 8, 2016. http://data.worldbank.org/indicator/SP.URB.TOTL.IN.ZS.

Young, Iris Marion. 1990. *Justice and the Politics of Difference.* Princeton: Princeton University Press.

Part II

STRUCTURAL APPROACHES TO SOCIAL JUSTICE

Chapter Six

Intersectional Organizing as an Approach to Social Justice

Lessons from Brazil's Domestic Workers' Movement

Caitlin M. Alcorn

In his foundational text, *A Theory of Justice,* John Rawls (1971) argues that "the basic structure of society . . . is the primary subject of justice because its effects are so profound and present from the start" (7). This "basic structure," he explains, results from "the way in which the major social institutions distribute fundamental rights and duties" and in turn, locate members of society in different (unequal) social positions (7). With a focus on the basic structure, that is, "the background social framework within which the activities of associations and individuals take place," Rawls proposes a kind of moral dualism to evaluate separately the actions of individuals and the institutions of the basic structure (Rawls 2001 cited in Young 2006, 91). Rawls's theory of justice, often shortened to "justice as fairness," fits within a larger context of political philosophy that conceptualizes justice in terms of distribution. This "distributive paradigm," as political theorist Iris Marion Young (1990) calls it, focuses the subject of social justice on the distribution of resources or social positions within a society.

For the purposes of this chapter, I will draw from the extensive work of Iris Marion Young (1990, 2000, 2006, and 2011) in which she reformulates Rawls's "basic structure" in order to better account for the relationship between individual and collective action and social structures. Young's reformulation proposes a theory of justice that broadens the concerns of justice to those beyond distributive issues. After exploring these ideas in more detail, I apply them to my research on the paid domestic service sector in Brazil. Young's critical theory of justice informs my argument for conceptualizing paid domestic service as a major social institution, and for framing the domestic workers' movement as a struggle not for "particularist," identity-based wins, but rather for a more just Brazilian society.

Extreme economic inequality, lingering racial hierarchies, and women's subordination continue to restructure Brazilian society. Despite improvement in recent years, Brazil remains one of the most unequal countries in the world. Between 2006 and 2012, for example, the richest one percent of the population accrued 25 percent of all incomes (Medeiros et al. 2015). Though long characterized as a "racial democracy" (Freyre 1986 [1933]), racial hierarchies of white supremacy are evident in nearly every sector of Brazilian society. Afro-Brazilian (*preta ou parda*, "black or brown") households are overly represented among the poorest ten percent of the population (76.2 percent) while white households are overly represented among the wealthiest one percent of the population (79.5 percent) (*Instituto Brasileiro de Geografia e Estatística* [IBGE] 2015). In a number of indicators of well-being and quality of life, Afro-Brazilians are worse off than their white neighbors, including in access to running water and a working septic system, internet, food security, and formal education (IBGE 2015).

While Brazil has witnessed major improvements in measures of gender equality in the last decade, women continue to experience discrimination in nearly all aspects of life. Women remain significantly underrepresented in public office at all levels of government. They also continue to be constrained to the lowest paid jobs in the service sector and earn significantly lower wages on average than men at all levels of education (World Bank 2016; IBGE 2016). Looking at race and gender together reveals racial hierarchies among women as well. Afro-Brazilian women earn lower wages and experience higher rates of labor informality than white women, leaving them less protected by labor legislation (World Bank 2016).

All of these hierarchies converge within the domestic service sector in Brazil. Over six million predominantly working-class women of color perform the devalued and often invisibilized labor of cooking, cleaning, and caring for children and elders in the homes of white middle- and upper-class families. Nearly one in five employed black women in Brazil works as a domestic worker, which is defined by the Ministry of Labor and Employment as anyone over the age of eighteen who provides services of a continuous nature and of a noncommercial purpose to a person or family within their residence including cooks, housekeepers, nannies, chauffeurs, and elderly companions, among others. Domestic workers earn lower wages, experience higher rates of discrimination, lower rates of unionization, and higher rates of abuse and sexual harassment than nearly every other occupation (UN Women 2013). They were also excluded from most labor protections until winning the passage of *Emenda Constitucional 72* (*Projeto de Emenda Constitucional das Domésticas* or PEC 72), a constitutional amendment that extended additional labor rights for domestic workers (*domésticas*) and regulations on employers (*patrões*) in 2013. Steeped in the vestiges of slavery, domestic ideology, and class exploitation, the domestic service sector has influenced Brazilian social life since the beginning of colonization in the sixteenth century, though its significance is often overlooked.

In their book *Cultures of Servitude*, Ray and Qayum (2009) make clear that in societies "with long, unbroken histories of domestic servitude, the institution can be seen as central to understanding self and society" (Ray and Qayum 2009, 2). If we conceptualize paid domestic service not just as an occupational category or a sector of employment, but as an institution that reflects and reproduces social injustice, both on a daily and generational time scale and across so-called "private" and "public" spaces, then we are called to take seriously the organizing principles of paid domestic service, along with attempts at remaking them.

In this chapter, I aim to do just that by historicizing the significance of the paid domestic service sector and its role as a social institution in Brazil, and then offering an analysis of the movement that is attempting to remake that institution in a more just way. Just as the axes of gender, race, and class power interact to shape the devaluation and invisibility of the domestic worker, so too do they inform their particular modes of political mobilization (Bernardino-Costa 2014). By tackling the systems that at once contribute to the devaluation of domestic work and structure Brazilian society as a whole, the domestic workers' movement has been able to achieves specific legislative advances for its members, while simultaneously unsettling "broad patterns of social positions and relationships in the society" (Young 2011, 97).

In the next section, I briefly lay out Young's reformulation of Rawls's "basic structure" and the theory of justice it informs, after which I present the methods and materials used for this study. In the following analyses, I draw on Young's theorization to detail the current and historical significance of the institution of paid domestic service, and to frame domestic worker organizing as not only a struggle for more rights, but as a restructuring of this unjust social institution. Finally, I present the impacts of domestic worker organizing, highlighting the public dialogues and wider social changes they have sparked. I aim to demonstrate the ways in which domestic worker organizing is disrupting longstanding race, gender, and class-based structural hierarchies and contributing to a more just Brazilian society.

YOUNG'S THEORY OF JUSTICE

In *Inclusion and Democracy*, feminist political theorist Iris Marion Young (2000) lays out four basic aspects of her reformulated concept of "structure."

First, social structures consist in the connections and relationships between determinate social positions that condition the opportunities and life chances of the people in those positions. Importantly, the unit of analysis in these positions is not individuals, but what Young calls "structural social groups," that is, "a collection of persons who are similarly positioned in interactive and institutional relations" (2000, 97). Second, social structures are recursively produced through the actions of social actors, but (thirdly), not *only* from individual action. Young argues that social structures do not exist as already wholly formed entities; rather, they "exist only in the action and interaction of persons" in accordance to rules and expectations (2000, 95). However, structures are also comprised of sociohistorical conditions that are the collective outcomes of previous actions. Fourth, the collective actions and interactions between actors in different social positions are not only informed by past actions, they also have unintentional results that inform future actions. In her later work, Young (2011) uses the term "social-structural processes" in place of "structures" to emphasize the dynamism of structures and the ways in which the structurally informed actions of those in one social position reinforce the rules and resources available to those in other positions.

This reformulated notion of "the basic structure of society" informs Young's interventions into theorizing social justice. Drawing on Marx's critique of liberal conceptions of justice, Young argues that the subject of social justice is much broader than the distribution of resources or social positions (1990, 2006). Theories of justice within the "distributive paradigm," therefore, ignore "nondistributive" issues of justice such as "those concerning the social division of labor, structures of decision-making power, and processes that normalize behavior and attributes of persons" (Young 2006, 91). Such theories also tend to focus on the distributive outcomes of institutions, rather than the institutions themselves. Promoting social justice, Young argues, requires an intervention in "the institutional processes and individual actions and interactions," so as to remake those very institutions and relationships that determine distributive patterns (Young 2001, 18; Young 2011). Young's theory of justice thus encourages a deeper engagement with the social institutions that make up the basic structure of society and enables a conceptualization of injustice in the more relational terms of oppression and domination (Young 1990). It also incorporates a more active role of individuals and structural social groups, calling us to account for them as actors and agents within structural processes, rather than just recipients or consumers of those processes' outcomes.

Young's more comprehensive theory of justice enables us to better understand the devaluation and legal exclusion of domestic workers as a structural issue, an injustice, not just a pattern of individual moral wrongs. It also enables the conceptualization of the paid domestic service sector as a social institution, the relations in which contribute to (and are informed by) wider social-structural processes.

METHODOLOGY

I undertook a qualitative approach to researching the significance of the domestic service sector and the impacts of domestic worker organizing in Brazil. Such an approach allows for a deep interrogation into the meaning of the changing social structure by answering questions of why and how these changes are happening, and to what effect. My analysis in this chapter is grounded in information drawn from three main data sources: existing interviews with Creuza Maria de Oliveira, former president of the National Federation of Domestic Workers; a variety of major national news media sources; and datasets available through the *Instituto Brasileiro de Geografia e Estatística* (Brazilian Institute of Geography and Statistics or IBGE).

Throughout the chapter, I cite three interviews with Creuza Oliveira, who was president of the *Federação Nacional das Trabalhadoras Domésticas* (the National Federation of Domestic Workers or FENATRAD) when the constitutional amendment was approved. These interviews were conducted between 2013 and 2015 by the *Secretaria de Políticas de Promoção da Igual-dade Racial* (the Special Secretary for the Promotion of Racial Equality or SEPPIR), *Oxfam Brasil*, and *Tarde*, a daily newspaper. Though I did not conduct the interviews myself, they provide critical insight into the movement's goals and intersectional analysis. I also draw from a public lecture Oliveira gave at the 2017 National Meeting of Working Women hosted by *Central dos Sindicatos Brasileiros* (Brazilian Union Center or CSB).

As a way to measure the broader impacts of changes in the domestic service sector, I conducted content analysis of popular news media coverage of PEC 72. Media content analysis is a nonintrusive research method that enables the researcher to "identify popular discourses and their likely meanings" (Macnamara 2005, 6). Popular news media both influences and reflects popular opinion, thus providing an important window through which to understand and interpret social changes. My sources for this analysis are widely circulated daily newspapers *Folha de São Paulo*, *O Globo*, and *O Estado de S. Paulo (Estadão)*, as well as top-selling weekly magazines *Veja* and *IstoÉ*. All of these sources largely target middle- and upper-class readers and have both print and digital versions. Through preliminary analysis of the sources, I noted that mainstream media tended to focus on the legislation and its impacts, rather than the organizing that led to its passage. For this reason, I narrowed my focus to the news media discourse around PEC 72. By conducting the keyword search *"PEC das domésticas"* on each publication's website, relevant articles published between April 1, 2013 (the month PEC 72 was passed), and May 1, 2018, were used. These articles were then coded along three broad categories of analysis: (1) how the legislative changes are broadly framed (positive, negative, or neutral); (2) whose perspective is highlighted (worker or employer); and (3) anticipated outcomes, consequences, or responses to the legislation (both within the domestic service sector and beyond).

Finally, I conducted descriptive data analysis on datasets from IBGE's annual *Pesquisa Nacional por Amostra de Domicílios* (National Household Sample Survey or PNAD), which measures a range of socioeconomic and employment indicators including number of domestic workers, labor card status (indicator of formal employment), and race and gender breakdowns of the labor force. This analysis was used to offer a fuller understanding of the domestic service sector, and to provide additional empirical evidence of the societal changes suggested in the popular news media.

It is important to note here the many ways in which I am an "outsider" to the subjects of this research. I have lived in Brazil for some time and am fluent in Portuguese, but as a white, middle-class, North American woman, my life experiences are likely more clearly reflected in the experiences of the women who hire domestic workers than the domestic workers themselves. By acknowledging my own positionality within hierarchies of power and privilege, I do not intend to explain them away or reinscribe the "essentialist nature of social categories," but instead hope to make visible the ways in which these social categories influence my analysis and the knowledge this analysis ultimately produces (see Nagar 2014, 84).

ANALYTICAL REVIEW OF DOMESTIC WORK AND DOMESTIC WORKER ORGANIZING

In this section I bring the interdisciplinary literature on paid domestic work, specifically Brazilian feminist scholarship on domestic work and domestic worker organizing (Saffioti 1978; Souza 1980; Melo 1989; Rezende and Lima 2004; Pinho and Silva 2010; Silva 2010; Brites 2014; Pinho 2015) into conversation with Iris Marion Young's theorizations of social justice. I argue for the conceptualization of the paid domestic service sector as fundamental social institution through which wider social injustices are reproduced and potentially undone. I also draw extensively from the rich historical literature on domestic worker organizing in Brazil and highlight the critical alliances formed with feminist, black, and labor movements (Oliveira et al. 1989; Garcia Castro 1993; Motta 1999; Gonçalves 2010; Bernardino-Costa 2011, 2014). Again, drawing from Young's work, I frame this process of intersectional organizing as not only a struggle for labor rights, but also a struggle to restructure a critical social institution in a more just way.

Paid Domestic Work as a Social Institution

The institution of paid domestic service is one of fundamental significance in Brazilian society, reproducing gender, race, and class-based inequalities and notions of servility (Souza 1980; Rezende and Lima 2004; Brites 2014). Its insidious power to reproduce such hierarchies stems from the organizational reach across both time and space. That is, in the daily performance of work deemed "dirty" and unskilled, and in the generational performance of raising children, relations of servitude are reinforced and normalized. Middle- and upper-class children are raised being served by working-class black and brown women, learning their place in the existing hierarchies of Brazilian society (Brites 2014). Similarly, as Valentine (2007) reminds us, "power operates in and through particular spaces to systematically (re)produce particular inequalities" (19). In the private space of the home, hidden amongst acts of domination and affection, wider social hierarchies are reproduced and depoliticized. Exploitation is often clouded in the sentiments of family and friendship associated with the homespace.

The presence of a large "servant class"[1] has been fundamental to the development of Brazilian society and the economy and has shaped individual and class relations from the era of Portuguese colonialism to present day. For nearly three and a half centuries black women worked as slaves in the homes of white slave owners. When Lei Áurea (Golden Law) was passed in 1888, it legally ended slavery but provided no remuneration to the former slaves (Saffioti 1978). Many women simply continued performing the same duties they had carried out as slaves, going "from their slave quarters straight into remunerated domestic service" (Melo 1989, 249). At the turn of the twentieth century, "over 70 percent of the economically-active former-slave population was engaged in domestic work" (ILO 2016a, 4).

The era of slavery in Brazil left the white middle-class with "a repugnance for manual and domestic work, as well as the custom of taking for granted the ethos of servility, expecting to be 'naturally' served by those considered inferior and powerless" (Garcia Castro 1993, 20). Such a cultural expectation was able to flourish throughout the twentieth century in an economic environment characterized by an abundance of cheapened female labor and high levels of inequality (Souza 1980; Casagrande 2008). The maintenance of the major organizing principles of paid domestic service from its roots in slavery to present day are evident in the widespread expectation among Brazilians to have a domestic worker at their disposal (Casagrande 2008; Pinho 2015).

Today, domestic work remains a highly racialized and feminized occupation. Of the 6.4 million domestic workers in Brazil, over 90 percent are women, and 64 percent are black women (ILO 2016a). Using Young's theorizations, we can see the recursive relationship between the processes and interactions within the institution of paid domestic work and those in other social institutions. The continued availability of such a large supply of cheapened female labor, institutionalized through intentional State policies, has shaped Brazilian society far beyond the domestic employment relationship (Alvarez 1990; Beese 1996). Specifically, it has contributed to a stalled renegotiation of traditional gender divisions of labor in the home as well as to limited state provision of social services (Souza 1980). These effects then reinforce the dependency (both real and perceived) of the middle and upper-classes on the low-wage labor of domestic workers. Writing about Brazil toward the end of the twentieth century, Herdita Pereira de Melo (1989) explains,

> Brazil does not have the infrastructure that would allow women of the upper, middle, and lower classes to free themselves from domestic chores. This lack can be explained by the traditional social inequality pervading Brazilian history, where slaves and, later, domestic workers were always available to take care of household duties for the ruling class. . . . The abundance and low cost of these human resources have made it possible to incorporate middle- and upper-class women into the labor market without having to pressure society into providing social services such as day-care centers and full-time schooling, partially freeing women from child rearing. (Melo 1989, 247–58)

The inadequacies of the social system contribute to and are able to continue because of the presence of a servant class who take on these arduous tasks in place of a more efficient system (Nett 1966). The lack of state-provided social services is thus built on and reproduces the same racial, gender, and class hierarchies that sustain the paid domestic service in its unjust form. "Such a mutually reinforcing process," Young (2000) would argue, "means that the positional relations and the way they condition individual lives are difficult to change" (98). I now turn my focus to the movement struggling to bring about that change.

Domestic Worker Organizing in Brazil

There is a long and rich history of domestic worker organizing in Brazil that dates back to the establishment of the Santos Professional Association of Domestic Employees in 1936 (Gonçalves 2010; Bernardino-Costa 2011,

2014; FENATRAD 2018). From the very beginning, achieving labor rights and recognition from the state were core objectives of the movement. What distributive theories of justice might interpret as simply a struggle for a more just distribution of labor rights, Young's (2011) more comprehensive theory interprets as a struggle for the restructuring of an unjust social institution. Throughout their decades of organizing, domestic workers formed alliances with labor unions, black movements, and later feminist movements to advance their cause. In the process, they sharpened their own intersectional analysis and broadened the scope of these allied movements (Bernardino-Costa 2014). Together, they have brought about not only changes to the domestic service sector, but also broader changes in Brazilian society. For the purposes of this chapter, I highlight a few key moments in the movement's history and focus on their legislative wins and losses. In this way I aim to emphasize the ways in which the movement articulates particularist interests and experiences to achieve specific rights for its members, but in doing so is able to put forward wider claims of justice. In the words of Iris Marion Young (2000), "by criticizing the existing institutions and policies . . . they appeal to a wider public for inclusion, recognition, and equity" (110).

The Santos Professional Association of Domestic Employees worked closely with the Brazilian Black Front, a militant black women's group, to mobilize domestic workers around the struggle for labor rights and recognition equal to other workers (Gonçalves 2010; Bernardino-Costa 2014). These first struggles for labor rights, however, were met with stark losses. Early labor legislation like the Consolidation of Labor Laws (*Consolidação das Leis do Trabalho* or CLT) decree of 1943 excluded domestic work altogether (Brazil 1943, *Decreto-Lei 5.452* 1943; Saffioti 1978; Bernardino-Costa 2011). Through this exclusion the state established a highly exploitable sector of women and reaffirmed the social hierarchies that funneled women to this sector in the first place. Such exclusions also informed domestic worker organizing efforts at the time for increased recognition by the state as members of the working class.

In the late 1950s to 1960s, the domestic workers' movement deepened its ties with the black rights movement and began working with organized labor as they established a number of associations in cities throughout the country (Bernardino-Costa 2014). In 1972, domestic workers experienced their first major legislative victory with the passage of Law 5.859 (Domestic Workers Law), which extended access to social security, the right to paid vacation, and the right to a *carteira de trabalho assinada*, a signed work card, which is necessary in order to access labor protections (Brazil 1972, *Lei 5.859* 1972; Saffioti 1978; Souza 1980; FENATRAD 2018).

Domestic workers sought to seize upon the return to democracy in the late 1980s and pushed for a number of labor rights to be included in the new

Constitution of 1988 (Garcia Castro 1993; Motta 1999). The newly reestab-
lished democratic state, however, did little to change its role of maintaining
a sector of flexible, cheapened, female-dominated labor. The 1988 Federal
Constitution reaffirmed and expanded a number of labor rights established
by the CLT of 1943, but once again excluded domestic workers from the
majority of those rights. The Constitution thus served to reaffirm and even
strengthen existing race and gender hierarchies as many Brazilians were
guaranteed a fuller framework of rights and citizenship based on their status
as productive workers, while domestic workers, whose very labor sustained
and reproduced their employers' productive capacity, remained marginalized. Importantly though, with the 1988 Constitution domestic workers
gained the right to unionize (Brazil Const, art. 7, 1988).

The National Federation of Domestic Workers (*Federação Nacional das
Trabalhadoras Domésticas* or FENATRAD), which brought all of the local
domestic worker unions together into one network, was founded in 1997 and
a year later became affiliated with the national trade union center, *Central
Única dos Trabalhadores* (Central Workers Union or CUT) (Gonçalves
2010). FENATRAD brought major changes to union organizing, broadening
CUT's scope beyond traditional labor advances. Terezinha Gonçalves explains, "What was in the past a space for class struggles has become a space
that has given rise to active engagement in shaping policies for gender and
race equality in Brazil" (Gonçalves 2010, 66).

In 2003, due to public pressure from domestic workers and their allied movements, the federal government established the Special Secretary of Women's
Policies (SPM) and the Special Secretary for the Promotion of Racial Equality
(SEPPIR), formally acknowledging that race and gender inequalities existed in
Brazilian society (Gonçalves 2010). FENATRAD has been deeply involved in
these ministries, using them to develop and implement a number of programs
and policies aimed at improving the situation of domestic workers in Brazil,
including the 2013 Constitutional Amendment 72 (*Proposta de Emenda à
Constituição* or PEC 72) (Gonçalves 2010). FENATRAD worked with legislators to draft the legislation and in April 2013 the Brazilian Congress passed
PEC 72, extending nearly full labor rights to domestic workers. In June 2015,
Congress approved *Lei Complementar 150* (Enabling Law 150 or LC 150) to
formalize many of the rights extended in PEC 72.

Today, FENATRAD includes twenty-six unions across fifteen states and
describes itself as an "*organização de classe*," a class organization, but also
emphasizes that their members are predominantly women of color (FENA-
TRAD 2018). The FENATRAD website states,

> Women are the majority in domestic work. . . . FENATRAD works alongside
> other movements and institutions that defend the equal rights of women and

combat gender discrimination. The majority of workers and domestic workers are black. Hence, the trade unions and associations maintain a strong dialogue with organizations of the black movement. These alliances are very important for trading experiences and developing actions that help everyone.[2] (FENATRAD 2018)

Throughout their history, the domestic workers' movement navigated alliances with labor, feminist, and black movements, and as a result achieved specific legislative advances for their own members and strengthened the operations of allied groups. Through direct engagement with state institutions, the domestic workers' associations have institutionalized channels of communication and influence for themselves and other social movements to shape future government decisions. Their intersectional analysis and everyday lived experiences as working-class black women enabled them to see the ways in which systems of power and domination interlock in particular ways. Creuza Maria de Oliveira (2017), former president of FENATRAD made this clear when she said in a public lecture, "Our struggle is not just for labor rights. We also fight for the rights of women, for black women. We need housing, education, healthcare, daycare for our children. It is also necessary to think about society, in this wealth that is divided in an unequal way, in which few have so much, and many have almost nothing." In remaking this foundational social institution, the impacts of the movement can be felt far beyond the domestic employment relationship as they contribute to a more just Brazilian society.

RESULTS AND DISCUSSIONS

PEC 72 represents a marked shift in the state's relationship to paid domestic work, recognizing it for the first time as a professional category. The significance of this recognition is captured by Creuza Oliveira's statement that "the approval of this law is a matter of reparation for this category [of workers] that for more than 500 years has contributed to the Brazilian economy, contributed to Brazilian homes and has not had the same rights as other workers. We understand that it is a matter of justice to have equal rights to other workers" (SEPPIR 2013).

Changes within the domestic service sector are slow coming and have been hindered by the wider economic downturn in Brazil that started in early 2014. Additionally, PEC 72 applies only to domestic workers who work a minimum of three days per week in the same household, leaving part-time *diaristas* (day workers) unprotected. Informality remains a key limitation within the sector and will no doubt be a focus of ongoing domestic worker organizing to ensure oversight and compliance with the legislation. A limited focus on the specific legislative changes, however, leaves the broader impacts of domestic worker organizing unacknowledged. It is to these broader impacts that I turn now.

Evidence of Social Change

PEC 72 has been a huge topic of public dialogue within Brazil's most popular newspapers and magazines, largely targeted at middle- and upper-class readers. In the days and months following the legislation's passage, *Folha de São Paulo, O Globo, Veja, IstoÉ,* and *O Estado de S. Paulo* filled their pages with warnings of the major implications for Brazilian society stemming from the extension of domestic workers' labor rights. One article, "The Time Bomb in Domestic Work," published days before PEC 72 was even passed, warned that "in the medium and long term, the country will undergo a profound revolution in its society" (*IstoÉ* 2013). An article in *Veja,* the leading weekly publication in the country, stated plainly, "nothing will be the same" (Diniz 2013).

In this section, I draw on a textual analysis of mainstream media coverage of PEC 72 and LC 150, which reveals the beginnings of three key shifts in Brazilian society attributed to domestic workers' legislative successes. One, a renegotiation of the gendered division of labor within the home; two, a renewed push for better public services; and three, a shift away from the cultural expectation of racialized servitude. I then supplement the claims from media sources with data from the Brazilian Institute of Geography and Statistics. Together, these changes represent a forceful disruption to longstanding hierarchies that have organized Brazilian society.

First, popular media points to the legislation's role in disrupting middle-class domestic life, particularly the traditional gender division of labor, which has historically left women responsible for the bulk of household tasks[3] (Souza 1980). *Veja* published an issue on the day the legislation passed with a cover image of a white man with a forlorn expression in business clothes under an apron, washing dishes. The caption read, "You tomorrow: The new labor rules of maids are a mark of civilization for Brazil—and a sign that soon the domestic tasks will be divided among the whole family" (Diniz 2013). The accompanying article detailed the ways in which PEC 72 will result in "a radical rearrangement of family habits," including the increased participation of men and children in household chores and expanded use of household appliances (Diniz 2013). Similarly, an article published the following week in *Veja* titled, "PEC das Domésticas: Out with the Maid, in with the Dishwasher," concluded, "The house needs to be cleaned and the dishes and laundry washed. The main difference is that, now, the woman is not the only one in charge" (Ritto 2013).

Government data supports these predictions about the coming renegotiation of the gendered division of household labor. In 2012, the year before PEC 72 went into effect, only 48.2 percent of employed men indicated that they performed housework, compared to 89.8 percent of employed women. By 2015, the percentage of men performing housework had increased to 53 percent, while the percentage of women had increased only slightly to 91 percent (IBGE 2016). Though a five-percentage point increase in three years might not seem like much, it stands in stark contrast to the two-percentage point increase in men's participation over the previous seventeen-year period (IBGE 2016). Women remain largely responsible for domestic tasks even as their participation in the formal workforce has increased, but men appear to be slowly taking on greater responsibility. Such a shift marks a significant deviation from past behavior where working women simply shifted their domestic burden onto a paid domestic worker who served "as a buffer in potential gender conflicts over housework" (Pinho and Silva 2010, 102–3). A renegotiation of the gendered division of household labor within the family where men take on more responsibility is a potential long-term impact of domestic workers' organizing wins.

Second, popular news media cites the passage of PEC 72 as a potential catalyst for sparking a renewed push for public services. The article, "Nothing Will be the Same," published in *Veja,* predicted the extension of labor rights to domestic workers "may intensify the collective public power for improvements in the daycare system, public transport and everything that contributes to making life better for those who work, who must take care of their homes and who, from now on, will have to rely less and less on professional help at home" (Diniz 2013). State investment in childcare, eldercare, and full-time schooling had not been a central issue for middle-class families who were long able to cheaply hire a domestic worker to care for their children and other family members. With the passage of PEC 72, that is changing and demand for such services is increasing, as evidenced by the following media pieces. Articles titled "Law Makes Mothers Exchange Nannies for Full-Time Schooling" (Deodoro 2013), "Without Nannies, Children Stay Longer at Daycare" (M. Alves 2013), and "Full-Time Schooling Grows with Parents' Lack of Time and PEC das Domésticas" (*Folha de São Paulo* 2014) highlight how the lack of affordable childcare and full-time schooling, long an issue for working-class families, has quickly become a topic of major concern for middle-class Brazilians.

An article published by *O Globo* just two months after the legislation's passage explained plainly, "New rights for domestic workers have raised the cost for families, and many have begun to change their habits and routines, shifting to full-time schools and daycare centers to deal with the problem" (Cabral 2013). From 2012 to 2015, the number of Brazilian children under the age of three-years-old attending daycare (*creche*) increased by 15 percent (compared to a 10 percent increase in the previous three-year period) (IBGE 2016). As middle-class families shift from nannies to daycare and full-time schooling for their childcare, the opportunity arises for solidarities between working-class and middle-class people in pressuring the state to address the lack of affordable child care and fulfill its promise to reach 50 percent enrollment in daycares by 2024 (Ministry of Education 2014).

Finally, Brazilian news media highlights the professionalization of the domestic service sector and the formalization of the domestic employment relationship resulting from the passage of PEC 72. An article published in *O Globo* in 2015 explains, "the relationship between employers and domestic workers has evolved. Rights and duties of both parties are [now] provided by law." Furthermore, articles like, "How to Register your Maid and Avoid a Fine of Two Minimum Wages" provide detailed instructions for employers on how to follow the new laws (Mantoan 2014). Such a recognition of domestic workers as "real workers," and in turn, *patrões* as "real employers" presents a strong challenge to the lingering master-servant ties and racialized servitude that have long characterized the domestic employment relationship (Kofes 2001; Azeredo 2002). And, in cases where employers are resistant to such change, domestic workers are increasingly drawing on their newfound legal empowerment to take their employers to court for unpaid wages and benefits now required by law (Mendes and Moraes 2015). Between 2015 and 2017, the Regional Labor Court in São Paulo saw a 237 percent increase in the number of lawsuits filed by domestic workers against their employers (Dyniewicz 2018).

Further evidence of this cultural shift away from expectations and acceptance of racialized servitude can be found in the changing representation of domestic workers in entertainment and social media. A number of films released in recent years including *Doméstica* (Housemaids 2012), *Casa Grande* (The Big House 2014), and *Que Horas Ela Volta* (The Second Mother 2015) center domestic workers as the protagonists and offer critical and nuanced analyses of the social hierarchies that characterize the domestic employment relationship. Similarly, declining social acceptance of such elitist attitudes can be seen in recently established social media pages. For example, a Twitter page established in 2014 called "*A Minha Empregada*" ("My Maid") shames users who post derogatory comments about their domestic workers. The page has over seventeen thousand followers and has been featured on major Brazilian news sites like *O Globo*, *Fórum*, and *HuffpostBrasil*. The Facebook page, *"Eu Empregada Doméstica"* ("I, Domestic Worker") was established in 2016 to share personal stories of domestic workers and their experiences with employers to its more than 160,000 followers. The shifting portrayal and the greater voice of domestic workers in popular media and entertainment reflects the changing position of domestic workers in the Brazilian social imaginary. It also reflects a wider critique of the race, gender, and class hierarchies that have long devalued their work and that permeate Brazilian society more broadly.

CONCLUSION

Paid domestic work is a key institution through which gender, race, and class power structures are reinforced, reproduced, and potentially subordinated through day-to-day and generational relationships across private and public spaces. Recognizing it as such enables us to more fully account for the wider impacts of changes to the institution and the significance of the movement leading those changes. Iris Marion Young (2011) explains, "Structural injustice is a kind of moral wrong distinct from the wrongful action of an individual agent or the repressive policies of a state. Structural injustice occurs as a consequence of many individuals and institutions acting to pursue their particular goals and interests, for the most part within the limits of accepted rules and norms" (Young 2011, 52). The domestic workers movement does in fact seek to change repressive state policies and the individual actions that influence the lives of domestic workers. However, through their intersectional organizing, domestic workers unions are simultaneously able to address wider social hierarchies that inform the "rules and norms" of Brazilian society. PEC 72 was a historic win for domestic workers but, as Creuza Oliveira makes clear, its full impact can be seen in the transformation it has sparked in "the mentality of society" (P. Alves 2013). Such a transformation is evident in popular news media's coverage of PEC 72.

The domestic workers' movement engages in an approach to social justice that connects intimate interactions in the private space of the home with state actors and regional and international movements for dignity and justice. Just as the causes of the devaluation of domestic workers are long-term and structurally reproduced, so too are their interventions and organizing strategies. Oliveira often highlights the potential PEC 72 presents for disrupting the generational legacy of slavery that permeates through domestic work. Speaking in an interview with Oxfam Brasil about the legislative changes she explains,

> Historically, this category [of workers] comes from slave labor, the relationship between the Big House and the senzala [slave quarters]. . . . My great-great

grandmother was a slave; my grandmother, my mother and I were domestics. I became a domestic worker at the age of 10 and I didn't have the opportunity to study. Today, to know that there are young people going to college, that the number of young people in domestic work has fallen, for me, this is a very important victory. We need generations that are also in other areas of the labor market. She can be a domestic worker if she wants, but this cannot be the only open door or her destiny. (Oxfam Brasil 2015)

The struggle of the domestic workers' movement in Brazil is far from over, but the achievement of labor rights for domestic workers after over eighty years of organizing serves as a significant win and rallying point from which to gain momentum for continued organizing. As Eliana Gomes Menezes, then director of the Union of Maids and Domestic Workers of Greater São Paulo explained in an interview with National Public Radio about the legislation, "[O]ur victory is not the end, it's only the beginning. We have to make that law have value. It's a question of social justice" (Garcia-Navarro 2013).

In this chapter, I have centered my analysis on the paid domestic service sector in Brazil, and its historical and current significance in this particular context. It is important to note, though, that domestic work accounts for as much as 14 percent of waged female employment in Latin America (ILO 2016b). Globally, the ILO estimates there are over 67 million domestic workers aged fifteen years and older, nearly a third of whom are completely excluded from the scope of national labor legislation (ILO 2016b). Examining the institution of paid domestic work in any context affords a unique opportunity to explore the ways in which systems of race, gender, and class power intersect and are reified in intimate relationships and spaces. Furthermore, working with nondistributive theories of justice like the one proposed by Young enables us to better account for the broader significance of the extension of labor rights to domestic workers, and to understand the movements struggling for these rights not as articulating particularist interests but instead as promoting social justice through the restructuring of unjust institutions and relationships.

ACKNOWLEDGMENTS

I would like to thank Robert Anderson, Ross Doll, Kim England, Mónica Farías, Victoria Lawson, and Elizabeth Shoffner for their feedback on earlier drafts of this chapter. The research presented in the chapter was funded in part by the Harry Bridges Center for Labor Studies and the Department of Geography at the University of Washington. This material is based upon work supported by the National Science Foundation under Grant Number 1833330.

Any opinions, findings, and conclusions or recommendations expressed in this material are those of the author and do not necessarily reflect the views of the National Science Foundation.

NOTES

1. The term "servant class" is an intentionally provocative one that is used to emphasize the ways in which reproductive labor is often incorporated into markets as poorly paid, low-status work. Feminist labor geographers have used the term more specifically to refer to those who perform such work in the private homes of others (McDowell 2008, 2014; Lowe and Gregson 1989). The term implies a certain level of inequality within a society and is useful for capturing the essence of the lower "place" of domestic workers in the social hierarchy.

2. All translations done by author.

3. According to a 2017 report from the *Instituto Brasileiro de Geografia e Estatística* (IBGE), women in Brazil dedicate an average of 20.9 hours per week to household chores, compared to men's 10.8 hours.

REFERENCES

Alvarez, Sonia E. 1990. *Engendering Democracy in Brazil: Women's Movements in Transition Politics*. Princeton: Princeton University Press.

Alves, Maria Elisa. 2013. "Sem babás, crianças ficam mais na creche." *O Globo*, May 25. Accessed January 3, 2019. https://oglobo.globo.com/rio/sem-babas-criancas-ficam-mais-na-creche-8500813.

Alves, Paula Janay. 2013. "Se a PEC das Domésticas existisse, não teria sofrido tanto." *A Tarde*, June 1. Accessed January 23, 2019. http://atarde.uol.com.br/economia/noticias/1507901-se-a-pec-das-domesticas-existisse-nao-teria-sofrido-tanto.

Azeredo, Sandra. 2002. "A Ânsia, o Sino e a Transversalidade na Relação entre Empregadas e Patroas." *Cadernos Pagu* 19: 323–34.

Beese, Susan. 1996. *Restructuring Patriarchy: The Modernization of Gender Inequality in Brazil, 1914–1940*. Chapel Hill: The University of North Carolina Press.

Bernardino-Costa, Joaze (translated by Paulo Simoes). 2011. "Destabilizing the National Hegemonic Narrative: The Decolonized Thought of Brazil's Domestic Workers' Unions." *Latin American Perspectives* 38 (5): 33–43.

———. 2014. "Intersectionality and Female Domestic Workers' Unions in Brazil." *Women's Studies International Forum* 46: 72–80.

Brazil. 1943. "Aprova a Consolidação das Leis do Trabalho." *Decreto-Lei 5.452*. Executivo. Portal do Planalto. http://www.planalto.gov.br/ccivil_03/decreto-lei/del5452compilado.htm.

———. 1972. "Dispõe sobre a profissão de empregado doméstico e dá outras providências." *Lei 5.859*. Executivo. Portal de Planalto.

————. 1988. Constituição da República Federativa do Brasil, title II, chapter II, art. 7.

————. 2013. *Emenda Constitucional 72*. Legislativo. Portal de Planalto. https://www.planalto.gov.br/ccivil_03/constituicao/Emendas/Emc/emc72.htm.

Brites, Jurema. 2014. "Domestic Service, Affection and Inequality: Elements of Subalternity." *Women's Studies International Forum* 46: 63–71.

Cabral, Renata. 2013. "Escolas em horário integral custam até R$ 800 a mais por mês." *O Globo*, June 18. Accessed January 14, 2014. https://oglobo.globo.com/economia/escolas-em-horario-integral-custam-ate-800-mais-por-mes-8719138.

"*Cartilha do Trabalhado Doméstico*." Brasília: Ministério do Trabalho e Emprego, 2013.

Casagrande, Cassio. 2008. *Trabalho doméstico e discriminação*. Boletim. Rio de Janeiro: Centro de Estudos de Direito Economia e Social (CEDES).

Deodoro, Juliana. 2013. "Lei faz mães trocar babás por escola integral." *O Estado de S. Paulo*, April 28. Accessed January 5, 2019. https://www.estadao.com.br/noticias/geral,lei-faz-maes-trocar-babas-por-escola-integral,1026454.

Diniz, Laura. 2013. "Nada será como antes." *Veja*, April 1. Accessed January 7, 2019. http://www.eb.mil.br/web/imprensa/resenha/-/journal_content/56/18107/2754031;jsessionid=8EB8160C0DF845B829A6BC25BBD2F08B.lr2?refererPlid=18115#.XEQD6y2cbOQ.

Dyniewicz, Luciana. 2018. "Três anos depois de lei, 70% das domésticas estão na informalidade." *O Estado de S. Paulo,* August 12, 2018. Accessed January 5, 2019. https://economia.estadao.com.br/noticias/geral,tres-anos-depois-de-lei-70-das-domesticas-estao-na-informalidade,70002444821.

Federação Nacional das Trabalhadoras Domésticas (FENATRAD). 2018. "Institucional." Accessed June 27, 2018. http://www.fenatrad.org.br/site/?page_id=112.

Folha de São Paulo. 2014. "Ensino integral cresce com falta de tempo dos pais e PEC das domésticas." *Folha de São Paulo*, March 9. Accessed January 7, 2019. https://www1.folha.uol.com.br/cotidiano/2014/03/1422971-ensino-integral-cresce-com-falta-de-tempo-dos-pais-e-pec-das-domesticas-veja.shtml.

Freyre, Gilberto. 1986 [1933]. *The Master and the Slaves (Casa-Grande e Senzala).* Berkeley: University of California Press.

Garcia Castro, Mary. 1993. "The Alchemy Between Social Categories in the Production of Political Subjects: Class, Gender, Race and Generation in the Case of Domestic Workers' Union Leaders in Salvador-Bahia, Brazil." *The European Journal of Development Research* 5 (2): 1–22.

Garcia-Navarro, Lulu. 2013. "'We Are Not Valued': Brazil's Domestic Workers Seek Rights." NPR, May 27, 2013. https://www.npr.org/sections/parallels/2013/05/27/186722882/Brazils-Domestic-Workers-Continue-Fight-For-Fair-Treatment.

Gonçalves, Terezinha. 2010. "Crossroads of Empowerment: The Organisation of Women Domestic Workers in Brazil." *IDS Bulletin* 41: 62–69.

Instituto Brasileiro de Geografia e Estatística (IBGE). 2015. *Pesquisa Nacional por Amostra de Domicílios (PNAD)*. Rio de Janeiro: Instituto Brasileiro de Geografia e Estatística.

————. 2016. *Pesquisa Nacional por Amostra de Domicílios (PNAD)*. Rio de Janeiro: Instituto Brasileiro de Geografia e Estatística.

————. 2017. "Mulheres continuam a cuidar mais de pessoas e afazeres domésticos que homens." *Agência de Notícias IBGE.* Accessed January 7, 2019. https://agenciadenoticias.ibge.gov.br/agencia-noticias/2012-agencia-de-noticias/noticias/20912-mulheres-continuam-a-cuidar-mais-de-pessoas-e-afazeres-domesticos-que-homens.

————. 2018. *Pesquisa Nacional por Amostra de Domicílios (PNAD) Contínua.* Rio de Janeiro: Instituto Brasileiro de Geografia e Estatística.

International Domestic Workers Federation (IDWFED). 2018. "Brazil: Following Years of Campaigning by Domestic Workers, the Government in Recent Days Ratified the ILO C189." *IDWFED*, February 8, 2018. http://www.idwfed.org/en/updates/brazil-following-years-of-campaigning-by-domestic-workers-the-government-in-recent-days-ratified-the-ilo-c189.

International Labour Organization. 2016a. *Initial effects of Constitutional Amendment 72 on Domestic Work in Brazil.* Conditions of Work and Employment Series No. 79. Geneva: ILO.

————. 2016b. *Formalizing Domestic Work.* Geneva: ILO.

IstoÉ. 2013. "A bomba-relógio no trabalho doméstico." *IstoÉ,* March 28. Accessed August 20, 2018. https://istoe.com.br/286696_A+BOMBA+RELOGIO+NO+TRABALHO+DOMESTICO/

Kofes, Suely. 2001. *Mulher, Mulheres: Identidade, Diferença e Desigualdade na Relação entre Patroas e Empregadas Domésticas.* Campinas: Editora da Unicamp.

Lowe, Michelle, and Nicky Gregson. 1989. "Nannies, Cooks, Cleaners, au Pairs . . . New Issues for Feminist Geography?" *Area* 21 (4): 414–17.

Macnamara, Jim. 2005. "Media Content Analysis: Its Uses, Benefits and Best Practice Methodology." *Asia Pacific Public Relations Journal* 6 (1): 1–34.

Mantoan, Victória. 2014. "Como registrar sua empregada e evitar multa de dois salários mínimos." *O Estado de S. Paulo*, April 16. Accessed January 7, 2019. https://economia.estadao.com.br/noticias/geral,como-registrar-sua-empregada-e-evitar-multa-de-dois-salarios-minimos,182280e.

McDowell, Linda. 2008. "The New Economy, Class Condescension and Caring Labour: Changing Formations of Class and Gender." *NORA-Nordic Journal of Feminist and Gender Research* 16 (3): 150–65.

————. 2014. "Roepke Lecture in Economic Geography—The Lives of Others: Body Work, the Production of Difference, and Labor Geographies." *Economic Geography* 91 (1): 1–23.

Medeiros, Marcelo, Pedro Herculano Guimarães Ferreira de Souza, and Fábio Ávila de Castro. 2015. "A Estabilidade da Desigualdade de Renda no Brasil, 2006 a 2012: Estimativa com Dados do Imposto de Renda e Pesquisas Domiciliares." *Ciência & Saúde Coletiva* 20, no. (4): 971–86.

Melo, Hildete Pereira de. 1989. "Feminists and Domestic Workers in Rio de Janeiro." In *Muchachas No More: Household Workers in Latin America and the Caribbean,* edited by Elsa M. Chaney and Mary Garcia Castro, 245–67. Philadelphia: Temple University Press.

Mendes, Giulia, and Tatiana Moraes. 2015. "Cresce o número de domésticas que vão à justiça para solucionar impasses." *Hoje em Dia*, August 23. Accessed January 6, 2019. https://www.hojeemdia.com.br/primeiro-plano/cresce-o-número-de -domésticas-que-vão-à-justiça-para-solucionar-impasses-1.320543.

Ministério da Educação (MinistryofEducation). 2013. *Planejando a Próxima Década: Conhecendo as 20 Metas do Plano Nacional de Educação.* Ministério da Educação / Secretaria de Articulação com os Sistemas de Ensino (MEC/ SASE).

Ministério de Trabalho e Emprego (Ministry of Work and Employment). "Recurso de Revista 776.500/2001." *Trabalho Doméstico*. Accessed November 11, 2013. http:// www3.mte.gov.br/trab_domestico/trab_domestico_situacoes.asp

Motta, Alda Britto da. 1999. "Doing Housework for Pay: Political Struggles and Legal Rights of Domestic Workers in Brazil." In *Women, Development and Labor of Reproduction: Struggles and Movements,* edited by Mariarosa Dalla Costa and Giovanna Franca Dalla Costa, 117–133. Asmara, Eritrea: Africa World Press, Inc.

Nagar, Richa. 2014. *Muddying the Waters: Coauthoring Feminism across Scholarship and Activism.* Indianapolis: University of Illinois Press.

Nett, Emily M. 1966. "The Servant Class in a Developing Country: Ecuador." *Journal of Inter- American Studies* 8 (3): 437–52.

O Globo. 2015. "Aumentam as ações trabalhistas movidas por empregadas domésticas." *O Globo,* August 31. Accessed January 5, 2019. http://g1.globo.com/bom -dia-brasil/noticia/2015/08/aumentam-acoes-trabalhistas-movidas-por-empregadas -domesticas.html.

Oliveira, Creuza Maria de. 2017. "Palestra de Creuza de Oliveira." *Central dos Sindicatos Brasileiros.* Lecturepresentedat Encontro Nacional da Mulher Trabalhadora da CSB, Brasília, March 9. Accessed January 8, 2019. http://csbbrasil.org .br/blog/2017/03/16/palestra-de-creuza-de-oliveira-encontro-nacional-da-mulher -trabalhadora-da-csb-9-de-marco2017/.

Oliveira, Anazir Maria de, and Odete Maria da Conceição with Hildete Pereira de Melo. 1989. "Domestic Workers in Rio de Janeiro: Their Struggle to Organize." In *Muchachas No More: Household Workers in Latin America and the Caribbean,* edited by Elsa M. Chaney and Mary Garcia Castro, 363–71. Philadelphia: Temple University Press.

Oxfam Brasil. 2015. "Trabalho doméstico não pode ser o único destino." Accessed on March 14, 2017. https://www.oxfam.org.br/noticias/trabalho-domestico-nao -pode-ser-o-unico-destino.

Pinho, Patricia de Santana. 2015. "The Dirty Body that Cleans: Representation of Domestic Workers in Brazilian Common Sense." *Meridians* 13 (1): 103–28.

Pinho, Patricia de Santana, and Elizabeth B. Silva. 2010. "Domestic Relations in Brazil: Legacies and Horizons." *Latin American Research Review* 45 (2): 90–113.

Rawls, John. 1971. *A Theory of Justice.* Cambridge, MA: Harvard University Press.

Ray, Raka, and Seemin Qayum. 2009. *Cultures of Servitude: Modernity, Domesticity, and Class in India.* Stanford: Stanford University Press.

Rezende, Cláudia Barcellos, and Márcia Lima. 2004. "Linking Gender, Class and Race in Brazil." *Social Identities* 10 (6): 757–73.

Ritto, Cecilia. 2013. "PEC das domésticas: sai a empregada, entra a lava-louça." *Veja,* April 13. Accessed January 6, 2019. https://veja.abril.com.br/economia/pec-das -domesticas-sai-a-empregada-entra-a-lava-louca/.

Saffioti, Heleieth. 1978. *Emprego Doméstico e Capitalismo.* Petrópolis, RJ: Editora Vozes Ltda.

Secretaria de Políticas de Promoção da Igualdade Racial (SEPPIR). 2013. "Creuza de Oliveira fala sobre aprovação da PEC das domésticas." *ÚltimasNotícias,* March 27. Accessed March 11, 2014. http://www.seppir.gov.br/noticias/ultimas_noti cias/2013/03/creuza-de-oliveira-fala-sobre-aprovacao-da-pec-das-domesticas.

Silva, Elizabeth. 2010. "Maids, Machines and Morality in Brazilian Homes." *Feminist Review* 94 (1): 20–37.

Souza, Julia Filet-Abreu. 1980. "Paid Domestic Service in Brazil." *Latin American Perspectives* 7 (1): 35–63.

UN Women. 2013. *Domestic Workers Count Too: Implementing Protections for Domestic Workers.* New York and Brussels: UN Women and ITUC.

World Bank. 2016. *A Snapshot of Gender in Brazil Today Institutions, Outcomes, and a Closer Look at Racial and Geographic Differences.* http://elibrary.worldbank .org.offcampus.lib.washington.edu/doi/pdf/10.1596/25976.

Young, Iris Marion. 1990. *Justice and the Politics of Difference.* Princeton: Princeton University Press.

———. 2000. *Inclusion and Democracy.* New York: Oxford University Press.

———. 2001. "Equality for Whom? Social Groups and Judgments of Injustice." *The Journal of Political Philosophy* 9 (1): 1–18.

———. 2006. "Taking the Basic Structure Seriously." *Perspectives on Politics* 4 (1): 91–97.

———. 2011. *Responsibility for Justice.* Oxford: Oxford University Press

Chapter Seven

Freedom, Justice, and Space

Infrastructure as a Key Driver of Spatial Freedom?

Luis Emilio Cecchi

Have you ever accepted an onerous labor contract because it was the only way of getting a job to pay the bills? Were you forced to study for the career your parents wanted? Have you suffered intra-marital violence? If the answer to any of these questions is yes, then you have experienced what domination is. Iris Marion Young in *Justice and the Politics of Difference* (Young 1990) shows that domination is not a distant problem affecting exclusively developing societies. Domination happens every day among us all the time, sometimes so naturally that we do not even recognize it.

The understanding related to linkages of freedom, justice, and space has been generally overlooked by the literature. Thus, this research aims to explore and further the understanding of the relationships among these concepts. In order to link freedom with justice, I employ the neo-republican concept of freedom as non-domination that I claim cares about justice, since freedom as non-domination is a necessary condition for people to enjoy justice in a significant way. In doing so, this work connects the neo-republican conception of freedom (Pettit 1997, 2012, 2014) and the spatial justice approach (Harvey 2010; Soja 2010) to develop what I define as a "neo-republican spatial agenda." To be free under the neo-republican conception of freedom means that no person should have to depend on the arbitrary decision of others when deciding their life plans, keeping open as many meaningful options as possible for personal development. In this sense, I argue that a "neo-republican spatial agenda" promotes policies that foster material infrastructure, strengthen social capital, and maximize what I call "spatial freedom."

This chapter has three main objectives. The first is to fill a gap in the theoretical research related to freedom, justice, and space. The second and main objective is to theoretically develop and define a "neo-republican spatial agenda" that can be a useful guideline for public authorities and policy makers to design spatial public policies as well as a yardstick for social movements, civil society organizations, and citizens. Finally, the third objective of this chapter is to demonstrate the applicability of the theoretical concepts developed in this work. The case study I utilize to do this is the "Transit-Oriented Development Corridors" program in Johannesburg, South Africa. While a full analysis of this case study will be presented in future research, I use this case in the current work to demonstrate how the original concept of the "neo-republican spatial agenda" and the concept of "spatial freedom" can be applied to a concrete policy example by identifying how it conforms to the six criteria I defined as a key part of the agenda. I also discuss the challenges the Corridors Program faces in fully adhering to the agenda.

LINKING FREEDOM, JUSTICE AND SPACE

Freedom as Non-Domination

In this work, the concept of neo-republican freedom developed by Philip Pettit (1997, 2008b, 2012, 2014) provides the fundamental approach for understanding freedom. This concept takes justice into account concerning both the individual and the social dimensions from the local to the transnational level (Pettit 1997, 2012, 2014). Space and infrastructure had a tangential, although not absent, role in neo-republican theory. Freedom as non-domination is the unifying theme of the republican tradition of thought that can be traced back to the Roman republic (Pettit 2013, 1997; Skinner 2012). Two other core values remain in the contemporary version of republicanism constructed by Pettit: the separation and balancing of powers (defined as *mixed constitution*) and the existence of a contestatory citizenship (1997, 68). Active citizens controlling and being able to contest public decisions that go against their interests play a central role in neo-republicanism (1997, 277).

Freedom as non-domination reappeared at the end of the twentieth century as an alternative to Isaiah Berlin's (1969) mainstream freedom as non-interference conception. In Berlin's liberal terms, freedom as non-interference was defined as the

[a]bsence of obstacles to possible choices and activities—the absence of obstructions on roads along which a man can decide to walk. Such freedom ultimately depends not on whether I wish to walk at all, or how far, but on how many doors are open, how open they are, upon their relative importance in my life. (Berlin 1969, 32)

In this sense, "non-interference" entailed the "absence of restraint" (Long 1977; Hart 1971) and a private sphere (Constant 1988) in which citizens can choose to act as they please.

The neo-republican version introduced the term *domination* in contrast to freedom as non-interference. Domination exists when someone, either an individual or a collective agent, has the capacity to interfere on an arbitrary basis in certain choices that another person is in a position to make. To be considered as domination, this capacity to interfere should be intentional and have negative consequences for the other person. Domination can entail coercion of the body or the will. There are different resources that can give a person power over another: physical strength, political authority, social capital, access to key information, or having a privileged position, among others (Pettit 1997). Domination's *extent* and *intensity* can vary. It increases when it affects larger ranges of choices and more meaningful activities and vice versa.

If the three necessary conditions for domination are fulfilled (a person has the capacity to interfere on an arbitrary basis in certain choices that the other is in a position to make), this will lead to a situation of "common knowledge" between the parties involved. The two parties (the one in the dominant position and the one dominated) know that one of them has a dominating power over the other, and any others in society who know what is going on are also aware of that. This is key for the republican conception because it shows the intersubjective and social dimension of non-domination and its relationship with a subjective self-image, the capacity to look the other in the eye, what Pettit calls the "eyeball test."

Figure 7.1 shows a two-by-two matrix where there are two dimensions: neo-republicans and liberals. As shown in figure 7.1, each dimension is subdivided into two sets of binomials: domination/non-domination and interference/non-interference. Domination can happen without actual interference: it requires only the capacity for interference. This situation can be labeled as the "non-interfering master" case. It could be the case, at the extreme, of a slave with a benign master that lets him do what he wants. While in terms of non-interference this slave would be totally free, in neo-republican terms, he

		Liberals (L)	
		Interference	*Non-interference*
Neo-Republicans (NR)	*Domination*	UNFREE (NR and L)	*Non-interfering Master* UNFREE (NR) / FREE (L)
	Non-Domination	*Non-mastering interferer* FREE (NR) / UNFREE (L)	FREE (NR and L)

Figure 7.1. Matrix of Neo-Republicans and Liberals (Comparison between the ideals and freedom as non-interference and non-domination).

Source: Author elaboration based on Pettit 1997

would still be dependent on the good will of his master. This master could act with impunity and would not be penalized in case of interfering.

On the other hand, republicanism also considers that interference may occur without domination: the "non-mastering interferer" case. If an interference tracks the interests of the affected actors, this interference is not arbitrary. If the interference is not arbitrary, then it will not dominate. The main example favored by republicans to illustrate this case is the interferences made by public laws in citizens' lives. If public laws track citizen's interests, this is a way of promoting non-domination. Even when public laws set some limits to people's actions, if they track their interests, they offer some kind of protection or safeguards providing them security against the powerful in a robust and resilient way. Again, proponents of non-interference reject this view.

Freedom and Justice

Freedom as non-domination shown in figure 7.1 is at the center of the neo-republican theory of justice. But what does a neo-republican theory of social justice entail? As a general feature, it would pursue the expressive equal enjoyment of non-domination for every citizen. This means that a free citizen should be able to enjoy certain "basic liberties"; public laws and norms should protect and guarantee the exercise of that fundamental range of choices; and, the government should provide the necessary resources and protections until each person is capable of "walking tall among their fellow citizens" (Pettit 2014, 77). The "eyeball test" is of primary importance not only to determine the level of resources and protections that should be provided for given choices, but also to define the range of choices that should be protected. The necessary condition of giving resources to those people who need them the most shows the expressively egalitarian characteristic of the neo-republican justice conception. Under this conception, the state has a special commitment to helping the worse-off to enable them to enjoy the basic freedoms implied by freedom as non-domination (Pettit 2014, 1997; Lovett and Pettit 2001).

The neo-republican approach to social justice fosters a single freedom centered principle to elaborate demands of justice. "If we look after freedom properly, then justice and democracy will look after themselves. . . . [T]he domestic ideals of justice and democracy, on this account, derive from freedom, where freedom is given the depth and breadth demanded by republicanism" (Pettit 2014, 77–78). Freedom in this sense is the "gateway good" whose realization will foster the achievement of other valuable social goods. If the conditions for enjoying non-domination are fulfilled, then people will have the necessary resources to enjoy the status of the *free citizen*. Following this line of argument, a minimum level of freedom as non-domination is necessary to enjoy justice.

Every society will have to decide which specific freedoms are part of its fundamental freedoms and the way in which they will be incorporated to the cultural, legal, and political matrix of protection and empowerment (Pettit 2008a,103–4). Important differences can be easily spotted if we compare this list with how society looked like some centuries ago and even if we compare different cotemporary societies.

Spatial Justice and Infrastructure

In the last years, the neo-republican approach has been applied to new topics such as multiculturalism (Bachvarova 2014; Laborde 2008; Lovett 2010a); distributive justice (Dagger 2006; Lovett 2009); conservation and the environment (Slaughter 2008); international relations and global justice (Bachvarova 2013; Bohman 2008; Laborde 2010; Lovett 2010b; Pettit 2010); migration (Honohan 2014); bioethics (Durante 2009); and aboriginal peoples (Francis 2000). In this work, I apply the neo-republican conception to the spatial dimension.

The spatial justice theory provides a conception of space intimately entrenched with justice. It enables neo-republicanism to transit the path from its normative theory to the more challenging realities of the real world. It offers specific strategies and repertories to further the neo-republican concepts in the participation and control of public decisions.

David Harvey (2005, 2010), Edward Soja (1989, 1996, 2000, 2010) and Henri Lefebvre (1991, 1996, 2003) are the main references for the spatial justice approach. This conception shares common features with republicanism and can provide innovative tools to extend the republican theory. The spatial justice approach advocates for a "new spatial consciousness" that conceives space as a complex and collectively created social product that defines the geography in which we all live. In this regard, "the geographies in which we live can intensify and sustain our exploitation as workers, support oppressive forms of cultural and political domination based on race, gender, and nationality, and aggravate all forms of discrimination and injustice" (Soja 2010, 19).

The spatial justice approach and republicanism share the goal of reducing injustice. While the spatial justice approach aims to play a role in reducing infrastructure differences among neighborhoods and urban-rural areas, republicanism aims to lessen "domination relationships." The second point in common is the importance that they give to public space and place-based politics. Both approaches stress the creation of shared public spaces, such as public squares, green areas, markets, and so forth, where citizens can get together and develop a sense of community. At the same time, both approaches aim to be a yardstick for civil society groups and the citizenry in general to identify the injustices that they suffer in their daily lives and to speak out against them in the name of freedom as non-domination or spatial justice.

Nonetheless, the main difference between the two approaches is that while Soja claimed that the concept of justice is superior to freedom in its effectiveness to gain appeal across different social groups (Soja 2010, 21), Pettit affirms that freedom is the most important value, and that justice requirements can be accommodated under the republican conception.

My stance agrees with Pettit in that "freedom as non-domination allows us to see all issues of justice as issues, ultimately, of what freedom demands: what it demands in our social relations with one another, in our political relations with our government, and in the relations between the different societies on earth" (Pettit 2014, xxi). Nonetheless, I think that the spatial justice conception has a lot to offer to the republican approach, particularly the notion of "right to the city" (Lefebvre 1996). What is important about this conception is that it can help citizens claim their right to urban space and reclaim more democracy from those who have been using it to maintain their advantageous positions in society.

Infrastructure is a central concept for neo-republicanism. It is a key policy-making area to assure justice in society. That is why it is necessary to have a deeper understanding of infrastructure dynamics in order to construct what I define as a "neo-republican spatial agenda." In the last decades, there has been a prolific production of literature on urban infrastructure. McFarlane (2010) and McFarlane and Rutherford (2008) shed light on "the inherently political nature of networked urban infrastructure." Angelo and Hentschel state that people's small-scale interactions with infrastructure act as foundations for larger patterns of social interaction and fragmentation and (un)even geographical interactions (Angelo and Hentschel 2015, 307). In this regard, I adopt this revalorization of the concept of infrastructure as a prominent phenomenon affecting everyday people's lives and the political system as whole. My research uses this infrastructural approach to develop what I define as "spatial freedom" as a guide for the development of my "neo-republican spatial agenda."

The number of studies analyzing neighborhood effects has also flourished in the last years (Atkinson and Kintrea 2001; Bauder 2002; Durlauf 2004; van Ham et al. 2012). Spatial segregation and local neighborhoods can have a great impact in life-long developments of a person's life. Chetty and Hendren (2016) found that in the United States, the postal zip code turned out to be an accurate predictor of children's future outcomes in life. Such a geographically-caused discrepancy is illustrated by Galster and Sharkey (2017, 1) who state that the variations in geographic context across multiple scales (neighborhood, jurisdiction, metropolitan region) . . . affects the socioeconomic outcomes that individuals can achieve in two ways by altering the payoffs that will be gained from the attributes individuals have during any given period and the bundle of attributes that individuals will acquire (both passively and actively) during their lifetimes. (Galster and Sharkley 2017)

These kinds of analyses are promising for considering freedom related issues from a spatial perspective. They both add to the development of the infrastructural and the subjective/dignity components of my "spatial freedom" concept, as it will be explained in the next section.

In terms of policy, there are three main policy-making areas that guide the republican project: (a) *infrastructure*, that involves those institutions that would ensure to the general population the enjoyment of a meaningful range of choices; (b) *insurance*, those instruments fundamental to bolstering people who fall on difficult times; and (c) *insulation*, defense mechanisms to confront those dangers created by asymmetrical relationships and criminal activities. These instruments aim to provide resources and protection to citizens defending them from domination and injustice (Pettit 2014, 83).

ADVANCING A COMPREHENSIVE THEORETICAL FRAMEWORK

Toward a Neo-Republican Spatial Agenda

Such as republicanism defines freedom as the opposite of domination, I define the concept of "spatial freedom" as the opposite of "spatial domination." Further, I posit that "spatial freedom" has two main dimensions: *material infrastructure* and *dignity*. When these dimensions are both present, a person is considered spatially free or not spatially dominated. In this sense, a neo-republican conception of space fosters the equal distribution of "spatial freedom" among all citizens through policy initiatives that advance material infrastructure and dignity. The State is the responsible actor for implementing these policies while citizens should be able to participate in the design, and in contesting the public decisions that go against their interests. This "theory of space" that I have presented is the theoretical spatial counterpart of the policy-oriented "neo-republican spatial agenda." There are six fundamental policy areas that make up my "neo-republican spatial agenda": (a) transportation and mobility; (b) public spaces; (c) environment and sustainability; (d) basic public services networks; (e) affordable housing; and (f) citizen participation.

Transportation and mobility focus on developing infrastructure frameworks that are accessible to every citizen in order to enable them to manage their time and movement through the city in a bearable way, considering the two mentioned dimensions of "spatial freedom" (material infrastructure and dignity). Next, the creation and recuperation of public spaces in urban and rural areas is key. This becomes particularly important in vulnerable neighborhoods, which are the ones that on average have fewer green spaces and gathering places (Astell-Burt et al. 2014). Access to parks, streets, walkable public places, rethinking the city to balance the space dedicated to cars and traffic, and increasing spaces for citizen uses are just some examples of these initiatives. These are the kind of places where people can meet and share their experience in the city.

The spatial decisions involved in the "neo-republican agenda" must be environmental friendly and foster sustainable and circular policies. This involves the use of renewable energies, recycling policies, fostering the transition toward a circular economy and the minimization of risks to people's health. In addition, the basic public services network consists in the State's responsibility of extending basic public services such as roads, gas/fuel, electricity, water, and Internet services to the most vulnerable areas and improving their quality where they already exist. Inspired by the idea of expressive egalitarianism, education, health, administrative attention, and security institutions are also part of these basic services.

Affordable housing policies and innovative land use regulations also play an important role. Precautions on the impact of these measures on property prices should be considered in order to avoid reinforcing segregation processes. Finally, citizen participation entails the obligatory existence of instances of participation in the design (ex-ante) and control (ex-post) of public policies. This is a key element of the "neo-republican spatial agenda," which provides the citizenry and social movements the opportunity to take part of spatial policy decision-making processes. Public authorities in charge must be open to receiving proposals from civil society regarding the social use of certain spaces. This is of central importance because it treats people as citizens and not as mere consumers; also, it gives citizens as much control as possible over the acts of government in general.

The Concept of Spatial Freedom

The notion of space under republicanism is an underdeveloped topic. Most of the attention has been devoted to analyzing the relation between space and its role in furthering civic virtue and strengthening social bonds: what I call the "citizenship-civic virtue line" (Dagger 2001; Duany, Plater-Zyberk, and Speck

2000; Putnam 2001). In this section, I will analyze what I define as the two central dimensions of "spatial freedom": "material infrastructure" and "dignity."

"Material infrastructure" has an impact in people's freedom and a role in fostering their enjoyment of spatial non-domination[1]. The analysis of material infrastructure is a new way of addressing the analysis of space in neo-republicanism. This is what I call the "neo-republican material infrastructure line" (Cecchi 2016). Neo-republicanism considers any damage committed to the environment as an attack on our basic liberties,[2] as an assault to the "range of our undominated choice" (Pettit 1997, 139). If the damage is caused by a specific agency, this actor is clearly dominating those affected by its actions. Following this line of thought, when replacing the environment as such for "man-made space" or, more specifically, the material infrastructure created to live in a society, it is possible to identify the resemblance between the two arguments. Those actions or omissions (by specific agencies) that bring about deficient or inexistent basic infrastructures exercise spatial domination over those who are affected. As figure 7.2 shows, spatial domination entails either the existence of deficient material infrastructure or the lack of it. Thus, it is fair to claim that the absence of basic material infrastructure is an indicator of liability to domination.

For example, a person who lives in a precarious house in a peripheral urban slum without any official basic services such as water, electricity, gas, or sewer system suffers from spatial domination. Someone who cannot go to work on a rainy day because of lack of appropriate roads or means of transport or a person who suffers health diseases as a consequence of living in a contaminated territory are also being spatially dominated. In this regard, I claim that it is possible to remove this domination through appropriate infrastructure. Implementing adequate infrastructure to solve these basic problems is a necessary condition to spatially liberate these persons or at least to reduce their level of spatial domination.

Spatial domination consists of those spatial (infrastructural) conditions that contribute to making a person depend on another person's arbitrary decision. Regarding the example at the urban slum, living in such precarious conditions exposes this person to be dependent on the good will of her employer when the latter is deciding to sanction her for being absent, or by potentially

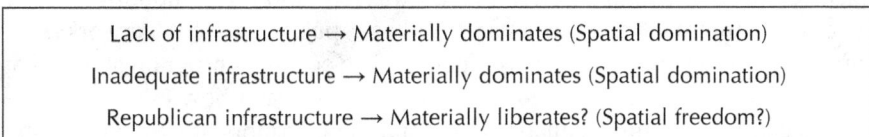

Lack of infrastructure → Materially dominates (Spatial domination)

Inadequate infrastructure → Materially dominates (Spatial domination)

Republican infrastructure → Materially liberates? (Spatial freedom?)

Figure 7.2. Spatial Damage through Material Infrastructure Scheme.
Source: Author elaboration based on Pettit.

using that absence to justify a future decision of firing her. This situation will always be an extra negotiation asset in favor of the employer when negotiating salary improvements, promotions, or other benefits like choosing vacation dates. The worker will always start the conversation with a liability on her side. This liability could be used as an extra argument in case of being fired, or as a threat in case the employee starts to participate in labor union activities. Another aspect of the vulnerability of a person who inhabits this kind of slum has to do with another type of domination menace: the danger of depending on the arbitrary favor of local clientelist brokers to access those services that the State is not properly providing.

To this respect, although I have argued for a central importance to material infrastructure aspects, I acknowledge that this is only one part of the domination menace that citizens should be protected from. The second dimension of spatial freedom is "dignity." The policies included in a neo-republican spatial agenda should provide citizens with the necessary resources to be non-dominated. Dignity has a central role in being able to pass the *eyeball test* and being able to speak to other persons as an equal without fear or necessity of contenting them. Going back to the example of the person in the slum, an infrastructural advancement in transportation would enable her to spend less time going from the periphery to her workplace. All the defined policy areas in the neo-republican spatial agenda add to people's dignity. Being able to move through the city in a timely and cost-effective way; having access to basic services; living in a proper house; or taking part in the policy-making process either in planned events or in public demonstrations, are all situations that reinforce a person's dignity and confidence.

Spatial Transformation: The Corridors in Johannesburg

South African cities are among the most extreme cases of planned spatial segregation during a colonization process (Soja 2010). Johannesburg is an emblematic example of this. Aiming to reconnect and enable formerly segregated communities, the "Transit-Oriented Development Corridors" program, originally named "Corridors of Freedom," is a concrete policy example that includes the six key policy components of the "neo-republican spatial agenda" defined earlier, which include transportation and mobility, public spaces, environment and sustainability, basic public services networks, affordable housing, and citizen participation. The corridors program shows that space can have tangible consequences in daily life, and how enduring these effects can be over time. Johannesburg and the Corridors are an emblematic example of how the neo-republican spatial agenda can offer new tools to analyze and design empirical public policies. Under the Apartheid system, most

South Africans were forced to live on the outskirts of cities and villages. They were considered "temporary sojourners" having the right to only offer their cheap labor to industrial and commercial activities.

Although the democratic transition in 1994 brought great changes in political freedoms, racial segregation spatial patterns are still in place. Roads, rivers, buffer zones of empty land and other barriers were constructed to keep people separated, and are still problematic when it comes to sharing common public spaces and commuting between different areas of the city (Rubin and Appelbaum 2018; Chapman 2015; City of Johannesburg [CoJ] 2014b).

The corridors were defined by the city government as a "new spatial vision for the city in line with the Growth and Development Strategy 2040 (GDS 2040), based on corridor Transit-oriented Development" (City of Johannesburg 2014b). The government identified that for too long the city had been shaped by its apartheid past. Today the city is still divided into rich and poor areas, black and white areas, and townships and suburbs. Black people are the most disadvantaged, living far away from their workplaces, their children's schools, and most avenues for leisure (Rubin and Appelbaum 2018; Chapman 2015; CoJ 2014b). The project consists of the construction of "well-planned transport arteries linked to mixed-use development nodes with high-density accommodation, supported by office buildings, retail developments and opportunities for education, leisure, and recreation" (CoJ 2014b). All those activities are gradually being located within the same geographical nodes. Social infrastructure, such as parks, local shops, local schools, clinics, and police stations are being located along the corridors too (CoJ 2014b).

It is possible to identify in the corridor's objectives some of the components mentioned as relevant for a neo-republican spatial approach. For example, the provision of new transportation material infrastructure that aims to reverse urban sprawl tendencies and to reduce the commuting time in a city where 1.3 million people spend more than two hours a day commuting from home to work (CoJ 2014a). The extension of basic public services such as education, security, and leisure are also in line with republican ideas. The corridors also have a commitment toward sustainability, aiming to reduce carbon emissions by replacing private transportation with the use of "affordable and convenient" buses and by constructing cycling and pedestrian paths, providing affordable and social housing along the Bus Rapid Transit (BRT) development corridors (CoJ 2014a). Achieving mixed-use development nodes with high-density accommodation close to office buildings, retail developments, schools, hospitals, and opportunities for leisure and recreation are also part of the plan (CoJ 2014b).

The corridors program, at least in its spirit, encompass all that has been previously explained. In particular, one of the objectives of the project is to increase residents' "freedom of movement as well as economic freedom—liberating them from apartheid spatial legacy characterized by informal settlements, poor schooling and limited recreational spaces" (CoJ 2014b, 1). The corridors aim to treat people like citizens instead of treating them like consumers when affirming that it "will give rise to a people centered city where the needs of communities, their safety, comfort and economic well-being are placed at the core of planning and delivery processes" (CoJ 2014b).

Although a thorough assessment of the program will be carried out in a future work, several challenges can be already identified at this stage. Even when the provision of basic services in Johannesburg is comparatively high (about 95 percent of households enjoy piped water, flush toilets, and electricity), there is a striking contrast in informal settlements where less than half of the households have access to basic sanitation (CoJ 2018b). Lack of access to and low-quality basic services reinforce processes that particularly affect the most vulnerable communities who are therefore suffering spatial domination. A vital challenge regarding basic infrastructure extension and affordable housing construction is the risk of displacement and increased vulnerability that can be generated by the improvement of services and the related rise in land prices. Another key challenge required for the success of the program is how to reengage and include local communities in the implementation of the project. Community participation was limited at the policy design stage and protests and conflicts have led to long policy implementation deadlocks (Chapman 2015). A key lesson that the neo-republican spatial approach can bring to the corridors program is that infrastructure interventions must be supplemented with social development and engagement strategies that cope with the multidimensional aspects of marginalization in order to achieve the full potential of the corridors policy and improve well-being.

CONCLUSION

Throughout this work I have explored the relation between freedom, justice, infrastructure, and space from an innovative perspective by endorsing the neo-republican conception of freedom and connecting it with the spatial justice approach to develop a neo-republican spatial agenda. The agenda aims to serve as a theoretical basis to guide public officials in the design of public policies and civil society actors to recognize everyday life instances of spatial domination. This awareness should ideally serve as a way to organize political actions and frame collective claims. Before getting to this instance, it was necessary to explore what "freedom as non-domination" entails as a concept of freedom in itself, as the base for the neo-republican theory of justice and as the source of inspiration for a spatial policy agenda. The concepts of spatial justice and infrastructure were also explored as central inputs to the neo-republican spatial agenda. A neo-republican conception of space implies the equal distribution of "spatial freedom" among all citizens through policy initiatives that foster material infrastructure and dignity. A neo-republican conception of space considers the existence of deficient material infrastructure, or the total lack of it, as an indicator of liability to spatial domination. In this regard, I argue that it is possible to remove spatial domination through infrastructure. Implementing adequate infrastructure is a necessary condition to spatially liberate people or at least to reduce spatial domination. Nonetheless, in order to achieve what I defined as "spatial freedom," another condition should be met. This second necessary dimension is dignity. The policies included in a neo-republican spatial agenda provide citizens with the necessary resources to be able to feel as an equal with others, to be able to fulfill the eyeball test, to be non-dominated.

The analysis of the Transit-Oriented Development Corridors program example, although preliminary, shows that the neo-republican spatial agenda can serve as a constructive tool for analyzing public policy characteristics. It is clear in the analysis of the corridors that infrastructure interventions are not enough in themselves to bring about the transformations intended in the policy's goals. Failing to address several social problems such as the causes of poverty cycles, drug abuse, crime, or unemployment, threatens to undermine the fulfillment of the policy's goals. It is at this point that investing in the development of people's capacities and providing the necessary resourcing will have an impact in their dignity and in their subjective conception of their standing regarding their fellow citizens. A neo-republican spatial agenda would encourage the provision of such fundamental infrastructure but would strongly recommend complementing these initiatives with social policies that can strengthen people's abilities. At the same time, citizen participation channels should be improved at the design and implementation stages of the public policy. These actions should be implemented as equally as possible in spatial terms by reducing negative infrastructure externalities and should start with the consideration of the most vulnerable groups and areas in order to foster spatial freedom and non-domination.

The corridors are one of the most ambitious and systematically addressed projects to transform the spatial dynamics in South African cities. Their importance is as big as the challenge they are trying to reverse: decades of planned segregation that still have a strong impact. In upcoming works, an in-depth analysis of the corridors case will serve to define potential indicators to empirically address the "neo-republican spatial agenda." More should be said about the "politics of infrastructure," the power relations behind these kinds of policy making processes and the social collective action protests. Borrowing McFarlane's (2008, 366) statement, it might serve us well to remember the following: "What is often at stake here is not simply the provision of infrastructure, but the conceptualization of the city, and the nature of social justice."

NOTES

1. I am grateful to Philip Pettit for his commentaries on this topic. For more on this issue see Pettit (2014, 2012, 2008).

2. The issue of identifying what the specific content of the basic liberties is has not been directly addressed in the literature besides in Rawls's (1973) and in H. L. A. Hart's (1973) works (Pettit 2008b). Nonetheless, Pettit advances a list of concrete basic liberties under neo-republicanism that fulfill the three conditions mentioned before. These are freedom to think what you like; freedom to express what you think; freedom to practice the religion of your choice; freedom to associate with those willing to associate with you; freedom to own certain goods and to trade in their exchange; freedom to change occupation and employment; and freedom to travel within the society and settle where you will (Pettit 2012, 103).

REFERENCES

Angelo, Hillary, and Christine Hentschel. 2015. "Interactions with Infrastructure as Windows into Social Worlds: A Method for Critical Urban Studies: Introduction." *City* 19 (2-3): 306–12. doi:10.1080/13604813.2015.1015275.

Astell-Burt, Thomas, Richard Mitchell and Terry Hartig. 2014. "The Association between Green Space and Mental Health Varies across the Lifecourse: A Longitudinal Study." *Journal of Epidemiol Community Health*, 68, no. 0: 578–83.

Atkinson, Rowland, and Keith Kintrea. 2001. "Disentangling Area Effects: Evidence from Deprived and Non-deprived Neighborhoods." *Urban Studies* 38 (12): 2277–98.

Bachvarova, Mira. 2013. "Non-domination's Role in the Theorizing of Global Justice. *Journal of Global Ethics* 9(2): 173–85.

Bachvarova, Mira. 2014. "Multicultural Accommodation and the Ideal of Non-domination." *Critical Review of International Social and Political Philosophy* 17 (6): 652–73.

Berlin, Isaiah. 1969. *Four Essays on Liberty*. Oxford: Oxford University Press.

Bohman, James. 2008. "Non-domination and Transnational Democracy." In *Republicanism and Political Theory*, edited by Cecile Laborde and John Maynor, 190–216. Malden, MA: Blackwell Publishing.

Carter, Ian, Matthew H. Kramer, and Hillel Steiner. 2007. *Freedom: A Philosophical Anthology*. Malden, MA: Blackwell Publishing.

Cecchi, Luis Emilio. 2016. "Freedom and Spatial Justice. Towards a Republican Agenda of Spatial Freedom." PhD dissertation. Hamburg University.

Chapman, Thomas Patrick. 2015. "Spatial Justice and the Western Areas of Johannesburg." *African Studies* 74 (1): 76–97.

Chetty, Raj, and Nathaniel Hendren. 2016. The Impacts of Neighborhoods on Intergenerational Mobility: Childhood Exposure Effects. *NBER Working Paper No. 23001*. The National Bureau of Economic Research. Accessed July 5, 2018. https://www.nber.org/papers/w23001.

City of Johannesburg. 2010. *Consolidated Johannesburg Town Planning Scheme of 2010*. Accessed April 10, 2018. http://www.joburgarchive.co.za/2010/pdfs/town_planning_2010.pdf.

———. 2014a. *Louis Botha Avenue Development Corridor Strategic Area Framework*. https://www.joburg.org.za/departments_/Pages/City%20directorates%20including%20departmental%20sub-directorates/development%20planning/Corridors%20folder/Strategic-Area-Frameworks.aspx . Accessed August 7, 2019.

———. 2014b. *Corridors of Freedom: Re-stitching Our City to Create a New Future*. Accessed July 15, 2014. https://www.joburg.org.za/images/pdfs/corridors%20of%20freedom_s.pdf.

———. 2018. *Draft Integrated Development Plan 2018/ 2019 Review*. Accessed July 5, 2018. https://www.joburg.org.za/documents_/Documents/Intergrated%20Development%20Plan/idp%20documents/IDP%20for%20Council%20(2).pdf.

———. 2018a. *Spatial Development Framework 2040*. Accessed June 12, 2018. https://unhabitat.org/books/spatial-development-framework-2040-city-of-johannesburg-metropolitan-municipality/.

———. 2018b. *Climate Change Strategic Framework City of Johannesburg*. Accessed May 2, 2018. https://www.globalcovenantofmayors.org/wp-content/uploads/2015/06/CCSF-CoJ-Final.pdf.

Constant, Benjamin.1988. *Constant: Political Writings*. Cambridge, UK: Cambridge University Press.

Dagger, Richard. 2001. "Republicanism and the Politics of Place." *Philosophical Explorations* 4 (3): 157–73.

———. 2006. "Neo-republicanism and the Civic Economy." *Politics, Philosophy & Economics* 5 (2): 151–73.

Duany, Andres, Elizabeth Plater-Zyberk, and Jeff Speck. 2000. *The Rise of Sprawl Suburban and the Decline of Nation the American Dream*. New York: North Point Press.

Durante, Chris. 2009. "Republicanism in Bioethics?" *The American Journal of Bioethics* 9 (2): 55–56.

Durlauf, Steven N. 2004. "Neighborhood Effects." *Handbook of Regional and Urban Economics*. Vol. 4. Elsevier. 2173–242.

Francis, Mark. 2000. "Republicanism and Aboriginal Peoples." *Journal of Australian Studies* 24 (64): 153–65.

Galster, George, and Patrick Sharkey. 2017. "Spatial Foundations of Inequality: A Conceptual Model and Empirical Overview." *The Russell Sage Foundation Journal of the Social Sciences* 3 (2), Spatial Foundations of Inequality (February 2017), 1–33.

Hart, Herbert Lionel Adolphus. 1971. "Rawls on Liberty and its Priority." *The University of Chicago Law Review* 40 (3): 534–55.

Harvey, David. 2005. *Neoliberalization: Towards a Theory of Uneven Geographical Development*. 93–115. Stuttgart, Germany: Franz Steiner Verlag.

Harvey, David. 2009. *Social Justice and the City*. Athens and London: University of Georgia Press.

———. 2010. *A Brief History of Neoliberalism*. Oxford: Oxford University Press.

Honohan, Iseult. 2014. "Domination and Migration: An Alternative Approach to the Legitimacy of Migration Controls. *Critical Review of International Social and Political Philosophy* 17 (1): 31–48.

Laborde, Cécile. 2008. *Critical Republicanism: The Hijab Controversy and Political Philosophy*. Oxford: Oxford University Press.

———. 2010. "Republicanism and Global Justice: a Sketch." *European Journal of Political Theory* 9 (1): 48–69.

Lefebvre, Henri. 1991. "The Production of Space," translated by Donald Nicholson-Smith. Malden, MA: Blackwell Publishing.

———. 1996. *Writings on Cities*, vol. 63, no. 2. Oxford, UK & Malden, MA: Blackwell Publishers Inc.

———. 2003. *The Urban Revolution.* Minneapolis: University of Minnesota Press.

Long, Douglas C. 1977. *Bentham on Liberty*. Toronto: University of Toronto Press.

Lovett, Frank. 2009. "Domination and Distributive Justice." *The Journal of Politics* 71 (3): 817–30.

———. 2010a. "Cultural Accommodation and Domination." *Political Theory* 38, no. 2: 243–67.

———. 2010b. *A General Theory of Domination and Justice*. Oxford: Oxford University Press.

Lovett, Frank, and Philip Pettit. 2001. "Neo-republicanism: A Normative and Institutional Research Program." *Annual Review of Political Science* 12 (1): 11–29. doi:10.1146/annurev.polisci.12.040907.120952.

McFarlane, Colin. 2010. "Infrastructure, Interruption, and Inequality: Urban Life in the Global South." In *Disrupted Cities: When Infrastructure Fails*, edited by Stephen Graham, 131–44. New York and London: Routledge Taylor & Francis Group.

McFarlane, Colin, and Jonathan Rutherford. 2008. "Political Infrastructures: Governing and Experiencing the Fabric of the City." *International Journal of Urban and Regional Research* 32 (2): 363–74.

Pettit, Philip. 1997. *Republicanism: A Theory of Freedom and Government*. Oxford: Oxford University Press.

———. 2008a. "The Basic Liberties" In *The Legacy of H. L. A. Hart: Legal, Political and Moral Philosophy*, edited by Matthew Kramer, Claire Grant, Ben Colburn, and Anthony Hatzistavrou, 201–24. Oxford: Oxford University Press.

———. 2008b. "Republican Freedom: Three Axioms, Four Theorems." *Republicanism and Political Theory* 104: 45–56.

———. 2010. "A Republican Law of Peoples." *European Journal of Political Theory* 9 (1): 70–94.

————. 2011. "The Instability of Freedom as Noninterference: The Case of Isaiah Berlin. *Ethics* 121(4): 693–716.

————. 2012. *On the People's Terms: A Republican Theory and Model of Democracy*. Cambridge, UK: Cambridge University Press.

————. 2013. "Two Republican Traditions." In *Republican Democracy: Liberty, Law and Politics*, edited by Andreas Niederberger and Philipp Schink, 169–204. Edinburgh: Edinburgh University Press.

————. 2014. *Just Freedom: A Moral Compass for a Complex World.* New York and London: WW Norton & Company.

Putnam, Robert D. 2001. *Bowling Alone: The Collapse and Revival of American Community*. New York: Simon and Schuster.

Rawls, John. 1971. *A Theory of Justice*. Cambridge, Massachusetts: Belknap Press, Harvard University.

Rubin, Margot, and Alexandra Appelbaum. 2018. "Spatial Transformation through Transit-Oriented Development in Johannesburg Research Report Series." *South African Research Chair in Spatial Analysis and City Planning*, 2016. Accessed August 24, 2018. https://issuu.com/sacpwits/docs/1_synthesis_report.

Skinner, Quentin. 2012. *Liberty before Liberalism*. Cambridge, UK: Cambridge University Press.

Slaughter, Steven. 2008. "The Republican State and Global Environmental Governance." *The Good Society* 17 (2): 25–31.

Soja, Edward. 1989. *Postmodern Geographies: The Reassertion of Space in Critical Social Theory*. London and New York: Verso.

————. 1996. *Journeys to Los Angeles and Other Real-and-Imagined Places*. Malden, MA: Blackwell.

————. 2000. *Postmetropolis: Critical Studies of Cities and Regions*. Oxford, UK & Malden, MA: Blackwell Publishers Inc.

————. 2010. *Seeking Spatial Justice*, vol. 16. Minneapolis: Minnesota Press.

Van Ham, Maarten, David Manley, Nick Bailey, Ludi Simpson, and Duncan Maclennan. 2012. "Neighborhood Effects Research: New Perspectives." In *Neighborhood Effects Research: New Perspectives,* edited by Maarten van Ham, David Manley, Nick Bailey, Ludi Simpson, and Duncan Maclennan, 1–21. Heidelberg, London and New York: Springer Dordrecht.

White, Stuart, and Daniel Leighton. 2008. *Building a Citizen Society: The Emerging Politics of Republican Democracy*. London: Lawrence & Wishart Ltd.

Young, Iris Marion. 1990. *Justice and the Politics of Difference*. Princeton, NJ: Princeton University Press.

Chapter Eight

AIDS and Aid in Uganda

PEPFAR—Social Justice or Structural Violence?

Vandana Wadhwa and Poojitha Kondabolu

Uganda's HIV/AIDS epidemic makes for a compelling study, transitioning from one of the most severe in the 1980s to one with steadily declining HIV-prevalence rates in the 1990s. This decline was largely ascribed to firm political commitment, an open multisectoral approach, and an aggressive public health campaign stressing safe sexual behavior. The U.S. President's Emergency Plan for AIDS Relief (PEPFAR) was announced in 2003 to address continuing high AIDS-related mortality in Uganda and similarly affected countries. However, rates of new HIV infection rose in Uganda during PEPFAR phase-I (PEPFAR-I 2003–2008), primarily from rising new HIV infections (Barrett 2007; Kinsman 2010; UN General Assembly Special Session on Drugs [UNGASS] 2012). This opens PEPFAR's approach to question given its dominant role in funding Uganda's HIV/AIDS programming.

Converging multiple data sources within a case-study approach, we use "theory building" (Yin 2009) to situate Uganda's experience with PEPFAR within a "structural violence" framework (Galtung 1969). Despite PEPFAR's socially just intent of increasing anti-retroviral therapy (ART) access (De Cock, Mbori-Ngacha, and Marum 2002; Farmer et al. 2001; Kenworthy and Parker 2014), we contend that the unmindful overlay of PEPFAR's ideological and governance structures onto Uganda's existing inequitable socioeconomic structures resulted in structural violence by increasing or maintaining inequitable healthcare access among already disadvantaged groups. We particularly highlight an oft-neglected facet of structural violence—the consideration of consequence rather than of intent in determining guilt on the charge of structural violence (Galtung 1969).[1]

Our work contributes to the understanding of social (in)justice in two major ways: First, we add to theoretical body of literature on social justice by examining and highlighting *consequences* of structural interplays within a structural violence framework, and second, we contribute to a greater understanding of the structural and operational mechanisms of social justice approaches and their pitfalls that may result in social injustice. We hope to illustrate the necessity of politicizing and examining aid structures (Seckinelgin 2008) to promote greater analytical engagement with health policy and of mindfully prioritizing consequence over intent.

Below, we provide a study context by briefly outlining Uganda's HIV/AIDS epidemic and the various interventions and sociocultural and political-economic structures that influenced its trends. While a "historically deep" examination (Farmer 1996) would include the impact of colonialism and Uganda's civil war on the epidemic, the scope of this background is limited to more recent history. PEPFAR is also introduced, particularly in reference to its ideological and governance structures. Next, we provide the methodology and data sources, explaining their role in helping build the consequent analysis and case for how foreign aid structures placed over existing place-based structures created a situation of harm despite their just intent.

We note that our study was conducted in 2010 and evaluates the impact of PEPFAR-I and some of the U.S. congressionally reauthorized phase II (2009–2013). The study is therefore retrospective and thus, much of the supporting data and literature are from the 2004 to 2011 timeframe spanning PEPFAR-I and part of phase II. The value of such a study emanates from more than the benefit of hindsight: as presented in the conclusion, PEPFAR's more recent phases include many improvements, but most have either come too late or are hostage to volatile shifts in U.S. political ideologies and funding climate (American Foundation for AIDS Research [amfAR] 2019; Gostin 2013; Merson 2012; Oliver 2012). This leaves us with PEPFAR's early versions as the only complete picture to examine and draw warnings and lessons from on the unjust consequences of an otherwise well-intended program.

AIDS AND AID: THE UGANDAN CONTEXT

AIDS was first diagnosed in Uganda in 1982 in Rakai District bordering Lake Victoria. Diffusing primarily through heterosexual transmission along major transportation routes, HIV/AIDS became a generalized epidemic and the leading cause of adult mortality by 1986. Tackling the epidemic became President Yoweri Musaveni's high administrative priority—early strategies comprised a multisectoral approach to comprehensive information, education, and communication. However, HIV prevalence rates peaked close to 22 percent by 1990–1992, prompting a behavior modification campaign addressing socially contextual risk networks, emphasizing abstinence/late sexual debut, "zero-grazing" or faithfulness, and partner reduction. Pressure from health workers finally wore down the ideological resistance against condom promotion from Musaveni and religious leaders by the latter half of the 1990s. The resulting three-pronged approach is often called "ABC" (*A*bstinence, *Be* faithful; if neither, use *C*ondoms). Specific behavioral modification efficacy and Uganda's HIV-epidemic data accuracy remain heavily contested, but most credit the comprehensive ABC approach for lowering HIV prevalence rate to 5 percent by 2000–2001 (Barrett 2007; Green, Halperin, Nantulya, and Hogle 2006; Ibembe 2009; Kinsman 2010; Parkhurst 2013; Stoneburner and Low-Beer 2004; Tumushabe 2006; UNGASS 2012).

From 1989 to 2000, major encouraging trends included rises in age of sexual debut for all youth aged fifteen to nineteen years, in abstinence rates among female youth and in condom use rates for women and men. Extra-marital sex almost halved among men from 23 percent to 12 percent (Uganda AIDS Commission, MEASURE Evaluation and Republic of Uganda Ministry of Health [UAC et al.] 2003).

HIV/AIDS and Uganda's Sociocultural and Political-Economic Structures

Despite the above encouraging trends, women's HIV prevalence rates, women's HIV prevalence rates consistently remained higher than men's and peaked at younger ages, indicating their higher vulnerability, especially earlier in life. By the mid-2000s, women bore 60 percent of Uganda's HIV/AIDS burden, with a 1:4 male-female ratio of new infections among youth aged fifteen to twenty-four years (Neema, Musisi, and Kibombo 2004; Parikh 2007; UAC et al. 2003). These figures reflect Uganda's patriarchal social structure wherein early marriage, polygamy, and multiple partnerships, sexual violence and coercion, lower access to education and paid work, weak land rights and attendant practices of "widow-inheritance." These lead to low personal and financial autonomy, limited ability to negotiate safe sex, and promote engagement in transactional or commercial sex to survive. All these factors elevate women's vulnerability to HIV infection, particularly at young ages. Violent conflict also placed women in greater situations of vulnerability to infection (Clark, Bruce, and Dude 2006; Ibembe 2009; Kalipeni and Oppong 1998; Neema et al. 2004; Parikh 2007; UAC et al. 2003; UNGASS 2012).

Moreover, the systemic marginalization, stigmatization, and criminalization of "sexual others" including commercial sex workers (CSWs), men who have sex with men (MSMs), and lesbian, gay, bisexual, transgender, queer, and intersex (LGBTQI) communities places them in situations of abuse, violence, socioeconomic disadvantage, and hinders access to healthcare services (Hladik et al. 2012; Johnson 2007; King et al. 2013; Kiapi 2010; UNGASS 2012). Unsurprisingly, HIV prevalence among these groups was significantly higher in Uganda at approximately 13.7 percent for MSMs and 35 percent for CSWs (UNGASS 2012).

Musaveni's early adoption of neoliberal policies, open approach toward the epidemic, and appeals for external aid won him considerable international funding for HIV/AIDS programming, including for anti-retroviral drugs (ARVs). However, structural adjustment programs (SAPs) weakened invest-ment in public healthcare systems, creating issues of physical and financial inaccessibility, human and other resource shortages, and low-quality care. ARV supply chains were fragmented, and the drugs were still out of reach for most, despite the cheaper generics available by the early 2000s. Nega-tive impacts on agriculture and the economy due to the epidemic and SAPs made livelihoods and food security more tenuous. In such conditions, women may turn to commercial, intergenerational, or transactional sex, and men to seasonal migration or mobile work, creating bridges and relays of infection transmission (Barnett and Blaikie 1992; Ibembe 2009; Kalipeni, Semu, and Asalele Mbilizi 2012; Parik, 2007; Parkhurst and Lush 2004; Pfeiffer and Chapman 2010; Seckinelgin 2008; Tumushabe 2006).

Throughout the 1990s, AIDS-related mortality remained consistently high, underscoring the need for treatment and care. Uganda's HIV/AIDS efforts of the 1990s had cost $180 million (Kinsman 2010; UAC et al. 2003), but treatment and care would require larger and more dedicated outlays than were then available to Uganda. Additionally, Uganda's inequitable socio-political-economic structures exacerbated the epidemic but were in turn affected by it, heightening vulnerability to HIV/AIDS and depressing healthcare access and creating situations of (structural) violence (Craddock 2009; Rao Gupta et al. 2008; Seckinelgin 2008; White, Pope, and Malow 2009).

PEPFAR: Scope and Structures

In 2003, President George W. Bush announced the five-year, $15 billion-dollar U.S. President's Emergency Plan for AIDS Relief (PEPFAR-I, 2003–2008) for low-resource countries. It emphasized treatment and care, but also sexual transmission prevention modeled after the Ugandan ABC approach (US Government Accountability Office [GAO] 2006; United States Leader-ship Against HIV/AIDS, Tuberculosis, and Malaria Act of 2003 [Leader-ship Act]). PEPFAR's ideological structure was heavily influenced by U.S. religious conservatives, apparent in various special provisions, earmarks for abstinence, and be faithful components (known as AB), and preferred fund-ing of faith-based organizations (FBOs). These resonated well with Ugan-dan sociopolitics surrounding HIV/AIDS, itself influenced by evangelical ideology (Evertz 2010; Gusman 2013; Jones and Norton 2010; Oliver 2012; Santelli, Speizer, and Edelstein 2013). PEPFAR's vertical (project-specific) governance structure and emphasis on treatment scale-up was a mix of "humanitarianism," institutionalized "best practices" and evidence (ARTs as treatment-plus-prevention), fund recipient capacity, and U.S. security and economic interests (Cohen 2008; Dietrich 2007; Ingram 2010; Kenworthy and Parker 2014; Office of the Global AIDS Coordinator [OGAC] 2005a; Tumushabe 2006). PEPFAR funds flow from its major coordinating agencies to Prime Implementing Partners and then local and nonlocal subpartners in the focus country. Healthcare delivery is predicated on a "network model," a centralized healthcare design modified from Uganda's own system. Technical support and commodities flow from specialized core to peripheral areas that provide basic services. In turn, referral systems link advanced-services patients back to higher tier facilities at or proximal to the core (Institutes of Medicine [IOM] 2007; Ooman, Bernstein, and Rosenzweig 2007).

Ironically, since PEPFAR's introduction, Uganda's HIV/AIDS prevalence rates rose above 7 percent, partly because more people survived but largely due to a rise in new HIV infections (UNGASS 2012). As Uganda's largest single funder and policy shaper for HIV/AIDS programming (Ooman et al. 2007; GAO 2006), PEPFAR's inability to reverse, slow down, or simply arrest the trend of rising new infections gives cause for examination.

METHODOLOGY

This descriptive case study (Yin 2009) is primarily based on textual data from academic literature, statistical, and other reports including electronically archived materials, supplemented by field data (in-depth interviews and site observations) from a PEPFAR case study in Uganda conducted by the second author in July 2010 (Kondabolu 2010). Stakeholders for the eight in-depth interviews were selected for their ability to act as key informants and their representativeness across PEPFAR's major governance tiers, program areas and geographic sites.[2]

Stakeholders were apprised of the study and questions, and informed consent was obtained. Semi-structured interviews asked stakeholder perspectives on PEPFAR's structure, program areas, successes and weaknesses, and insights regarding PEPFAR's future and sustainability. Interviews were conducted in English (median length was two hours), and field notes later fleshed out—therefore, stakeholder perspectives are paraphrased unless expressly denoted otherwise. Anonymity was guaranteed—stakeholders are identified by randomly allocated letters, and potential identifiers of affiliations, roles, and geographic locations have not been disclosed. Field observations were recorded at interview locations and additional urban and rural ART sites to which the second author was provided access due to her affiliation with a parallel donor institution. The study conformed to the London School of Economics (LSE) Departmental Research Ethics Policy (LSE n.d.).

Interview data from Kondabolu's (2010) original case study on aid sustain-ability also pointed to often-problematic imposition of PEPFARs ideological and governance structures onto Uganda's existing inequitable healthcare con-text without adequately addressing the latter. Such stakeholder perspectives germinated the seed for the current interpretation and analysis. The presented themes correspond to stakeholder concerns, which were cross-checked and cross-referenced with existing reports and academic literature to build our critical analysis—In turn, stakeholder perspectives provided a valuable sense of "ground reality" to the literature. Converging data from these sources, we utilized theory building, a method that continuously and seamlessly loops through and reconciles findings from field data, theory, and relevant literature rather than analyzing them distinctly from one another (Dooley 2002; Eisen-hardt and Graebner 2007; Yin 2009). Doing so allowed us to build upon the "structural violence" framework presented below.

DEBATING SOCIAL JUSTICE AND STRUCTURAL VIOLENCE: AN ANALYSIS

A Framework for Violence

Johan Galtung coined the term "structural violence" (SV) to describe "indi-rect" violence where the violence or harm is embedded in social, political, and economic structures. It manifests as unequal distribution of power and resources and can be understood as "social injustice." Importantly, its deter-mination must be linked to consequence not intent (Galtung, 1969).

Critiques of the SV framework include its limitations in parsing out types of violence and structures (Cameron 2011; "Comments" in Farmer 2004). More nuanced conceptualizations such as a "continuum of violence" and alternate conceptualizations of violence and inequitable structures exist in literature (Brown and Moon 2012; Craddock 2009; King 2010; Lee 2016a; Sharp, Campbell, and Laurie 2014; Scheper-Hughes and Bourgois 2004). Descriptions of violence-causative unequal power relations in the political economy of aid include notions of "Empire," imperialism, neocolonialism, and neoliberalism (Basu 2004; Oliver 2012; Sastry and Dutta 2013), govern-mentality, security, and assemblage (Brown, Craddock, and Ingram 2012; Ingram 2010), governance and "scale-up politics" (Kenworthy and Parker 2014; Seckinelgin 2008). However, these robust frameworks lack the ex-plicit considerations of intent/consequence originally presented by Galtung (1969). Further, the SV framework captures a broad spectrum of structures, highlights insidious, hidden, and "ordinary" forms of violence and their consequent "suffering and harm" (Farmer 1996; Galtung 1969; Lee 2016b).

Finally, health-related scholarship and health geography have effectively used SV to conceptualize elevated risk/vulnerability to HIV/AIDS resulting from structural barriers (e.g., Argento et al. 2011; Farmer 2004; Loyd 2009; Mukherjee 2007; Wadhwa 2012; White et al. 2009).

SV's systemic nature requires it to be addressed by broad-reaching structural approaches (Rao Gupta et al. 2008). PEPFAR's aim of addressing AIDS mortality in low-resource settings through wide-spread access to ARTs and broad preventive measures certainly fits the intent of a socially just structural approach many have called for (De Cock, Mbori-Ngacha, and Marum 2002; Farmer et al. 2001). However, although PEPFAR's many documents reflect a cognizance of Uganda's underlying structural issues and inequalities, namely, inadequate health infrastructure, and social structures that disadvantaged women and marginalized groups, PEPFAR's implementation of its treatment and prevention components were fraught with issues (OGAC 2005b; Oliver 2012).

The Analysis

In the critical analysis below, we demonstrate how PEPFAR's ideological and governance structures interacted with each other and with Uganda's socio-political-economic structures to heighten or maintain vulnerability to HIV/AIDS for already disadvantaged populations through unequal and depressed healthcare access. As mentioned, Uganda's disadvantaged populations include women, vulnerable/high-risk groups such as CSWs, MSMs, and alternate sexualities/genders but also general populations in lower income groups and rural areas who lack easy financial and/or physical access to healthcare. Each theme below presents issues and barriers, followed by harmful consequences.

Follow the Money: Fund Disbursement Mechanisms

At the core of PEPFAR-I's structural issues was its fund disbursement mechanism. More than half the stakeholders mentioned that PEPFAR's vertical funding flow through Prime Implementing Partners and subpartners created parallel governance structures that bypassed the host country's health system and health priorities, significantly weakening both general and HIV-related healthcare. Just over half of all PEPFAR-committed funds for Uganda went to large, international nongovernmental organizations (NGOs) in 2005. Allocation to Ugandan government health entities was a meager 6 percent, and PEPFAR's non-coordinated budget timetable made it difficult to coordinate healthcare investments with national plans. Thus, most of PEPFAR's significant infusion into Uganda's health sector was unavailable for comprehensive healthcare and national healthcare priorities such as essential medicines, health delivery facilities, and importantly, health personnel training (Oliveira-Cruz and McPake 2011; Ooman et al. 2007; Nabyonga-Orem, Ssengooba, and Okuonzi 2009).

Additionally, PEPFAR-I's governance and ideological structures often intertwined, determining the direction, scope, and thrust of funding. Stakeholder A pointed out that part of PEPFAR politics was the underlying "moral ideology" that often negatively affected program efficacy, and how the ABC model is emphasized. PEPFAR funding expressly supported FBOs as subpartners: The 2006 estimated budget for Uganda awarded over 40 FBOs special grants for AB activities, and for providing linkages between prevention, care, and treatment (OGAC 2005b), giving them significant presence. PEPFAR's special provisions such as the "anti-prostitution pledge," and "gag-rule" disallowed funding to entities serving CSWs, or those offering even information on abortion, respectively. The related "conscience clause" allows PEPFAR funded entities to opt out of providing services in case of moral/religious objections to certain persons or practices (e.g., commercial sex or homosexuality; Dietrich 2007; Evertz 2010; Oliver 2012).

Consequence: The above issues lead to important considerations of where funds did *not* flow. Both governance and ideological structures had heavy negative impacts on healthcare access for CSWs, MSMs, and LGBTQIs. Ugandan FBOs are prominent in all areas of HIV programming due to PEPFAR's funding structures. Their increased reach and additional power to legally deny services through special provision clauses severely constrained healthcare access for these groups, compounding the sheer lack of existing government-funded services for them (Evertz 2010; Gusman 2013; UNGASS 2012). CSWs were told outright that lifesaving ARVs are wasted on them (Kiapi 2010), and MSMs and LGBTQI often opted to forgo needed services due to discriminatory attitudes from health workers (King et al. 2013). Moreover, an entire range of comprehensive reproductive, family planning, and HIV/STI-prevention services catering to women and families in general and to CSWs, LGBTQI, and MSMs specifically, also bore the financial brunt of the restrictive special provisions (Dietrich 2007; Evertz 2010; GAO 2006; Ingram 2010; Oliver 2012). Resultantly, over 75 percent of CSWs did not have access to such services in 2009 (UNGASS 2012). The PEPFAR-cosponsored 2008 HIV Implementer's Forum expressly excluded representation and healthcare access demands from MSMs and LGBTQI groups, further marginalizing an already disadvantaged group (Hladik et al. 2012; Mugisha and Mukasa 2008). Further, a systematic inherent bias was visible in lower PEPFAR funding allocated to countries with higher proportions of "risk populations," countries including Uganda (Grosso, Tram, Ryan, and Baral 2012)

The Medicinal "ARTs": Politics of Scale(up)
and ART Provision

PEPFAR's rapid scale-up strained Uganda's healthcare system already weakened by earlier neoliberal policies. Due to weak funding investments, PEPFAR's "network model" of healthcare delivery did not function as envisioned. Shortage of trucks and transport made distribution of ARVs and CD4 (infection-fighting white blood-cells) testing kits from the core inefficient. Fragmented linkages for timely blood-sample transport to labs rendered any Early Infant Diagnosis (EID) capacity moot. These issues were only addressed by a pilot project as late as 2013 (Kiyaga et al. 2013).

PEPFAR did bring about some "horizontal" capacity increase (Merson 2012), but it was inadequate, a duality apparent in stakeholder feedback. According to Stakeholder B, PEPFAR provided valuable access to EID and CD4 testing kits and funded a central diagnostics laboratory. However, Stakeholder E said, "the central lab never materialized." The planned lab was eventually launched in 2011, halfway through PEPFAR-II (UNGASS 2012). Other stakeholders (A, C, D, H) echoed similar observations; PEPFAR did invest in some labs, public hospitals and healthcare personnel training, but not enough. Each stakeholder specifically mentioned inadequacy in human resource investment, especially the lack of new personnel to address the scaled-up needs for testing, ART administration and monitoring, and care/support. They highlighted the internal brain-drain from other important healthcare areas such as TB and primary care to PEPFAR's programs due to its increased need and higher salaries. Reduced TB and primary care negatively affected not only healthcare delivery in general, but also the efficacy of PEPFAR's own treatment components. Field observations noted heavy shortages of medical equipment and trained medical staff at all levels. HIV-positive patients formed long lines at clinics even before sites opened or arrived throughout the day in a steady stream.

ARV procurement and distribution is the most significant aspect of PEPFAR's treatment component, but supply chain and distribution structures were based primarily on U.S. political-economic interests rather than humanitarianism or cost efficacy (Dietrich 2007; Windisch et al. 2011). Stakeholders A and G spoke of problems arising from using only U.S. commodities and drugs, including higher costs and shortages. Using expensive brand-name drugs approved by the Food and Drug Administration (FDA) cost PEPFAR 10–40 times more than using generic formulations pre-qualified by WHO, which would have ensured greater speed and volume of procurements. Under pressure from activists, FDA adopted an "expedited review" system, but approved only two generic ARVs by 2004 and had spent only 27 percent of ARV funds on low cost generics by 2006. The slow pace of the FDA's review of generics caused additional delays, leading to problematic stock-outs of these lifesaving drugs (Dietrich 2007; IOM 2007; Merson 2012; Windisch et al. 2011).

Consequences: Four stakeholders (C, D, E, H) mentioned such stock-outs, reporting that ARV and testing-kit supplies had been inconsistent over the years, noting that interruptions started anywhere from a few months to three years after the first wave of supplies. All four stakeholders mentioned having to turn away ART eligible and enrolled patients. Stakeholder D said, "[Twelve] patients came in yesterday—they had to be turned away to other centers." On the other side of this scenario was Stakeholder F, whose agency was fielding such patients:

> There is a large unmet need—about 20 patients come in a day from other centers—they are in desperate need of treatment, but we are forced to turn them away. We have no slots for treatment provision. Next fiscal year, we have to use a quota system [restriction on numbers of new enrollees], which will make things worse—this is a highly successful program going backwards.

The capping or quota system was reversed in 2010 under pressure from activists who feared the caps had already placed too many lives in jeopardy ("PEPFAR Makes U-Turn in Uganda" 2010). Stakeholder D mentioned that sending patients from one site to another presented additional access issues for much of the Ugandan population, approximately 85 percent of which was rural and not well linked by transportation routes (IOM 2007). Field notes reflected these access issues: patients typically walked, bicycled, or used *bodas* (light motorized scooters) to get to these ART sites, many of which were only connected by roads resembling wide dirt tracks.

All stakeholders reported that fragmented service delivery, weak referral systems from lower- to higher-tier facilities, and ART procurement and distribution issues severely limited people's access to health resources at every level and left them without access to life-saving ARTs, particularly children and those in rural communities. Although the Ugandan HIV/AIDS epidemic had largely been an urban phenomenon, HIV-prevalence rates reflected a closing gap at 8.4 percent and 7 percent for urban and non-urban areas, respectively (UNGASS 2012). The impact of the above issues on remote and rural communities was worsened by their lack of both financial and physical access. More than three-quarters of Uganda's urban population fell in the top two quintiles of the wealth index, while almost half the rural population fell in the two lowest quintiles, indicating their lower levels of financial access (Uganda Bureau of Statistics [UBOS] 2012). Physical access to healthcare also presented issues—less than half the population lived within five kilometers (approximately three miles) of a healthcare facility in 2011 (Uganda AIDS Indicator Survey [UAIS] 2012). Most ART-accredited sites were higher-level hospitals and Health Centres IV (county level), located in cities and towns. Even by 2011, only 6 percent of sub-county level Health Centres III were offering ART services. Access was even more problematic for the epidemic's hardest-hit remote populations like fishing communities (UNGASS 2012).

Weak healthcare networks and problematic ART procurement and distribution generally resulted in slow uptake of treatment and related activities during the first few years. By 2006, just over 20 percent of adults had tested for and received HIV results, only 12 percent of HIV-positive pregnant women received Prevention of Mother to Child Transmission (PMTCT) therapy, and only 39 percent of all those in urgent need of ART were receiving it from any source (UBOS 2012; UNGASS 2010). Appropriate comprehensive care was also not available to keep children and adults healthy for effective ART uptake. The situation was worse in rural areas, where children were twice as likely to be undernourished (15 percent versus 7 percent for urban children), have lower access to improved water sources (65 percent versus 90 percent) and improved sanitation (26 percent versus 72 percent; UBOS 2012). Field observations noted that extremely low CD4-counts were very common among children at pediatric ART sites, but not all eligible children were receiving ART—there was no way to know if some children in the sites' health charts had since died or were too sick to come in.

HIV-Prevention Issues: Emphasis on ART and The Trouble with "ABC"

PEPFAR-I's treatment component was its largest with a mandated allocation of 55 percent of received funds (modified to 50 percent for treatment and care during PEPFAR-II). The emphasis placed on treatment at the expense of other programs was questioned by some stakeholders, given that HIV/AIDS resurgence in Uganda was due to rising new infections, which outpaced AIDS deaths and the numbers placed on ART (UNGASS 2012).

Stakeholder F explained, "PEPFAR is making itself unsustainable because while they were emphasizing treatment scale-up, the virus is outstripping our capacity." PEPFAR reports showed a flatlining, even downtrend in funding since 2008; stakeholders reported uncertainty in the funding climate that affected their provision of services, particularly ART. A financially and epidemically sustainable response was seen as an imperative given the emphasis on expensive treatment with inadequate attention to prevention. Stakeholder C: "Driving the cost and epidemic is adult infection—there is a need to turn off the tap . . . and to prioritize prevention, not just treatment—behavior change, prevention, and treatment must all go together."

"The PEPFAR strategy for preventing sexual transmission of HIV is largely shaped by the ABC model and the abstinence-until-marriage spending requirement" (GAO 2006, i). The mandated allocation of 66 percent expenditure of sexual transmission prevention funding on AB activities (GAO 2006) was secured through concerted lobbying from U.S. and Ugandan evangelical groups and a U.S. Congressional testimony by "Uganda's First Lady [who] is a charismatic champion of AB programming" (OGAC 2005b, 109; also Kinsman 2010; Tumushabe 2006).

Abstinence was PEPFAR's favored strategy for adolescents and unmarried youths (aged ten to twenty-fours years; OGAC 2005a), but has limited application in a society where almost half of women are married by age eighteen and young girls may engage in transactional or transgenerational sex (Jones and Norton 2010; Neema et al. 2004; Parikh 2007). In 2006, half of all youth (fifteen to twenty-four years) had had sex before age nineteen—trends remained similar for women but increased among male youths by 2011 (UBOS 2012), revealing that large proportions of adolescents and youths were not provided relevant protective messaging.

The be-faithful component (the "B" in AB and ABC) was also problematic—serodiscordant partner transmission accounted for half the new infections in 2005 in Uganda (OGAC 2009). Marriage remains one of the largest risk factors for many Ugandan women due to their partners' risk behavior (Neema et al. 2004; Parikh 2007; UAC et al. 2003). Almost a quarter of married/cohabiting Ugandan men had risky casual sex in 2006 (Stephenson 2010), which remained unchanged in 2011 (UBOS 2012). Moreover, 60 percent of Ugandan women experience intimate partner violence, sexual coercion, and abuse (UNGASS 2012). Neither abstinence nor faithfulness applies to those subjected to such violence, which is linked to greater risk of HIV/AIDS infection (Cohen, Schleifer, and Tate 2005; Evertz 2010; Karagami et al. 2006; Neema et al. 2004; Parikh 2007; Stephenson 2010).

Similarly, neither prevention strategy applies to CSWs, LGBTQIs, and MSMs, who were left to access a severely under-resourced condom promotion component (Cohen et al. 2005; Evertz 2010; Johnson 2007). Uganda's healthcare system already does not cater to these groups or factor them into healthcare strategies. Asked for an explanation, James Kigozi, Uganda AIDS Commission spokesperson said, "There's no mention of gays and lesbians in the National Strategic Framework [for HIV/AIDS], because the practice of homosexuality is illegal" (New Humanitarian, 2007, para. 11).

PEPFAR's emphasis on AB programming ignored Uganda's social realities; about 15 percent of adolescents had had sex by age fifteen, and the teenage pregnancy rate was very high (UNGASS 2012; Jones and Norton 2010). Yet, OGAC instructs, "[A]lthough PEPFAR funds may be used to deliver age-appropriate AB information to in-school youths aged 10 to 14 years, the funds may not be used to provide information on condoms to these youths" (GAO 2006, 27). Misleading and inaccurate information in abstinence literature distributed by PEPFAR-funded sites also undermined program credibility, such as a PEPFAR-funded draft of a secondary-school HIV/AIDS curriculum that claimed that HIV could go through "small pores" in condoms (Cohen et al. 2005).

Condoms are also not always a viable solution in a culture, including Uganda (Higgins et al. 2010; Parikh 2007), but condom information and correct use are essential to any comprehensive HIV-prevention program. Stakeholders A, C, and H felt PEPFAR's HIV-prevention program was less than comprehensive, with condom promotion, microbicide gels, and male circumcision not given enough emphasis. PEPFAR-I policies largely restricted condom promotion to CSWs and "high-risk" groups (GAO 2006), despite *all* women's high vulnerability to HIV-infection from the generalized nature of the epidemic and high discordant partner transmission (OGAC 2009). Moreover, shortly after PEPFAR-I was announced with its emphasis on AB, President Musaveni reversed policy support for condom use. A condom recall followed suspiciously soon, resulting in a severe national shortage of the prophylactics (Barrett 2007; Epstein 2005; Gusman 2013; Ingram 2010; Jones and Norton 2010).

Consequences: The emphasis on ARTs did not address the growing epidemic's nature, which was fueled by new infections and was worsened by PEPFAR's incomprehensive prevention strategy that laid undue stress on AB. Resultantly, new infection incidence rose over PEPFAR-I's duration (UNGASS 2012). One of the severest consequences of the mandated AB spending allocation were cuts in PMTCT services (GAO 2006). One can infer the harm, given that approximately ninety-one thousand children were born to HIV-positive women but only half the women had access to PMTCT. Only a third of such women received any type of ART even by the end of PEPFAR-I, exposing an overwhelming number of children to HIV, and explaining why PMTCT accounted for over 20 percent of all HIV-transmission in Uganda (UNGASS 2010). Further, evidence overwhelmingly shows that AB-only programs elsewhere and during PEPFAR-I in Uganda have either been ineffective or have led to harmful outcomes such as unwanted pregnancies and sexually transmitted infections (Lo, Lowe, and Bendavid 2016; Santelli et al. 2013).

Through inadequate attention to condom promotion and other preventative measures, PEPFAR negated the right to full information about a complete range of HIV prevention methods for large parts of the population (Cohen et al. 2005; Evertz 2010; Oliver 2012; Santelli et al. 2013). Financial and physical access to condoms was also compromised. Condom distribution fell from 118 million to 69 million and men's condom use, particularly in risky situations, declined from 50 percent to half that level by 2011 (Gusman 2013; UNGASS 2012), which could undoubtedly contribute toward new infections. These contextually unsuitable emphases of the prevention component prompted Stakeholder A to echo the widely held belief among various PEPFAR stakeholders (not limited to those interviewed): "PEPFAR policy makers are confusing what [they think] is right with what is safe."

CONCLUSION

PEPFAR's positive impact was significant and inarguable in the light of prevention of thousands of deaths and new infections even during our study's timeframe (OGAC 2009; Walensky and Kuritzkes 2010). One can effectively argue that PEPFAR *reduced* structural violence by finally bringing about what advocates have called for since long—social justice in ART access (De Cock, Mbori-Ngacha, and Marum 2002; Farmer et al. 2001; Kenworthy and Parker 2014). However, our analysis demonstrates that such access to lifesaving ARVs excluded some of the most vulnerable populations, specifically, CSWs, MSMs, LGBTQI (or "key populations") as well as children and those from low-income groups and rural/remote areas. ART access barriers were created by funding flows that were preferential to FBOs, featured exclusionary special clauses, and did not coordinate with national health priorities for system strengthening and efficient ART scale-up. CSWs, MSMs, and LGBTQI, as well as many women and youth, were also excluded from access to an effective and/or contextually appropriate HIV-prevention strategy, contributing to the continued rise in new infections in these groups (UNGASS 2012).

We have argued that PEPFAR policies pushed the ideological agendas of the donor (albeit with a willing ally in the Musaveni administration) and the donor's governance interests, rather than looking to the vulnerabilities and barriers embedded within the Ugandan social and political-economic context to tailor an appropriate policy response (also Cohen 2008; Evertz 2010). Addressing underlying structural drivers of an epidemic is essential to effectively tackling the epidemic (Campbell, Cornish, and Skovdal 2012; Rao et al. 2008), but "therapeutic regimes outpaced attention to the broader social conditions of HIV infection" (Kenworthy and Parker 2014, 1).

While many of the ideological and governance structural barriers discussed in our analysis were addressed in subsequent PEPFAR phases, continued vigilance against any reversals is necessary. For example, special provisions and mandatory allocations were rescinded to varying degrees, but rollbacks were slow (Gostin 2013; Oliver 2012). In fact, the threat of their full reintroduction remains a reality with changing ideologies and funding priorities of successive U.S. administrative regimes, harming key vulnerable populations such as pregnant women and MSMs (American Foundation for AIDS Research [amfAR] 2019). Significant ART scale-up in recent years has led to coverage of almost three-quarters of persons living with HIV/AIDS (WHO 2019). Uganda reached the epidemiological "tipping point" by matching ART initiation with new incidence of HIV-infections in 2013, although this goal was reached a full decade after PEPFAR's inception. This lag is not surprising since PEPFAR budgets for system strengthening during this entire decade illogically bore negative correlations with HIV prevalence rates, lowering PEPFAR's efficacy (Moucheraud et al. 2016). Children under fifteen remain one of the least covered general population groups, new HIV-infection rates are still unacceptably high and declining trends have not always been steady, with young girls and women (ages fifteen to twenty-four) accounting for a quarter of all new infections among women (OGAC 2018; UAC 2015). Small scale settings reflected some encouraging trends in high-risk behavior modification and the success of scaled-up multipronged treatment and prevention strategies including PMTCT and male circumcision (Grabowski et al. 2017). However, broader studies show that AB programming has had virtually no positive impact on changing behaviors or reducing new infections (Lo, Lowe, and Bendavid 2016). Even PEPFAR reports acknowledge that reduction of new infections among adolescent girls and young women and male circumcision coverage has made slow progress in Uganda, as has ART and other coverage among children and key populations (OGAC 2018). Women still bear the brunt of the HIV-epidemic's burden, and prevalence rates are four times higher among women than men in the fifteen to twenty-four age group (WHO 2017). Recent HIV-prevalence rates for CSWs and MSMs (34 percent and 13 percent respectively) are still similar to mid-PEPFAR-II statistics (WHO 2019). The situation for these latter groups is likely to get worse with their continued preclusion from formal PEPFAR-funded healthcare coupled with a worsening national context, where Uganda's punitive legal system now expressly criminalizes homosexuality and the spread of HIV infection (Devi 2014; Hagopian et al. 2017).

PEPFAR's lack of contextuality resulted in lowering thresholds of HIV infection prevention and raising barriers to care and treatment for some of the most disadvantaged groups, and thus, in the commission of structural violence. As Galtung (1969) reminds us, intent is not material in determining guilt in the commission of structural violence—consequence is. Kirmayer (in Farmer 2004, 321) states, "Structural violence [SV] is a powerful metaphor that leads us to look for the brutality in taken-for-granted arrangements." Indeed, SV's label immediately draws attention to both mechanisms (socio-economic-political structures) and phenomena (inequities, harm, suffering). The "moral heat" (Waquant's critique in Farmer 2004) generated by SV's use here is intended to spark a greater debate on, and more reflexive engagement with historical and contemporary socio-political and economic contexts underlying the Ugandan HIV/AIDS epidemic (and epidemics elsewhere) and the global ideological and political-economic structures that overlay them. Paraphrasing Stakeholder D's words, there is a need to mitigate this ill-conceived donor funding where our lack of autonomy prevents us from determining a response based on local needs.

The lesson then, is that if, by force of human nature, we cannot divorce politics and health, then the very least we can ask of ourselves and our policy makers is a greater mindfulness of consequence on the most vulnerable, and a watchfulness against the "unanticipated consequences" of policy that Merton (1936) warned against. In sum, PEPFAR-I's policies effectively transgressed social justice adherence by rendering lifesaving HIV/AIDS services inaccessible because of sexuality, occupation, class, or geographical residence. While PEPFAR's ideological structures are still being dismantled, and its governance moving toward "country ownership," ongoing examination is *essential* to ensure that the former ideology is not tied to political regime shifts and the latter is more than mere aid-parlance for shifting accountability (Esser 2014). A continual critical lens on health programs is necessary to ensure that the "geopolitical economies of global health" (Ingram 2010) do not translate into the "political economy of brutality" (Farmer 1996).

NOTES

1. Here, our purpose is not to present stereotypes of a poor, 'third world' country, or of victimized/helpless communities, and villainous powers. We fully acknowledge the complexities, including Uganda's efforts towards building socioeconomic capacities, the agency of individual women/LGBTQI, power of its vibrant advocacy groups, and PEPFAR's largely positive intent to lower the HIV/AIDS burden. The purpose here is to examine intertwining structural interplays and their consequences to draw lessons for future social justice approaches and programs.

2. Stakeholders were representative of PEPFAR governance tiers, and worked with its coordinating offices, prime/implementing partners, and sub-partners. Two stakeholders were from a parallel donor institution working closely with PEPFAR who were interviewed for their in-depth yet "removed" perspectives. For maximum variation across PEPFAR program areas, stakeholders were selected across administrative, clinical (treatment and diagnostics), and advocacy roles, which often overlapped, providing a wide range of perspectives from each stakeholder. Six inter-

viewees served urban settings, and one each in peri-urban and rural settings, reflecting the distribution of PEPFAR funded sites. Time and resource constraints determined the final number of interviews (Baker and Edwards 2012; Guest, Bunce, and Johnson 2006), but yielded rich data that consistently fell along distinct themes.

REFERENCES

American Foundation for AIDS Research (amfAR). 2019. "The Effect of Expanded Mexico City Policy on HIV/AIDS Programming: Evidence from the PEPFAR Implementing Partners Survey." Issue Brief: Washington, DC: amfAR. https://www.amfar.org/uploadedFiles/_amfarorg/Articles/On_The_Hill/2019/IB-1-31-19a.pdf.

Argento, Elena, Sushena Reza-Paul, Roy Lorway, Jinendra Jain, M. Bhagya, Mary Fathima, S. V. Sreeram, Rahman Syed Hafeezur, and John O'Neil. 2011. "Confronting Structural Violence in Sex-Work: Lessons from a C-led HIV Prevention Project in Mysore, India." *AIDS Care* 23, no. 1: 69–74.

Baker, Sarah Elsie, and Rosalind Edwards.2012. *How Many Qualitative Interviews Is Enough?* Discussion Paper. NCRM. Accessed February 24, 2014. (Unpublished). http://eprints.ncrm.ac.uk/2273/.

Barnett, Tony, and Piers M. Blaikie. 1992. *AIDS in Africa: Its Present and Future Impact*. New York: The Guilford Press.

Barrett, H. R. 2007. "As Easy as ABC . . . ? Uganda's Fight against HIV/AIDS." *Geography* 92, no. 2: 154–57. Accessed January 12, 2014. http://www.jstor.org/stable/40574189.

Basu Sanjay. 2004. "AIDS, Empire, and Public Health Behaviorism." *International Journal of Health Service* 34, no. 1: 155–67. doi: 10.2190/UFAT-MU9G-9X39-JHG2.

Brown, Tim, Susan Craddock, and Alan Ingram. 2012. "Critical Interventions in Global Health: Governmentality, Risk, Assemblage." *Annals of the Association of American Geographers* 102, no. 5: 1182–89.

Brown, Tim, and Graham Moon. 2012. "Geography and Global Health." *The Geographical Journal* 178: 13–17. doi:10.1111/j.1475-4959.2011.00425.x.

Cameron, Drew. 2011. "The Consequences of Rationing Antiretroviral Treatment in SubSaharan Africa." *Journal of International Service* 20, no. 1: 1–18.

Campbell, Catherine, Flora Cornish, and Morten Skovdal. 2012. "Local Pain, Global Prescriptions? Using Scale to Analyse the Globalization of the HIV/AIDS Response." *Health & Place* 18: 447–52. doi:10.1016/j.healthplace.2011.10.006.

Clark, Shelley, Judith Bruce, and Annie Dude. 2006. "Protecting Young Women against HIV/AIDS: The Case against Child and Adolescent Marriage." *International Family Planning Perspectives* 32, no. 2: 79–88.

Cohen, Jonathan., Rebecca Schleifer, and Tony Tate. 2005. "AIDS in Uganda: The Human-rights Dimension." *The Lancet* 365, no. 9477: 2075–76. doi:10.1016/S0140-6736(05)66716-5.

Cohen, Jonathan. 2008. "The Great Funding Surge." *Science, New Series* 321, no. 5888: 512–19. Accessed January 1, 2014. http://www.jstor.org/stable/20054581.

Craddock, Susan. 2009. "AIDS and the Politics of Violence." In *HIV/AIDS: Global Frontiers in Prevention/Intervention*, edited by Cynthia Pope, Renee White, and Robert Malow, 279–291. London and New York: Routledge.

De Cock, Kevin M., Dorothy Mbori-Ngacha, and Elizabeth Marum. 2002. "Shadow on the Continent: Public Health and HIV/AIDS in Africa in the 21st Century." *Lancet* 360, no. 9326: 67–72. PMID:12114058.

Devi, Sharmila. 2014. "Uganda Takes 'Another Step Backward' with HIV Bill." *Lancet* 383: 1960. Accessed June 10, 2019. https://www.thelancet.com/pdfs/journals/lancet/PIIS0140673614609417.pdf.

Dietrich, John W. 2007. "The Politics of PEPFAR: The President's Emergency Plan for AIDS Relief." *Ethics & International Affairs* 21: 277–92. doi: 10.1111/j.1747-7093.2007.00100.x.

Dooley, Larry M. 2002. "Case Study Research and Theory Building." *Advances in Developing Human Resources* 4, no. 3: 335–54. doi: 10.1177/1523422302043007, http://adh.sagepub.com/content/4/3/335.

Eisenhardt, Kathleen. M., and Melissa E. Graebner. 2007. "Theory Building from Cases: Opportunities and Challenges." *Academy of Management Journal* 50, no. 1: 25–32. doi: 10.5465/amj.2007.24160888.

Epstein, Helen. 2005. *God and the Fight against AIDS*. The New York Review of Books 52, no. 7. Accessed July 18, 2013. http://www.nybooks.com/articles/archives/2005/apr/28/god-and-the-fight-against-aids/.

Esser, Daniel E. 2014. "Elusive Accountabilities in the HIV Scale-up: 'Ownership' as a Functional Tautology." *Global Public Health* 9, no. 1-2: 43–56. doi: 10.1080/17441692.2013.879669.

Evertz, Scott H. 2010. *How Ideology Trumped Science: Why PEPFAR Has Failed to Meet Its Potential*. Washington, DC: The Center for American Progress and the Council for Global Equality. Accessed July 5, 2013. http://www.americanprogress.org/issues/2010/01/pepfar.html.

Farmer, Paul.1996. "On Suffering and Structural Violence: A View from Below." *Daedalus* 125, no. 1: 261–83.

Farmer, Paul, Fernet Léandre, Joia S Mukherjee, Marie Sidonise Claude, Patrice Nevil, Mary C Smith-Fawzi, Serena P Koenig, Arachu Castro, Mercedes C. Becerra, Jeffrey Sachs, Amir Attaran, and Jim Yong Kim. 2001. "Community-based Approaches to HIV Treatment in Resource-poor Settings." *Lancet* 358: 404–9. Accessed July 15, 2014. http://www.who.int/whr/2004/media_centre/en/lancet.pdf.

Farmer, P., with comments by Philippe Bourgois and Nancy Scheper-Hughes, D. Fassin, Linda Green, H. K. Heggenhouen, Laurence Kirmayer, and Loic Wacquant. 2004. "An Anthropology of Structural Violence." *Current Anthropology* 45, no. 3: 305–25. Accessed January 18, 2014. http://www.jstor.org/stable/10.1086/382250?origin=JSTOR-pdf.

Galtung, Johan. 1969. "Violence, Peace, and Peace Research." *Journal of Peace Research* 6, no. 3: 167–91.

GAO. 2006. *Global Health: Spending Requirement Presents Challenges for Allocating Prevention Funding under the President's Emergency Plan for AIDS Relief* (GAO-06-395). Washington, DC: GAO.

Gostin, Lawrence, O. 2013. "PEPFAR's Antiprostitution "Loyalty Oath": Politicizing Public Health." *The Hastings Center Report*, 43, no 3: 11-2. https://doi.org/10.1002/hast.172.

Grabowski, Kate M., David M. Serwadda, Ronald H. Gray, Gertrude Nakigozi, Godfrey Kigozi, Joseph Kagaayi, Robert Ssekubugu, Fred Nalugoda, Justin Lessler, Thomas Lutalo. 2017. "HIV Prevention Efforts and Incidence of HIV in Uganda." *New England Journal of Medicine* 377: 2154–66. doi: 10.1056/NEJMoa1702150.

Green, Edward C., Daniel T. Halperin, Vinanda Nantulya, and Janice Alene Hogle. 2006. "Uganda's HIV Prevention Success: The Role of Sexual Behavior Change and the National Response." *AIDS Behavior* 10: 335–46.

Grosso, Ashley L., Khai Hoan Tram, Owen Ryan, and Stefan Baral. 2012. "Countries Where HIV Is Concentrated among Most-At-Risk Populations Get Disproportionally Lower Funding from PEPFAR." *Health Affairs* 31, no. 7: 1519–28. doi: 10.1377/hlthaff.2012.0216

Guest, Greg, Arwen Bunce, and Laura Johnson. 2006. "How Many Interviews Are Enough? An Experiment with Data Saturation and Variability." *Field Methods* 18: 59–82. doi:10.1177/1525822X05279903.

Gusman, Alessandro. 2013. "The Abstinence Campaign and the Construction of the Balokole Identity in the Ugandan Pentecostal Movement." *Canadian Journal of African Studies/La Revue canadienne des études africaines* 47, no. 2: 273–92. http://dx.doi.org/10.1080/00083968.2013.829941.

Hagopian, Amy, Deepa Rao, Aaron Katz, Sallie Sanford, and Scott Barnhart. 2017. "Anti-homosexual Legislation and HIV-Related Stigma in African Nations: What Has Been the Role of PEPFAR?" *Global Health Action* 10, no. 1306391: 1–10. doi: 10.1080/16549716.2017.1306391.

Hellen, Jacqueline P., and Vandana Wadhwa. 2015. "Sex [Work] and [Structural] Violence: A Study of Commercial Sex Workers in Budhwar Peth, Pune, India." In *Geographies of Health and Development,* edited by Isaac Luginaah and Rachel Bezner Kerr, 45–60. New York: Routledge Health Series.

Higgins, Jenny A., Susie Hoffman, and Shari Dworkin. 2010. "Rethinking Gender, Heterosexual Men, and Women's Vulnerability to HIV/AIDS." *American Journal of Public Health* 100, no. 3: 435–45. doi:10.2105/AJPH.2009.159723.

Hladik, Wolfgang, Joseph Barker, John M. Ssenkusu, Alex Opio, Jordan W. Tappero, Avi Hakim, and David Serwadda. 2012. "HIV Infection among Men Who Have Sex with Men in Kampala, Uganda–A Respondent Driven Sampling Survey." *PLoS One* 7: e38143. https://www.ncbi.nlm.nih.gov/pmc/articles/PMC3364961/.

Ibembe, Peter. 2009. "The Evolution of the ABC Strategy of HIV Prevention in Uganda: State and International Impact on Public Health." In *HIV/AIDS: Global Frontiers in Prevention/Intervention*, edited by Cynthia Pope, Renee White, and Robert Malow, 246–55. London and New York: Routledge.

Ingram, Alan. 2010. "Governmentality and Security in the U.S. President's Emergency Plan for AIDS Relief (PEPFAR)." *GeoForum* 41: 607–16.

Institutes of Medicine (IOM). 2007. *PEPFAR Implementation: Progress and Promise.* Committee for the Evaluation of the President's Emergency Plan for AIDS Relief (PEPFAR) Implementation. Accessed January 23, 2014. http://www.nap.edu/catalog/11905.html.

Johnson, Cary A. 2007. *Off the Map: How HIV/AIDS Programming Is Failing Same-Sex Practicing People in Africa*. International Gay and Lesbian Human Rights Commission. GM Printing, New York, NY. Accessed February 25, 2014. http://iglhrc.org/content/africa-map.

Jones, Shelley, and Bonny Norton. 2010. "Uganda's ABC Program on HIV/AIDS Prevention: A Discursive Site of Struggle." In *Language and HIV/AIDS*, edited by C. Higgins and B. Norton, 155–70. Bristol, UK: Multilingual Matters/Channel View Publications.

Kalipeni, Ezekiel, and Joseph Oppong. 1998. "The Refugee Crisis in Africa and Implications for Health and Disease: A Political Ecology Approach." *Social Science & Medicine* 46, no. 12: 1637–53.

Kalipeni, Ezekiel, Linda Semu, and Margaret Asalele Mbilizi. 2012. "The Brain Drain of Health Care Professionals from Sub-Saharan Africa: A Geographic Perspective." *Progress in Development Studies* 12: 153–71. DOI: 10.1177/146499341101200305.

Karamagi, Charles A. S., James K. Tumwine, Thorkild Tylleskar, and Kristian Heggenhougen. 2006. "Intimate Partner Violence against Women in Eastern Uganda: Implications for HIV Prevention." *BMC Public Health* 6: 284. doi:10.1186/1471-2458-6-284. Accessed January 26, 2014. http://www.biomedcentral.com/1471-2458/6/284.

Kenworthy, Nora J., and Richard Parker. 2014. "HIV Scale-up and the Politics of Global Health, Global Public Health." *An International Journal for Research, Policy and Practice* 9, no. 1-2: 1–6. DOI: 10.1080/17441692.2014.880727.

King, Brian. 2010. "Political Ecologies of Health." *Progress in Human Geography* 34, no. 1: 38–55.

King, Rachel, Joseph Barker, Sylvia Nakayiwa, David Katuntu, George Lubwama, Danstan Bagenda, Tim Lane, Alex Opio, and Wolfgan Hladik. 2013. "Men at Risk; a Qualitative Study on HIV Risk, Gender Identity and Violence among Men Who Have Sex with Men Who Report High Risk Behavior in Kampala, Uganda." *PLoS ONE* 8, no. 12: e82937. doi:10.1371/journal.pone.0082937.

Kinsman, John. 2010. "Working on a Hunch: A History of HIV Preventio in Uganda." In *AIDS Policy in Uganda: Evidence, Ideology and the Making of an African Success Story*. New York: Palgrave Macmillan.

Kiyaga, Charles, Hakim Sendagire, Eleanor Joseph, Ian McConnell, Jeff Grosz, Vijay Narayan, Godfrey Esiru, Peter Elyanu, Zainab Akol, Wiford Kirungi, Joshua Musinguzi, and Alex Opio. 2013. "Uganda's New National Laboratory Sample Transport System: A Successful Model for Improving Access to Diagnostic Services for Early Infant HIV Diagnosis and Other Programs." *PLoS ONE* 8, no. 11: e78609. doi:10.1371/journal.pone.0078609.

Koenig, Michael, Tom Lutalo, Fend Zhao, Fred Nalugoda, Fred Wabwire-Mangen, Noah Kiwanuka, Jennifer Wagman, David Serwadda Maria Wawer, and Ron Gray. 2003. "Domestic Violence in Rural Uganda: Evidence from a Community Based Study." *Bulletin of the World Health Organization* 81: 53–60. http://www.who.int/bulletin/Koenig0103.pdf.

Kondabolu, P. 2010. *PEPFAR I as a Tool for Sustainable HIV/AIDS Care and Treatment: Case Study, Uganda*. Unpublished master's dissertation. Department of Social Policy, London School of Economics and Political Science, UK.

Lee, Bandy X. 2016a. "Causes and Cures IX: Consequences of Violence." *Aggression and Violent Behavior* 30, no. 5: 110–14. doi:10.1016/j.avb.2016.06.013.

———. 2016b. "Causes and Cures VII: Structural Violence." *Aggression and Violent Behavior* 28, no. 3: 109–14. https://doi.org/10.1016/j.avb.2016.05.003.

Lo, Nathan C., Anita Lowe, and Eran Bendavid. 2016. "Abstinence Funding Was Not Associated with Reductions in HIV Risk Behavior in Sub-Saharan Africa. *Health Affairs* 35, no. 5: 856–63. doi:10.1377/hlthaff.2015.082.

Loyd, Jenna M. 2009. "A Microscopic Insurgent": Militarization, Health, and Critical Geographies of Violence." *Annals of the Association of American Geographers* 99, no. 5: 863–73. doi: 10.1080/00045600903253478. Accessed January 2, 2014. http://dx.doi.org/10.1080/00045600903253478.

LSE. n.d. *Research Ethics Policy and Procedures.* London: London School of Economics and Political Science. Accessed September 18, 2019. https://info.lse.ac.uk/staff/services/Policies-and-procedures/Assets/Documents/resEthPolPro.pdf.

Kiapi, Evelyn M. 2010. "Uganda: '*Why Waste ARVs on Sex Workers?*'" Inter Press Service, Kampala, December 3, 2010. Accessed February 27, 2014. http://www.ipsnews.net/2010/12/uganda-why-waste-arvs-on-sex-workers/.

Merson, Mary H. 2012. "Health Policy Brief: Assistance for Global HIV/AIDS." *Health Affairs*, July 13, 2012. http://www.healthaffairs.org/healthpolicybriefs/brief.php?brief_id=71.

Merton, Robert K. 1936. "The Unanticipated Consequences of Purposive Action." *American Sociological Review* 1, no. 6: 894–904. Accessed September 24, 2013. https://www.jstor.org/stable/2084615.

Moucheraud, Corrina, Susan Sparkes, Yoriko Nakamura, Anna Gage, Rifat Atun, and Thomas J. Bossert. 2016. "PEPFAR Investments in Governance and Health Systems Were One-Fifth of Countries' Budgeted Funds, 2004–14." *Health Affairs* 35, no. 5: 847–55. doi: 10.1377/hlthaff.2015.1445.

Mugisha, Frank, and Victor Juliet Mukasa. 2008. "Uganda: LGBT Arrested at International HIV/AIDS Meeting." *OutRight Action International.* June 5, 2008. Accessed June 9, 2019. https://www.outrightinternational.org/content/uganda-lgbt-arrested-international-hivaids-meeting.

Mukherjee, Joia S. 2007. "Structural Violence, Poverty and the AIDS Pandemic." *Development* 50: 115–21. doi:10.1057/palgrave.development.1100376.

Nabyonga, Orem Juliet, Freddie Ssengooba, and Sam Okuonzi. 2009. "Can Donor Aid for Health Be Effective in a Poor Country? Assessment of Prerequisites for Aid Effectiveness in Uganda." *The Pan African Medical Journal* 3, no. 9. http://www.panafrican-med-journal.com/content/article/3/9/full.

Neema, Stella, Nakanyike Musisi, and Richard Kibombo. 2004. *Adolescent Sexual and Reproductive Health in Uganda: A Synthesis of Research Evidence* (Occasional Report no. 14). New York: The Alan Guttmacher Institute. Accessed February 21, 2014. http://www.guttmacher.org/pubs/2004/12/20/or14.pdf.

New Humanitarian. 2007. "Stuck in the Closet: Gays Left Out of HIV/AIDS Strategy. Kampala. March 17, 2006. Accessed June 21, 2013. http://www.thenewhumanitarian.org/feature/2006/03/17/stuck-closet-gays-left-out-hivaids-strategy.

Office of the Global AIDS Coordinator (OGAC). 2005a. *Engendering Bold Leadership: PEPFAR 2009 Annual Report to Congress.* Washington, DC: OGAC. Accessed February 4, 2014. https://2001-2009.state.gov/s/gac/rl/c14961.htm.

———. 2005b. *PEPFAR Country Operational Report.* Washington, D.C.: OGAC. Accessed February 4, 2014. www.pepfar.gov.

———. 2009. *Celebrating life: PEPFAR 2009 Annual Report to Congress.* Washington, DC: OGAC. Accessed February 4, 2014. http://www.pepfar.gov.

———. 2018. *PEPFAR Progress Report 2018: PEPFAR Strategy for Accelerating HIV/AIDS Epidemic Control (2017–2020).* Washington, DC: OGAC. Accessed June 4, 2019. https://www.pepfar.gov/documents/organization/286448.pdf.

Oliver, Marcia. 2012. "The US President's Emergency Plan for AIDS Relief." *International Feminist Journal of Politics* 14, no. 2: 226–46. doi: 10.1080/14616742.2012.659848.

Oliveira-Cruz, Valeria, and Barbara McPake. 2011. "Global Health Initiatives and Aid Effectiveness: Insights from a Ugandan Case Study." *Globalization & Health* 7, no. 20. doi:10.1186/1744-8603-7-20.

Ooman, Nandini, Micheal Bernstein, and Steven Rosenzweig. 2007. *Following the Funding for HIV/AIDS.* Accessed January 23, 2014. http://www.cgdev.org/publication/following-funding-hivaids-comparative-analysis-funding-practices-pepfar-global-fund-and.

Parikh, Shanti A. 2007. "The Political Economy of Marriage and HIV: The ABC Approach, 'Safe' Infidelity and Managing Moral Risk in Uganda." *American Journal of Public Health* 97: 1198–1208. doi:10.2105/AJPH.2006.088682.

Parkhurst, Justin O. 2013. "The Subtle Politics of AIDS: Values, Bias and Persistent Errors in HIV Prevention." In *Global HIV/AIDS Politics, Policy, and Activism: Persistent Challenges and Emerging Issues,* edited by R. A. Smith, 113–142. ABC-CLIO.

Parkhurst, Justin O., and L. Lush. 2004. "The Political Environment of HIV: Lessons from a Comparison of Uganda and South Africa." *Social Science and Medicine* 59, no. 9: 1913–24.

"PEPFAR Makes U-Turn in Uganda." 2010. *Health-E*, August 4. Accessed Aug 23, 2014. http://www.health-e.org.za/2010/08/04/pepfar-makes-u-turn-in-uganda/.

Pfeiffer, James, and Rachel Chapman. 2010. "Anthropological Perspectives on Structural Adjustment and Public Health." *Annual Review of Anthropology* 39: 149–65 doi:10.1146/annurev.anthro.012809.105101.

Rao Gupta, Geeta, Justin Parkhurst, Jessica Ogden, Peter Aggleton, and Ajay Mahal. 2008. "Structural Approaches to HIV Prevention." *The Lancet* 372, no. 9640: 764–75. doi: 10.1016/S0140-6736(08)60887-9.

Santelli, John S., Ilene S. Speizer, and Zoe R. Edelstein. 2013. "Abstinence Promotion under PEPFAR: The Shifting Focus of HIV Prevention for Youth." *Glob Public Health* 8, no. 1: 1–12. doi:10.1080/17441692.2012.759609.

Sastry, Shaunak, and Mohan Jyoti Dutta. 2013. "Global Health Interventions and the 'Common Sense' of Neoliberalism: A Dialectical Analysis of PEPFAR." *Journal of International and Intercultural Communication* 6, no. 1: 21–39. doi: 10.1080/17513057.2012.740682.

Scheper-Hughes, Nancy, and Philippe Bourgois. 2004. "Introduction: Making Sense of Violence." *In Violence in War and Peace: An Anthology*, edited by Nancy Scheper-Hughes and Philippe I. Bourgois, 1–27. Malden, MA: Wiley-Blackwell.

Seckinelgin, Hakan. 2008. *International Politics of HIV/AIDS: Global Disease—Local Pain*. London: Routledge.

Semugoma, Paul, Chris Beyrer, and Stefan Baral. 2012. "Assessing the Effects of Anti-homosexuality Legislation in Uganda on HIV Prevention, Treatment, and Care Services." SAHARA J. 9, no. 3: 173–76. doi: 10.1080/17290376.2012.744177.

Sharp, Joanne, Patricia Campbell, and Emma Laurie. 2010. "The Violence of Aid? Giving, Power and Active Subjects in One World Conservatism." *Third World Quarterly* 31, no. 7: 1125–43. doi:10.1080/01436597.2010.518789.

Stephenson, Rob. 2010. "Community-Level Gender Equity and Extramarital Sexual Risk-Taking among Married Men in Eight African Countries." *International Perspectives on Sexual and Reproductive Health* 36, no. 4: 178–88. Accessed February 1, 2014. http://www.jstor.org/stable/41038665.

Stoneburner, Rand L., and Daniel Low-Beer. 2004. "Population-Level HIV Declines and Behavioral Risk Avoidance in Uganda." *Science* 304, no. 5671: 714–18.

Tumushabe, Joseph. 2006. *The Politics of HIV/AIDS in Uganda* (Social Policy and Programme Development paper no. 28). Geneva: United Nations Research Institute for Social Development.

UBOS and ICF International Inc. 2012. *Uganda Demographic and Health Survey 2011*. Kampala, Uganda: UBOS and Calverton, Maryland: ICF International Inc.

Uganda AIDS Commission (UAC), MEASURE Evaluation, and the Republic of Uganda Ministry of Health. 2003. *AIDS in Africa during the Nineties: Uganda—A Review and Analysis of Surveys and Research Studies*. Uganda AIDS Commission, MEASURE Evaluation and Government of Uganda. Accessed January 21, 2014. https://www.measureevaluation.org/resources/publications/sr-04-32/at_download/document.

Uganda AIDS Commission. 2015. *National HIV and AIDS Strategic Plan 2015/2016–2019/2020, An AIDS Free Uganda, My Responsibility!* Uganda AIDS Commission, Republic of Uganda. Accessed June 6, 2019. http://cquin.icap.columbia.edu/wp-content/uploads/2017/06/ICAP_CQUIN_National-HIV-and-AIDS-Strategic-Plan_2015-16-2019-20.pdf.

Uganda AIDS Indicator Survey (UAIS). 2012. *Uganda AIDS Indicator Survey: Key Findings*. Calverton, Maryland, USA: Uganda Ministry of Health and ICF International. Accessed July 10, 2014. http://health.go.ug/docs.

United States Leadership Against HIV/AIDS, Tuberculosis, and Malaria Act of 2003 (Leadership Act), H.R. 1298, 108th Congress (2003–2004). 2003. Retrieved January 1, 2014 from https://www.govtrack.us/congress/bills/108/hr1298.

UNGASS. 2010. *Country Progress Report Uganda—January 2008 to December 2009*. Government of Uganda: Kampala, Uganda, January 2008. Accessed February 27, 2014. http://data.unaids.org/pub/report/2010/uganda_2010_country_progress_report_en.pdf.

———. 2012. *Country Progress Report Uganda—January 2010 to December 2012*. Government of Uganda: Kampala, Uganda, January 2012. Accessed February 28,

2014 from http://files.unaids.org/es/dataanalysis/knowyourresponse/countryprog ressreports/2012countries/file.68583.es.pdf.

Wadhwa, Vandana. 2012. "Structural Violence and Women's Vulnerability to HIV/ AIDS in India: Understanding through a "Grief Model" Framework." *Annals of the Association of American Geographers* 102, no. 5: 1200–1208. doi:10.1080/00 045608.2012.659966.

Walensky, Rochelle P., and Daniel R. Kuritzkes. 2010. "The Impact of The President's Emergency Plan for AIDS Relief (PEPfAR) beyond HIV and Why It Remains Essential." *Clinical Infectious Diseases*, 50: 272–75 doi: 10.1086/649214. Accessed January 20, 2014. http://cid.oxfordjournals.org/.

WHO. 2017. *Uganda Population-Based HIV Assessment UPHIA 2016–2017.* Accessed June 6, 2019. https://www.afro.who.int/sites/default/files/2017-08/ UPHIA%20Uganda%20factsheet.pdf.

———. 2019. *Uganda: HIV Country Profile, 2017.* Accessed June 6, 2019. http://cfs .hivci.org/country-factsheet.html.

White, Renee T., Cynthia Pope, and Robert Malow. 2009. "HIV, Public Health, and Social Justice: Reflections on the Ethics and Politics of Health Care." In *HIV/ AIDS: Global Frontiers in Prevention/Intervention*, edited by Cynthia Pope, Renee T. White, and Robert Malow, 269–78. London and New York: Routledge.

Windisch, Ricarda, Peter Waiswa, Florian Neuhann, Florian Scheibe, and Don de Savigny. 2011. "Scaling up Antiretroviral Therapy in Uganda: Using Supply Chain Management to Appraise Health Systems Strengthening." *Globalization and Health* 7:25 http://www.globalizationandhealth.com/content/7/1/25.

Yin, Robert. K. 2009. *Case Study Research* (4th ed.). Thousand Oaks, CA: Sage Inc.

Conclusion

Reflections on "Tranquil Waters"

Vandana Wadhwa

Simply trying to capture the various ways that social justice has been conceived, conceptualized and defined would fill volumes. Here, I opt to trace its history briefly through both comprehensive and focused reviews while recognizing that the concept of social justice remains highly debated and contested. Its multifarious understandings in some form or another have spanned cultures and times. The formal term of social justice itself has evolved immensely, from its roots in Jesuit writings where it conformed to more conservative interpretations to various other conceptualizations as it became coopted by diverse schools of thought (libertarian, socialist, neorepublican, postmodern; Reisch 2014). In more recent times, it has been understood through its categorization of distributive, procedural, and interactional forms (Jost and Kay 2010), and has evolved from its distinct streams of redistributive versus recognition paradigms to a realization of the false dichotomy of the two (Fraser 1998). Through all this, a formal definition of social justice has been proffered by many, and yet a fully inclusive definition has been elusive. However, most definitions and conceptualizations of social justice research would fall within or be related to inequities and equality, barriers and access, poverty and privilege, individual rights and the collective good, and their implications for suffering. Social justice inquiry also includes taking a critical stance toward social structures and processes that shape individual and collective life" (Charmaz 2011, 359).

Perhaps, most of us can envision what a just society might look like. However, with its converse of social injustice being far more prevalent, we are perhaps rather more likely to recognize "social injustice." But are we? Galtung (1969) conceives of social injustice as the occurrence of "violence," where violence is interpreted as "aggression" or "harm" and which could be direct (personal) or indirect (structural, or where harm is entrenched in social structures of inequity and unequal power relations), and likewise, visible or invisible. As he explains,

> [I]t is not strange that attention has been focused more on personal than on structural violence. Personal violence *shows*. The object of personal violence perceives the violence, usually, and may complain[1]—the object of structural violence may be persuaded not to perceive this at all. Personal violence represents change and dynamism—not only ripples on waves, but waves on otherwise tranquil waters. Structural violence is silent, it does not show—it is essentially static, it *is* the tranquil waters." (Galtung 1969, 173; emphases by Galtung)

To follow a simple linear logic, if violence (injustice) is embedded in social structures, and social structures are reflected in "social spaces" (places as social constructs—see Lefebvre [1974] 1991), then examinations of society and space are productive ways to uncover social and spatial injustice. Geographers are uniquely equipped to discover such complexities of social (in)justice in space. Scholars in the discipline have produced a plethora of work on this topic (Heynen et al. 2018). Since the latter part of the twentieth century, geography has informed the understanding of "socio-spatial justice" (England 2014). The works of Harvey ([1973] 2009) and Soja (2010) are just two such signal examples.

Geographies of Intersectionality

Societies and spaces are dynamic and multidimensional, each itself is comprised of constantly shifting intersecting axes that further intersect again in the interplays between society and space. It is these intersectionalities attempt to uncover in this book. In this, we draw inspiration from Valentine's (2007, 19) directive to uncover the importance of spatial processes when researching "inequalities and power" in "multiple categories and structures" and from Hopkins's (2017) words that geography's attention to context, scale, and space-time relations can yield richer understandings of intersectionality.[2] We note that while none of the chapters here expressly invoke intersectionality, it is through these chapters' *amalgamation* within this book that both results in and exemplifies a variety of intersectionalities—each chapter attends to intersections between processes of power/resistance and parameters of identities, structures, scale, and time-space relations.

As social geographic studies, all chapters herein examine a manifestation of social (in)justice in a particular context over time or in a particular time and at a particular scale or scales, where context here translates as intersections of a particular structure, whether sociocultural and/or representing political economies, with identity and space. All chapters are also characterized by intersections between multiple scales of space, and/or multiple structures. For example, Myers et al. (chapter 1) address multiple scales of community and home, and further zoom-in to a focus on the micro-scale of the bathroom while considering the role of social structures of ableism and class when examining affordable, accessible housing for persons with disabilities in the U.S. Time-space relations are considerations for both Yogev and Alcorn in their respective chapters (chapters 2 and 6) that recount both survival and resistance—the former explores the long history of structural racism in marginalizing the presence and narratives of people of color in outdoor spaces, with a focus on America's National Park Service, while the latter traces the historical context of paid domestic workers in Brazil inhabiting the iniquitous, hierarchical structures of race/ethnicity, gender and class. Both chapters also trace these groups' activism and organizing for more just futures.

Chapters that examine a multiplicity of scales and/or structures include Samarasinghe's look at Sri Lankan migrant housemaids (chapter 3) affected by multiple levels of class-and-status-based masculine hegemonies embedded in national policies, as they traverse multiple scales from the local to the transnational; Eliot's application of "territorialization through violence" (chapter 4) views this process as the product of global, regional, national, and local sociopolitical power structures and of formal and informal political-economies affecting space (re)configurations at the local scale in Mumbai, India. Wadhwa and Pomeroy (chapter 5) examine interactions between dual conceptualizations of "social space," ("society as space" or society envisioned as a space itself and "space as a social construct") while exploring the multiple layerings of a continuum of violence in India's urban spaces. Cecchi's original formulation of a "neo-republican spatial agenda" and "spatial freedom" (chapter 7) demonstrates how these can be applied to dismantle and displace multiple oppressive structures of race and class using Johannesburg, South Africa, as a case in point. Finally, Wadhwa and Kondabolu's chapter (chapter 8) is an analysis of harm caused by "unmindful" overlays of the global political economies and ideological structures of foreign aid onto national sociocultural structures and political economies that impact healthcare access at local levels. In sum, this book uncovers complex processes and contexts, paying particular attention to geographic concerns of temporal and spatial fluxes.

Charting the "Now" and "What Lies Ahead"

This book's chapters and their cited works both reflect and indicate contemporary and future trends in social justice research and action. Conceptualizations and understandings of social and spatial justice are forwarded in this book through established, modified, and innovative theoretical frameworks. Modifying and integrating established conceptualizations to generate new understandings is also a visible trend in current literature on social justice, for example, Israel and Frankel's (2018) integration of Amartya Sen's capabilities approach with Pierre Bourdieu's ideas of field, capital forms, and habitus in order to generate a "metric notion" or measure of social justice. In terms of approaches and methods of examination, Hancock (2016) points to intersectionality, a covert yet key theme in all works here, as an "analytical framework for social justice" (Hancock 2016, quoted in Hopkins 2017, 2)—intersectionalities are likely to gain greater currency in future social justice inquiries as identities, spaces, and contexts collide, overlap, and interlace in an increasingly globalizing world.

As several works in this book attest, deploying mixed methodologies is likely a trend that will continue. Work in social justice relies on the combined strength of multiple approaches, tools, and/or data sources for robust inquiries into social justice. As in these chapters, the critical lenses afforded by gender/sexuality, race, class, and disability, and others will likely continue to aid incisive examinations of social (in)justice—these stances nurture insightful and powerful techniques and tools, for example, counternarrative and narrative analyses, autoethnographies, and photovoice. Armed with the sensitivities and sensibilities of critical perspectives, tools traditionally found in the positivist toolkit are also increasingly being pressed into use in social justice inquiries (for example, see Andrade et al. 2018).

Geography's longstanding engagement with society and space and questions of equity, equality, freedom, and justice are highlighted in the numerous studies in the pages of the 2018 *Annals of the AAG Special Issue* on Social Justice and the City and its editorial piece (Heynen et al. 2018). The works in this book seek to extend such geographic engagements with social justice, exploring a range of spatial and thematic areas. Spatially, they highlight "emergent spaces" of social (in)justice, where "emergent" encompasses the full gamut of its meanings. It encompasses the creation or rise of new tangible (physical) spaces resulting from processes of social (in)justice and new intangible spaces where such processes might play out. Importantly, emergent also encompasses those spaces where such hegemonies have long existed but where these continuing/extant injustices are now gaining a renewed prominence. The book's thematic diversity is apparent from chapter descriptions above—even with such richness and complexity, we have barely scratched the surface of social justice inquiries that look at intersections of space and society. Some marginalized spaces, groups, and societies have not been represented here because of the constraints that come with pulling together diverse perspectives in finite periods of time over limited networks of reach—intangible spaces (e.g., the cyberworld or mental/emotional scapes), rural geographies and various liminal spaces in between urban/rural polarities, perspectives of indigenous groups or representations of queer geographies, and embodied experiences are just a few salient examples. However, we have actively sought to investigate marginalized geographies that exist in interstitial spaces of everyday existences and those that are less visible when viewed through the lenses of dominant structures and mainstream narratives. We note that a strong effort has been made to adhere to the spirit of social justice even when collating this volume—the editors sought to include voices typically marginalized in mainstream Anglophone academic works, for example, those of non-native English speakers residing outside the Anglophone world, as well as graduate students and those who work outside or at the very margins of academia's formal structures.

An important consideration must always be how to move forward with all these understandings of social (in)justice. bell hooks (1990) observed that sites of injustice are also sites of resistance, and so it is that every social injustice recounted in these chapters also points directly to either an area of solution or an entire approach toward justice. Contemporary trends in social justice movements still reflect the power of such spaces of resistance (Langman and Benski 2019). Additionally, given the near-inevitability of intersectionality present in many lived experiences today, it may serve us well to equip ourselves with the understandings and strengths of the multipronged strategy of "plural resistance" (Piedalue 2017). Much work still remains to be done—one need only to look to contemporary literature (including works in the *Annals of the AAG Special Issue* 2018) and daily headlines to realize that current and future trends of social justice research and action are writ large. Age-old hegemonies of racism, sexism, ableism, classism, and further, the oppressions of homophobia, xenophobia, and myriad other "isms" and phobias will undoubtedly remain a continuing concern, with their renewed expressions around the globe through nationalist sentiments, tropes of security, ethnic purity, and "othering" (see for example, Hamilton and Foote 2018; Hinnant, Casert, and Cook 2019; Johnston 2018). The concurrent identification and critical examination of new/emergent spaces and processes of oppression and resistance become a pressing necessity in the pursuit of social justice—examples can be found in spaces of incarceration, zones of conflict, processes of climate change, and related movements for climate justice (McCauley, and Heffron 2018; Perrone 2019; Campion Young and Bohmert 2019). In today's societies of flux and change, many spaces and processes are fraught with tensions and polarities—the hidden/private spaces that harbor overt violence/injustice versus public spaces and their oft-invisible processes of marginalization and invisibilization. Some tensions and polarities, however, simultaneously bring promise as well as elevated risk/violence: for example, the freedoms and connections versus the pervasive violence of cyberspaces/cyberscapes; transnational and intranational mobilities that bring many possibilities yet elevate vulnerabilities to exploitation, violence, and death; the opportunities but also the multilayered tyrannies attendant to globalization (Al-Alosi 2017; Muñoz 2018; Perrone 2019; Radio Free Asia 2019; Swanson 2018). All of these trends call for cross-disciplinary examinations of social and spatial (in)justice, and we invite an intra- and inter-disciplinary collaboration of scholars, practitioners, and activists to further this agenda of exploring, exposing, and addressing the many forms of injustice present in societies and spaces today.

In conclusion, I return to the conceptualization of society as a space itself: perhaps the greatest utility of such an understanding is that it entails visualizing society (quite aptly, I believe) as a human-made built environment that necessitates navigating through its norms and structures built over time by the cultures that inhabit it. Each inhabitant has their own "place" within its horizontally segregated spaces and vertically hierarchic structures, a "place" typically delineated by the inhabitant's belonging to or affinity with a particular identity or intersecting identities. For those who are marginalized to the corners or lower orders of this social space, claiming a greater or more egalitarian share would require the modification, disruption, or destruction of its current built form. This book is one attempt in that direction. My hope here, in conclusion, is not only to disseminate a call to dismantle such active structures and expressions of injustice, but also to evoke a recognition of the insidious yet immense potential for violence inherent in the chokeholds of silences and the straitjackets of apathy.

NOTES

1. Galtung (1969) makes the attempt to clarify that personal violence may also be part of structural violence and thus indiscernable, but better justice to this concept can be found in other writings on the nature of violence. One such work with ready relevance to the idea of the normalization or "ordinariness" of such personal violence to where it is rendered "invisible" is Das (2008).

2. I am greatly indebted to Professor Peter Hopkins for sharing his valuable insights and clarifying the full scope and nature of intersectionality studies. Dr. Peter Hopkins is Professor of Social Geography, School of Geography, Politics and Sociology and University Dean of Social Justice at Newcastle University, Newcastle Upon Tyne, UK.

REFERENCES

Al-Alosi, Hadeel. 2017. "Cyber-Violence: Digital Abuse in the Context of Domestic Violence." *UNSW Law Journal* 40, no. 4: 1573–1603.

Andrade, Eli, Rene Leyva, Mei-Po Kwan, Carlos Magis, Hugo Stainez-Orozco, and Kimberly Brouwer. 2018. "Women in Sex Work and the Risk Environment: Agency, Risk Perception, and Management in the Sex Work Environments of Two Mexico-U.S. Border Cities." *Sexuality Research and Social Policy.* https://doi.org/10.1007/s13178-018-0318-0.

Campion Young, Brae, and Miriam Northcutt Bohmert. 2019. "Gender and Incarceration." In *Oxford Bibliographies.* Oxford: Oxford University Press. doi:10.1093/obo/9780199756384-0222.

Charmaz, Kathy. 2011. "Grounded Theory Methods in Social Justice Research." In *The SAGE Handbook of Qualitative Research—Strategies of Qualitative Inquiry,* edited by Norman K. Denzin and Yvonne S. Lincoln, 359–80. Thousand Oaks, CA: SAGE.

Das, Veena. 2008. "Violence, Gender, and Subjectivity." *Annual Review of Anthropology* 37: 283–99.

England, Marcia. 2014. "Social Justice." In *Oxford Bibliographies in Geography,* edited by Barney Warf. New York: Oxford University Press.

Fraser, Nancy. 1998. "Social Justice in the Age of Identity Politics: Redistribution, Recognition, Participation," WZB Discussion Paper, No. FS I 98–108, *Wissenschaftszentrum Berlin für Sozialforschung* (WZB), Berlin.

Galtung, Johan. 1969. "Violence, Peace, and Peace Research." *Journal of Peace Research* 6, no. 3: 167–91.

Hamilton, Aretina R., and Kenneth Foote. 2018. "Police Torture in Chicago: Theorizing Violence and Social Justice in a Racialized City." *Annals of the American Association of Geographers* 108, no. 2: 399–410. doi:10.1080/24694452.2017.1402671.

Harvey, David. (1973) 2009. *Social Justice and the City.* Rev. ed. Athens & London: The University of Georgia Press.

Heynen, Nik, Dani Aiello, Caroline Keegan, and Nikki Luke. 2018. "The Enduring Struggle for Social Justice and the City." *Annals of the American Association of Geographers* 108, no. 2: 301–316, doi:10.1080/24694452.2017.1419414.

Hinnant, Lori, Raf Casert, and Lorne Cook. 2019. "Europe-Wide Vote Fragments Center as Far-Right, Greens Gain." AP News. May 26, 2019. Accessed June 24, 2019. https://www.apnews.com/2c137002ee4844b7ac4d2f33e626419f.

hooks, bell. 1990. "Marginality as Site of Resistance." In *Out There: Marginalization and Contemporary Cultures,* edited by Russell Ferguson, Martha Gever, Trinh T. Minh-ha, and Cornel West, 341–43. Cambridge, Massachusetts: MIT Press.

Hopkins, Peter. 2017. "Social Geography I: Intersectionality." *Progress in Human Geography* XX, no. X: 1–11. https://doi.org/10.1177/0309132517743677.

Israel, Emil, and Amnon Frenkel. 2018. "Social Justice and Spatial Inequality: Toward a Conceptual Framework." *Progress in Human Geography* 42, no. 5: 647–65. https://doi.org/10.1177/0309132517702969.

Johnston, Lynda, and L. Johnston. (2018). "Gender and Sexuality III: Precarious Places." *Progress in Human Geography* 42, 6: 928–36. https://doi.org/10.1177/0309132517731256.

Jost, John T., and Aaron C. Kay. 2010. "Social Justice: History, Theory, and Research." In *Handbook of Social Psychology (vol. 3), edited by* S. T. Fiske, 1122–65. Hoboken, NJ: Wiley.

Langman, Lauren, and Tova Benski. 2019. "Global Justice Movements: Past, Present, and Future." In *The Palgrave Handbook of Social Movements, Revolution, and Social Transformation*, edited by B. Berberoglu, 301–24. Cham: Palgrave Macmillan.

Lefebvre, Henry. [1974] 1991. *The Production of Space.* Oxford: Blackwell Publishers.

McCauley, Darren, and Raphael Heffron. 2018. "Just Transition: integrating climate, energy and environmental justice." *Energy Policy* 119: 1–7 https://doi.org/10.1016/j.enpol.2018.04.014.

Muñoz, Solange. 2018. "Urban Precarity and Home: There Is No 'Right to the City.'" *Annals of the American Association of Geographers* 108, no. 2: 370–379. doi:10.1080/24694452.2017.1392284.

Perrone, Alessio. 2019. "Will Italy Prosecute Officials for the 2013 Shipwreck Disaster?" Al Jazeera. June 23, Accessed June 24, 2019. https://www.aljazeera.com/indepth/features/italy-prosecute-officials-2013-shipwreck-disaster-190623073318553.html.

Piedalue, Amy. 2017. "'Beyond Culture' as an Explanation for Intimate Violence: The Politics and Policies of Plural Resistance." *Gender, Place & Culture*, 24, no. 4: 563–74.

Radio Free Asia. 2019. "Myanmar Army Again Accused of War Crimes in Rakhine State." May 29, 2019. Accessed June 24, 2019. https://www.rfa.org/english/news/myanmar/myanmar-army-again-accused-of-war-crimes-05292019162057.html.

Reisch, Michael. 2014. *The Routledge International Handbook of Social Justice.* London: Routledge.

Soja, Edward. 2010. *Seeking Spatial Justice: Globalization and Community.* Minneapolis: University of Minnesota Press.

Swanson, Kate. 2018. "From New York to Ecuador and Back Again: Transnational Journeys of Policies and People." *Annals of the American Association of Geographers* 108, no. 2: 390–398. doi: 10.1080/24694452.2017.1368987.

Valentine, Gill. 2007. "Theorizing and Researching Intersectionality: A Challenge for Feminist Geography." *The Professional Geographer*, 59, no. 1: 10-21. doi 10.1111/j.1467-9272.2007.00587.x.

Index

About the Contributors

Jennifer Y. Pomeroy (PhD) is an assistant professor of geography in the Department of History and Political Science at York College of Pennsylvania. She earned her master's degree in geography/planning from the University of Akron and a PhD from the University of Maryland at College Park. She is a broadly trained geographer. She has published articles and books related to her research interests encompassing land use, land cover change and sustainability, and intelligence analysis and national security. Recently, she has expanded her research interests by focusing on coupled dynamic urban setting in the context of climate change and intersectionality of (in)equality and (in)justice. She has served as chair and other officer positions in the Asian Geography Specialty Group (AGSG) and Regional Development and Planning Specialty Group (RDPSG) of the American Association of Geographers (AAG).

Vandana Wadhwa (PhD) is the founder/CEO of Meridian R&C LLC. She consults for primarily educational and non-profit organizations regarding academic and applied research, securing grant funding, and organizational best practices and strategies. Her research interests lie at the intersection of social justice issues with health, medical, and disability geography, gender issues, and urban/regional development. She is the coeditor of *Malaria in South Asia* (Springer, 2010) and *Facets of Social Geography* (Foundation Press [Cambridge University Press], 2012), and has published numerous articles and chapters in major journals and books. She has served on a number of academic and community organizations in various capacities, including as board member of the Massachusetts Disability Policy Consortium and chair of several specialty groups of the American Association of Geographers (AAG). She is the recipient of the Distinguished Researcher Award of the Regional Planning and Development Specialty Group and the Distinguished Service Award of the Asian Geography Specialty Group of the AAG.

Caitlin M. Alcorn is currently a PhD candidate in the Department of Geography at the University of Washington. She holds a BS in food and resource economics from the University of Florida and an MA in international development and social change from Clark University. Her primary research interests include paid and unpaid care work, labor studies, urban inequality, and feminist theory and epistemologies. Her dissertation research is focused on the spatiotemporal reorganization of paid domestic work in urban Brazil, as the dominant employment arrangements shift from full-time, live-in work to live-out and part-time work.

Luis Emilio Cecchi is a policy analyst at the Organisation for Economic Co-operation and Development's Cities, Urban Policies, and Sustainable Development Division and a PhD candidate in the Department of Social Sciences at Hamburg University. He is currently working on the spatial dimension of social justice, sustainability, and cities to inform the development of innovative public policy agendas. He holds a master's degree in politics, economics, and philosophy from Hamburg University and a bachelor's degree in political science and government from Torcuato Di Tella University. He has worked as a consultant for the Argentinean National Government and as a research assistant for the Inter-American Development Bank, Yale, Syracuse, Pittsburgh, and Pennsylvania universities. In addition, he was a lecturer at Hamburg University, Torcuato Di Tella, and Osaka City University.

Emmanuel Eliot (PhD) is a professor and teacher at the University of Rouen-Normandy, France. His primary research interests lie in studying spatial diffusion of epidemics (HIV/AIDS in India, cholera in the nineteenth century in France). His current research focuses on contemporary sanitary reforms in India and France, and France's overseas territories. Using quantitative and qualitative methods, he explores the relationships between health and territorialization, particularly socio-geographical conditions and processes that underpin reforms and crises in different contexts. He has published articles and chapters in both French journals and English books. His work has been funded by various international scholarships including the Department for International Development (DFID), Indo-French programs (EHESS-ICSSR), and the COFUND Durham International Fellowship). He actively serves academic organizations at local, regional, and national levels in France.

Lillie Greiman received her MA in cultural geography from the University of Montana. She has been a research associate at the RTC: Rural (the Research and Training Center on Disability in Rural Communities) since 2012. She has directed national interventions on home usability for the Research and Training Center on Independent Living at the University of Kansas. Additionally, she has worked on several projects in housing, community living, demography of rural disability, geospatial analysis of pain, and community participation. Prior to her work with the RTC, Lillie was a Fulbright scholar in Fes, Morocco, where she conducted qualitative research investigating Moroccan women's relationships to food and the spaces of food production.

Brendan Hogg grew up in New England and earned his bachelor's degree in sport and exercise physiology from Plymouth State University. He is an ACSM (American College of Sports Medicine) certified exercise physiologist with experience in clinical settings as well as various research avenues such as sport psychology, exercise physiology, and disability research. He began working for RTC: Rural (the Research and Training Center on Disability in Rural Communities) as a graduate student in 2016 and was hired as a project coordinator after receiving his MS in health and human performance. He currently coordinates and implements interventions aimed at improving the quality of life of people with disabilities. Brendan often works face-to-face with people with disabilities in the gym and in their homes. He is a strong advocate for the importance of regular physical activity and aims to spread the known benefits of exercise and promote the belief that "exercise is medicine."

Poojitha (Pooja) Kondabolu serves as the global tax policy lead at Airbnb where she works cross-functionally on a range of indirect tax issues relating to online marketplaces and privacy. Prior to joining Airbnb, Pooja was an attorney advisor to the NYC Taxpayer Advocate where she sought legal and policy changes to ensure the fair and equitable tax treatment of all NYC taxpayers. Pooja began her legal career as an M&A tax associate at Ernst Young. Pooja holds a JD and BA from the University of Connecticut and a MSc in social policy and development from the London School of Economics where she studied issues ranging from managing humanitarian crises to child rights to providing basic education in the developing country context.

Andrew Myers is currently a research associate at the Research and Training Center on Disability in Rural Communities (RTC: Rural). He began working there in 2011 when he was a graduate student interested in human-environment interactions. After earning his master's degree in geography from the University of Montana, he was hired as a full-time research associate. Andrew's work with the RTC focuses on community participation, housing, geography, transportation, and ecological models of disability.

He currently directs multiple federally funded projects that focus on housing modifications, exercise interventions, transportation surveys, and rural disability research. He grew up in Bakersfield, California, and earned a bachelor's degree in city and regional planning from California Polytechnic State University, San Luis Obispo.

Craig Ravesloot (PhD) is a clinical psychologist and research professor of psychology at the University of Montana where he directs rural disability, health, and community living research for RTC: Rural (the Research and Training Center on Disability in Rural Communities). He has over thirty years' experience in research, program development, and evaluation of services for people with disabilities funded through the National Institute on Disability, Independent Living, and Rehabilitation Research (NIDILRR), the Centers for Disease Control (CDC), National Institutes of Health (NIH), and the Public Health Service (PHS). He was awarded the Disability and Health research scientist of the year award by the Southwest Conference on Disabilities and the Distinguished Service Award by the National Association of Rehabilitation Research and Training Centers. He has published numerous articles covering a range of topics including health, employment, housing, and independent living for people with disabilities.

Rayna Sage (PhD) is a rural sociologist who began working with RTC: Rural (the Research and Training Center on Disability in Rural Communities) in 2016. Prior to this, she worked as a home visiting social worker for rural low-income families with small children. After earning her PhD in sociology in 2012 from Washington State University, she served three years as a clinical assistant professor at WSU. Utilizing primarily qualitative methods, Dr. Sage conducts her research to study and combat gender and economic inequality and enhance the vitality of rural labor markets and community support systems. She spent most of her childhood in the rural mountains of Northern Idaho before moving with her timber family to rural western Washington State.

Vidyamali Samarasinghe (PhD) is a professor and the director of the International Development Program of the School of International Service at American University, Washington DC. She earned her BA (honors) in geography from the University of Sri Lanka, Peradeniya, Sri Lanka, and her PhD from Cambridge University, England, in economic geography. Her research is focused on gender issues relating to women's work in the Global South, feminization of migration and work, and critical analysis of conceptual and methodological issues relating to theories of gender in the Global South. Her regional expertise is on South Asia and South East Asia. She is the author of *Female Sex Trafficking in Asia: Resilience of Patriarchy in a Changing World* (2007), updated and published in paperback in 2009. She is also coauthor and coeditor of several academic books and monographs. Her publications also include numerous refereed journal articles and book chapters.

Yonit Yogev has lived in the Pacific Northwest for twenty-eight years. She graduated in June 2017 from the Evergreen State College with a master's in environmental studies after a twenty-five-year career in nursing. Yonit has been an avid outdoorsperson and environmentalist for most of her life, as well as a lifelong social justice and anti-racism activist. Her previous academic background includes a BA in sociology from Tufts University and a master's in nursing from the University of Washington. She hopes to inspire and encourage ongoing conversations about racism, implicit bias, and the depth of structural racism in society. She believes these conversations are a vital part of dismantling the roots of social inequity.

www.ingramcontent.com/pod-product-compliance
Lightning Source LLC
Chambersburg PA
CBHW050649280326
41932CB00015B/2843